Personalities in Power
The Making of Great Leaders

by
Florence Littauer

HUNTINGTON⬡HOUSE, INC.
P.O. Box 53788 Lafayette, Louisiana 70505

Huntington House, Inc.
P. O. Box 53788, Lafayette, Louisiana 70505

Library of Congress Catalog Card Number 88-083383

ISBN 0910311-56-0

Printed by Faith Press International Inc., Tyler, TX

**** **** * * * *

Table Of Contents

Prologue

Act I—The Past: 1932–1969

Act II—The Past: 1969–1988

Act III—The Campaign of 1988

Postscript: Personal Application

Prologue

— 1 —

Personality Potential

From the beginning of mankind, people have been interested in the lives of their leaders. Few of us can remember the dates of historical events, the causes of the great wars, or the details of documents, truces, and constitutions, but we all have a picture of the personalities who were in power. We don't remember principles and platitudes, but we know the people who made them and we are curious to know about their intimate lives and to find out how they made it to the top.

We've been fascinated with the lives of our leaders since Moses led his people out of Egypt, Julius Caesar controlled the Roman Empire, Jesus discipled 12 ordinary men, Constantine declared Christianity the official religion of the empire, Luther nailed his theses on the door at Wittenburg, the Pilgrims' John Alden proposed to Priscilla, Napoleon met his Waterloo, George Washington became our first president, Abraham Lincoln gave the Gettysburg Address, Teddy Roosevelt carried a big stick, FDR gave fireside chats, Ike won the war and the presidency, Nixon stood on the Great Wall of China, Jimmy Carter carried his own suitcase, and Reagan became the Great Communicator.

As we reflect upon these personalities in power, we might ask what makes someone a leader? Surely these people didn't look alike or think alike. They were from different backgrounds, countries, and political parties. They had unique personalities. What made them figures that will go down in history?

I have a T-shirt that says, "I must hurry and catch up with the rest for I am their leader." As I've taught leadership seminars, I've met all kinds of leaders. Some are running to catch up with the rest, some have firm control, some are so busy organizing they never get to leading, and some lead because no one else would do it.

To be a leader, by definition, a person must be in front, must march ahead of the others. No matter how bright or right a person may be, he can't be a leader if no one else chooses to follow. The elusive quality of leadership is the ability to inspire others to want to do your will. Without this appeal, the intentional leader is a captain without a ship, a king without a country.

What is the difference between a leader and a manager? The word manager means someone with his "hands on" the situation, a person who moves people around, handles them, puts them in the right spots. A capable manager can direct his programs with or without inspired magnetic leadership.

In our country we have longed for leadership, we've wanted a king, and we have often been willing to accept a lack of managerial skills or even mediocre performance if we could have a regal leader to inspire hopes beyond belief, to lead us toward an impossible dream.

Personally, we are all managers, but not all of us are leaders. Each one of us manages something. We direct some phase of life each day. We discipline children, employees, constituents or congregations. We move markers from square one to the winner's circle, but are we leaders? Do we inspire others to do it our way or do we just insist on obedience? Are we making the most of our leadership potential? Are we functioning in our strengths or plodding along in our weaknesses?

We can all be leaders no matter what our background, education or personality, if we can find a way to assess our abilities and learn to eliminate our negatives. Here is a plan of action and personal evaluation that combines self-analysis with real life examples from history. Here is a measuring stick with which you can examine yourself, your family, your co-workers, your church and your leaders, not to be judgmental, but to understand yourself and learn to get along with others that you might move from managing mediocre moments to leading your troops, whoever they might be, with inspiration and excitement.

Twenty years have passed since my first introduction to the simple personality analysis I will be explaining in this book. In that time, I've studied, taught, digested and written on the subject. I've conducted leadership training conferences, held Personality Plus seminars, appeared on T.V. talk shows, counseled hundreds of couples and written 14 books. I have used the knowledge of the four basic personalities to bring understanding to my own marriage, to my relationship with my children, to my business and civic associations, to the speaking profession, to my Christian ministry, and to the training of leaders. Several years ago, because of my lifetime personal interest in politics, I began to highlight all the descriptive words printed about candidates in newspapers and magazines. As I analyzed the personal strengths and weaknesses of celebrities, politicians and presidents, I cut out the articles and filed my clippings in a separate folder for each personality pattern. During the Watergate era, when the personalities of many politicians were being paraded before the T.V. cameras, I pulled out my research, added the daily exposures, and began to speak on "Personalities in Power." People loved the political application, and this analysis became a staple part of my seminars. Audiences were excited to know the personality differences of Powerful Nixon, Peaceful Ford, Perfect Carter and Popular Reagan.

As the interest in political personalities accelerated during the long primaries leading into the 1988 election, I was asked increasingly about presidents of the past and found that people who didn't even vote wanted to know about the lives of Roosevelt, Truman, Eisenhower, Kennedy and Johnson. Why were they elected? What made them tick? What kind of families did they have? Could I explain their personalities?

These questions led me into a further study of our past presidents, our living ex-presidents and some predictions of future possibilities. Soon I realized I should write a book on the four personality styles as they pertain to leadership using the lives of our presidents as examples.

I have aimed to instruct and entertain, to unite history and humor. I have taken the concept of personality analysis and have shown how we can use this to evaluate ourselves and to assist in selecting a mate, an employee, a pastor, or a president. There is no perfect person, for with each set of strengths there are accompanying weaknesses, but as we come into an understanding of our own personalities, we can see ourselves and our leadership potential and have a quick way to analyze others.

Over 2,000 years ago Hippocrates created a system of categorizing what he called the four basic temperaments. Many other personality analyses have been plotted out since then, but most of them have their roots in his theories. We will adapt his terms to fit our Personalities in Power.

Hippocrates	*Description*	*Our Terms*	*Example*
Sanguine	**Magnetic personality**	**Popular**	**Reagan**
Choleric	**Commanding personality**	**Powerful**	**Nixon**
Melancholy	**Analytical personality**	**Perfect**	**Carter**
Phlegmatic	**Pleasing personality**	**Peaceful**	**Ford**

Before going any further, turn to the Personality Profile in the back of the book and check off one word on each line that sounds the most like you. Transfer these marks to the same word on the scoring sheet and tally up your totals.

Are you a Popular Sanguine like Ronald Reagan who has a magnetic personality and inspirational leadership skills? Are you using your inborn ability to charm and challenge others? Are you living up to your potential or have you somehow failed to get your act all together at any one time?

Are you a Powerful Choleric like Richard Nixon who has a commanding personality and who is a born leader? Are you using your natural skills to direct and control in a positive way? Are you able to take charge of situations without becoming bossy or offensive?

Are you a Perfect Melancholy like Jimmy Carter who has an analytical personality and who can organize everything down to the last jot and tittle? Are you using your command of details to put you ahead of the others and your deep sensitive nature to heal the hurts of those in need? Are you able to relate on an emotional level without becoming depressed yourself?

Are you a Peaceful Phlegmatic like Gerald Ford whose leadership skills are in mediation, in bringing opposing forces into harmony? Are you using your pleasing personality to balance the more volatile natures around you? Are you able to use your inoffensive managerial skills to inspire others to peaceful co-existence without losing your own motivation?

Whichever personality you may have, you can be a leader. As you accept your strengths and talents and work to overcome your weaknesses, you will grow into your limitless potential and become the leader you were meant to be. As you begin to understand those other people who aren't a bit like you, you will learn that they aren't out to get you, they're just different.

This book combines the useful tool of personality analysis with examples of leaders that we have all known, but not necessarily understood. At the end of each biographical chapter is a chart giving the strengths and weaknesses of each president. As you read them over, check off any that sound like you as a second measure of personal evaluation.

In reading each chapter, you will become acquainted with new friends and will see that each one was a great man with some inborn weaknesses. Together we will learn to anticipate similar patterns in ourselves and others and be able to make future choices and changes with both knowledge and wisdom. An old Proverb says:

> *"Give instruction to a wise man and he will*
> *be yet wiser; teach a just man, and he will*
> *increase in learning."*

— 2 —

Political Theatre

So much of our perspective on people in the news comes through television that we often think of real life activities as media events. We begin to assume the White House is a painted backdrop created for the nightly news, that the First Ladies' ball gowns came out of some costume rental company, and that political campaigns have been cast with actors capable of pulling high ratings. As theatrical productions, presidential campaigns fill in the gaps between seasons of baseball and football and provide relief from crime and violence.

As we look at the Personalities in Power over the last 50 years, let's view our cast as real people playing their own roles, let's see the setting as our country, and let's enjoy the script as we would a miniseries on famous people. Let's settle back in our easy chairs and enjoy the show. Let's get acquainted with the cast: the presidents of the past, the present and the future. As we view their lives, and their limitations, we should realize that we are both the audience and the casting committee for we are the people who put them there.

Throughout the years as each new candidate has appeared, we have made him into an actor, endowed him with celebrity status, and put him on the stage of the political theatre. Sometimes after the choice has been made, we've become a fickle audience loving witty lines, clever turns of plot, glamorous designer costumes, low taxes and high benefits; but we've stopped applauding when our hero brought depression, war, civil unrest, scandal, apathy, hostages, and the Ayatollah onto the stage. We've sat in our balcony seats and watched presidents we adored fall off the pedestals on which we'd placed them, representatives we'd chosen reprimanded for fraud and embezzlement, a congressman jump into the Tidal Basin after a stripper, and a candidate get caught carousing in Bimini. We've been shocked by this cast engaged in "monkey business."

Doesn't it get confusing? Should we laugh or cry? We need program notes to give us a clear view of the past problems, of the present political predicaments, and of the predictions of the potential strengths and weaknesses of candidates auditioning for future roles.

We won't be taking sides, but observing people. We won't denounce Democrats or rebuke Republicans. Our drama is not for those who have blinders on and can only see value or virtue in their own cast. It's not for Democrats who would die if Richard Nixon came out of retirement, ran for the Senate and became chairman of the Ethics committee; or for Republicans who are still living in fear that Roosevelt will resurrect and run for a fifth term.

This theatrical review is for an audience that can look on the whole political scene with a sense of humor, that cares to observe the various personalities of the past, evaluate the leadership skills of the present, and find a simple way to make calculated choices in the future.

Using Personalities in Power as examples, we who put them there will also gain insight into our own patterns of behavior and an appreciation for other people who aren't a bit like us. We will learn Personality Principles, take our own Personality Profile, and chart out Personality Predictions for the future. Our script will include comedy, some drama and a little tragedy, so relax and enjoy the cast, those Personalities in Power, for we are the ones who put them there.

— 3 —

Personality Patterns

In order to understand the cast in any show, we read the program notes on each actor and actress. We see where they have all come from, what experience they have had, and what avocations they enjoy. It's important to keep in mind that we often have combined traits of two or more of the four basic personalities. The combinations tend to round us out and lend balance to our lives. Before we look at individual presidents, let's get acquainted with the four general personalities. Let's visit each of the families and learn of their background, motto, strengths, weaknesses and possibilities.

As we get to know the Popular family, we will see they all want to have fun, talk and go to parties. The Powerfuls want to be in control of all their relatives and friends. The Perfects want to get everything on a chart and do it correctly, and the Peacefuls want to smile and avoid conflict at all costs. Perhaps even in this brief introduction to the personalities, we will begin to see ourselves as others see us. To paraphrase Robert Burns,

> *Would the gift that God would give us to see ourselves*
> *as others see us.*

As you look at the Personality Patterns and read the family histories, think about yourself and your family. Double check the scoring you did on your Personality Profile as you become more familiar with the strengths and weaknesses of each personality type. Begin to analyze the people you live and work with, not to become an amateur psychiatrist, but to be aware of their differences so that you can accept them as they are, not as you had hoped they'd be.

Popular (Sanguine)

Strengths

- magnetic personality
- talker with sense of humor
- storyteller
- entertaining
- charming
- optimistic
- cheerful
- enthusiastic
- exciting
- friendly
- creative & colorful

- childlike emotions
- dramatic

Weaknesses

- compulsive talker
- exaggerates
- cannot remember details
- poor follow-thru
- undisciplined
- disorganized
- loses things
- immature
- interrupts

Peaceful (Phlegmatic)

Strengths

- cooperative
- diplomatic
- moderate
- patient
- well-balanced
- all-purpose
- agreeable
- inoffensive
- team-oriented
- administrative
- steady & easygoing
- hidden emotions

Weaknesses

- indecisive
- unenthusiastic
- fearful & worried
- compromising standards
- not self-motivated
- procrastinating
- underlying will of iron
- lazy & laid back
- dull & bland
- too accommodating

- mediator with listening skills
- low-key personality

Powerful (Choleric)

Strengths

- commanding personality
- worker with a business mind
- born leader
- excels in emergencies
- goal oriented
- logical thinker
- quick organizer
- takes control
- dynamic
- undeveloped emotions
- stimulates activity
- motivational
- confident

Weaknesses

- bossy
- impatient
- quick-tempered
- intolerant
- workaholic
- rude & tactless
- manipulative
- demanding
- not a team player
- end justifies means

Perfect (Melancholy)

Strengths

- sensitive to others
- philosophical & mystical
- artistic & musical
- organizes on paper
- long-range goals
- schedule oriented
- sees problems
- likes charts & graphs
- keeps emotions
- serious
- thoughtful
- intellectual
- detail conscious
- thinker with great reasoning power
- analytical

Weaknesses

- easily depressed
- bogged down
- too perfectionistic
- emphasis on negatives
- inflexible
- pessimistic
- moody
- suspicious
- too mysterious
- slow to action

— 4 —

The Populars
(Sanguines)

Family Motto: *"It's what's up front that counts."*
Family Hymn: *"Oh, For A Thousand Tongues"*
Family Verse: *A merry heart doeth good like a medicine.* Proverbs 17:22

The Populars started out in life with winning ways. The little girls knew how to charm their fathers and the boys knew how to roll their eyes toward mother. They talked early and constantly, said adorable things and seemed to attract doting attention. They managed to delight their teachers, gather a retinue of little friends, become class president and be voted the most likely to succeed. They starred in the Senior Class Play, became flamboyant athletes and cheerleaders, and were the life of every party. As adults they aimed at professions that emphasized glamour over work, creativity over routines, loose hours over schedules, and people over statistics. With their appealing personalities they were promoted quickly until they reached a plateau where more than an easygoing performance was required for advancement.

Many of the Populars went into teaching, acting, lecturing, radio and television—anyplace where they could talk for a living. Popular Willard Scott loves doing the weather on the *Today Show,* although he often loses his notes and sometimes can't find South Dakota on his weather map. Many Populars became sales people and it was the Popu-

especially motivated when the grand prize is a pink Cadillac or a trip to Hawaii.

Throughout history, the Populars have been drawn into politics because it combines talk and work, promises and patronage, personality and position, confidence and charm. Politics provides a platform, the role of favorite son, attention from a continuous audience, bands and banners, excitement and suspense. The campaign trip becomes a big board game where the candidates move from square to square and election night becomes the biggest party of all because the Populars are made to be winners and they are always reaching for a prize.

The Populars were brought up on fairytales where every princess marries Prince Charming and where everything turns out all right in the end. They tend to avoid harsh realities, turn the other way in times of trouble, and flee the pursuit of the "Bad News Bears."

As we begin to understand the Popular personality, we will see that with the charm and cheer comes the inability to remember details and to follow through. The Populars have light fluffy strengths and what they feel are trivial weaknesses. They expect everyone will love them, they enjoy center stage, they gravitate to spotlights and they all want to be the star of the show!

The Popular person is fascinated with himself and gets excited over any minor personal accomplishment. When my 6-year-old grandson Jonathan, a true Popular, kicked the ball into the wrong goal in his soccer game he came running off the field calling out, "Wasn't I great?" For people who don't understand the different personalities Jonathan's enthusiasm could be considered conceited, but for a Popular it's natural. Some people who can accept this personal praise when the Popular is a child can't accept the fact that this trait is for a lifetime not just for the moment. Self-adoration can be considered a weakness but it is also a part of the bubbling enthusiasm that gives the Populars their magnetic appeal.

When President Popular, Ronald Reagan, faced a group of newsmen in November 1988, he stayed true to form when he stated, "You're going to miss me." Who else could say that and get away with it?

Newsweek went on to say that even though much of the media disagreed with Reagan, they couldn't help but like him and they will miss him.

> *"During the Johnson, Nixon, Ford and Carter years, the presidency seemed to lose its luster. Reagan restored its dignity, and infused it with a sense of drama. Like FDR, he came along at a time when the nation needed to believe in itself again; and like FDR, he knew how to use his charismatic personality and the symbols of his office to restore America's confidence."* [1]

Newsweek is right; we will miss him.

Popular Summary
Let's do it the fun way

Desire: *Have fun*

Emotional needs: *Attention, affection, approval, acceptance*

Key Strengths: *Can talk about anything at any time at any place with or without information. Has a bubbling personality, optimism, sense of humor, storytelling ability, likes people*

Key Weaknesses: *Disorganized, can't remember details or names, exaggerates, not serious about anything, trusts others to do the work, too gullible and naive*

Gets Depressed When: *Life is no fun and no one seems to love them*

Is Afraid Of: *Being unpopular or bored, having to live by the clock or keep a record of money spent*

Likes People Who: *Listen and laugh, praise and approve*

Dislikes People Who: *Criticize, don't respond to their humor, don't think they are cute*

Is Valuable In Work: *For colorful creativity, optimism, light touch, cheering up others, entertaining*

Could Improve If: *They got organized, didn't talk so much and learned to tell time*

As A Leader They: *Excite, persuade and inspire others, exude charm and entertain, but are forgetful and poor on follow-through*

Tend to Marry: *Perfects who are sensitive and serious, but the Populars quickly tire of having to cheer them up all the time, and of being made to feel inadequate and stupid*

Reaction to Stress: *Leave the scene, go shopping, find a fun group, create excuses, blame others*

Recognized by: *Constant talking, loud volume, bright eyes, mov-*

The Powerfuls
(Cholerics)

Family Motto: *Do it my way, now!*

Family Hymn: *"Onward Christian Soldiers, Marching as to War"*

Family Verse: *Do all things decently and in order.*
I Corinthians 14:40

The first time the little Powerful babies yelled for a bottle and mother came running, they knew they could take control. It was not a matter of could they, or would they, but when could they take the whole house away from mother. The Baby Powerfuls invented "demand feeding." They soon found that adults were willing to let them have their own way, and if their wishes were not quickly fulfilled, they could get instant action by throwing themselves on the floor and screaming. This threat of a temper tantrum, especially in front of company or in supermarkets, would bring the entire family to its feet in obedience.

Once control had been established, the little Powerfuls only had to use manipulative skills when faced with defiance from family or friends. Because the Powerfuls were all born leaders, they dictated the rules for every game, made definitive choices for every hesitant person, and were put in charge when the teacher had to leave the room. The Powerfuls won the games and earned the letters; they were outstanding members of the debating team and could argue equally well for either side of any issue.

They always had projects underway, and from childhood they seemed to know how to make money. Because of their constant activities, they had little time for friends. While the Populars needed companions to form an audience and the Perfects needed supporters to cheer them up when they didn't quite reach their own high goals, the Powerfuls needed no one. They were self-sufficient, and often those other people just got in the way and slowed down their progress.

As adults, the Powerfuls looked for opportunities where they could exert control and preferred occupations where they could start at the top.

The Populars were voted most likely to succeed.

The Perfects were depressed for fear they wouldn't succeed.

The Peacefuls didn't care whether they would or wouldn't succeed.

The Powerfuls passed them all by and succeeded. They became the entrepreneurs, the president of Chrysler, the CEOs of the Fortune 500. It was a Powerful female family member who created the concept of women's lib, marched shoulder to shoulder with Bella Abzug, and started success magazines for the working woman and it was a Powerful woman, Phyllis Schlafly, who almost single-handedly stopped the passage of the Equal Rights Amendment.

Since the Declaration of Independence, the Powerfuls have been influential politicians. Because of their innate desire to lead, they took to political office like the proverbial duck to water. Imagine a whole district to dominate, a whole state to sublimate, a whole country to control!

The Powerfuls grew up with pragmatic principles. If it doesn't work, get rid of it. One Pastor Powerful produced an unwanted mutiny when his first move in a new position was to abolish the women's missionary society as "just so much dead wood."

Powerfuls don't want to spend time thinking about action, as the Perfects do, or talking about action, as the Populars do, or avoiding action, as the Peacefuls do. They want to act now and take a chance that their program will work. Powerfuls, such as Phil Donahue, promote controversy, thrive on opposition, and enjoy cutting comments. They are confident in leadership, often impulsive in decisions, and impatient with the dummies. They believe that work is the answer to all problems, and if only we'd get off our duffs, get down to business, and do it their way everything would turn out all right. Vacations and coffee breaks are for the weak and undisciplined who will never amount to much in life anyway.

Powerful Margaret Thatcher has been declared by columnist George E. Will as the democratic leader of the decade, the political woman of the century. "She is no intellectual but her considerable importance in the history of democracy derives from the degree to which she has sought and wielded power in the name of ideas.

"She has shown that a soothing personality is dispensable in a democracy."

She has a "porcelain personality—hard and a little bit brittle."

She has a "zest for up-an-at-'em enterprise" even though "many of her people want a quieter, less strenuous life than she has in mind for them." She keeps forging ahead, "neither taking nor allowing rest."[1]

Ex-Prime Minister Harold Macmillan, a Powerful himself, once called Margaret "a brilliant tyrant surrounded by mediocrities."[2]

Margaret Thatcher is an excellent example of a Powerful woman who has made it to the top in a field previously open to men only. Because of her dynamic personality, her drive and determination, she has succeeded as a respected leader.

A Powerful, such as Lee Iacocca, is a born leader with the desire to control and no need to rest. A Powerful, such as commentator Dan Rather or *Today's* Bryant Gumbel has loud, strong strengths and loud, noticeable weaknesses; with all the talent and ability the Powerful may possess, he occasionally may become bossy, opinionated, impatient, arrogant and rude.

In the theatrical productions of life the Powerfuls want to direct every drama or play the part of Superman. If they can't run the show, they won't play the game.

Powerful Summary
Let's do it my way.

Desire: *Have control*

Emotional Needs: *Sense of obedience, appreciation for accomplishments, credit for ability*

Key Strengths: *Ability to take charge of anything instantly, make quick, correct judgments*

Key Weaknesses: *Too bossy, domineering, autocratic, insensitive, impatient, unwilling to delegate or give credit to others*

Gets Depressed When: *Life is out of control and people won't do things their way*

Is Afraid Of: *Losing control of anything, such as losing job, not being promoted, becoming seriously ill, having rebellious child or unsupportive mate*

Likes People Who: *Are supportive and submissive, see things their way, cooperate quickly and let them take credit*

Dislikes People Who: *Are lazy and not interested in working constantly, who buck their authority, get independent or aren't loyal*

Is Valuable In Work: *Because they can accomplish more than anyone else in a shorter time and are usually right, but may stir up trouble*

Could Improve If: *They allowed others to make decisions; delegated authority, became more patient, didn't expect everyone to produce as they do*

As A Leader They: *Have a natural feel for being in charge, a quick sense of what will work and a sincere belief in their ability to achieve, but may overwhelm less aggressive people*

Tend To Marry: *Peacefuls who will quietly obey and not buck their authority, but who never accomplish enough or get excited over their projects*

Reaction To Stress: *Tighten control, work harder, exercise more, get rid of offender*

Recognized By: *Fast-moving approach, quick grab for control, self-confidence, restless and overpowering attitude*

— 6 —

The Perfects
(Melancholies)

Family Motto: *"If it's worth doing, it's worth doing right."*

Family Hymn: *"When the Roll is Called up Yonder, I'll Be There"*

Family Verse: *Be ye therefore perfect, even as your Father which is in Heaven is perfect.*

Matthew 5:48

The Perfects sensed from childhood that it was better to be right than popular. With an inbred sense of propriety and manners, they became model children who kept their rooms neat, their toys in even rows, and their Monopoly money in the box. To their neighbors they all seemed to be prodigies as they practiced the piano each morning from 6 to 7 and would rather conjugate French verbs than play video games.

They pleased their teachers by raising their hands before speaking, by passing in their papers on time, and by turning in the truants. Their parents bought them all computers where they stored the grades of their classmates (including the median mark for each exam), calculated the daily comparative value of the dollar, the *peso* and the *yen*, and mastered the complexities of the Federal Reserve System.

One of the Perfects was Valedictorian each year, and several received scholarships to Yale. As adults they chose careers that took intellectual depth, brilliance, talent and attention to details. Several of the Perfects became surgeons, some psychiatrists, professors, artists, musicians, accountants and tax attorneys.

Because of their perfectionistic natures and their pessimistic bent, the whole family could become easily depressed when people disappointed them and circumstances didn't turn out right. They wouldn't verbalize their feelings, and if you asked what the trouble was, they'd say, "Nothing."

Although they don't feel they are critical, and they wouldn't want to be quoted, I know they think the Populars are too noisy and superficial, the Powerfuls too bossy and insensitive, and the Peacefuls too compromising and indecisive. The Perfects didn't intend to be politicians—the whole system seems so unsystematic; yet as they looked at the shallow intellect of the available candidates, they felt a self-sacrificing call to save the nation from the collection of nit-wits trying to lead it nowhere in a hurry. Once involved, the Perfects couldn't leave the political parties unperfected, and they felt deeply about the punctuation of the platforms and the construction of the constitution. Because the Perfects have a passion for history, they see all present problems from a broad perspective, and because their minds think in columns, they can memorize dates, figures, details and allotments, making all those competing around them feel stupid and unprepared.

The Perfects were brought up in ivory towers, giving them a somewhat unrealistic view of the masses below. They believe in the basic goodness of each individual and idealistically look to the day when the slums are slammed shut, the castles closed up, and we all live happily ever after in the suburbs.

Walter Mondale, a member of the Perfect family, felt "he had been blessed with a rare opportunity to speak to America—to stand up for the old democratic principles that had nourished him and to cry out against what he saw as a new politics of selfishness and greed abroad in the land. His campaign, in its haunted last weeks, had become something more to him than a canvass for votes. It had become a witness, a kind of summing up, he said, of 35 years of public life. He paused then and turned away, gazing out at the sky above the clouds. It was as if he were seeing a time draw to an end."[1]

The Perfects are the dreamers and visionaries. They have high standards for themselves and others and sincerely believe that everyone wants to be Perfect like them, if only they knew how. As their strengths are deep, thoughtful and introspective, so their weaknesses are also deep, leading them into depression and despair when nothing seems to be going right.

Although they avoid drawing attention to themselves, the Perfects can become sensitive character actors for they have a unique ability to put themselves into the life of another person and portray their innermost feelings. We can easily picture a Perfect person playing the part of Hamlet, the melancholy Dane, standing on a turret of the Castle Elsinore, meditating deeply about the meaning of life and death, and musing, "to be or not to be, that is the question."

Perfect Summary
Let's do it the right way.

Desire: *Have it right*

Emotional Needs: *Sense of stability, space, silence, sensitivity and support*

Key Strengths: *Ability to organize, set long-range goals; have high standards and ideals, analyze deeply*

Key Weaknesses: *Easily depressed, too much time on preparation, too focused on details, remembers negatives, suspicious of others*

Gets Depressed When: *Life is out of order, standards aren't met and no one seems to care*

Is Afraid Of: *No one understanding how they really feel, making a mistake, having to compromise standards*

Likes People Who: *Are serious, intellectual, deep, and will carry on a sensible conversation*

Dislikes People Who: *Are lightweights, forgetful, late, disorganized, superficial, prevaricating and unpredictable*

Is Valuable In Work: *For sense of details, love of analysis, follow-through high standards of performance, compassion for the hurting*

Could Improve If: *They didn't take life quite so seriously and didn't insist others be perfectionists*

As A Leader They: *Organize well, are sensitive to people's feelings, have deep creativity, want quality performance*

Tend to Marry: *Populars for their personalities and social skills, but soon try to shut them up and get them on a schedule, becoming depressed when they don't respond*

Reaction To Stress: *Withdraw, get lost in a book, become depressed, give up, recount the problems*

Recognized By: *Serious, sensitive nature, well-mannered approach, self-deprecating comments, meticulous and well-groomed looks (Exceptions are hippy-type intellectuals, musicians, poets, who feel attention to clothes and looks is worldly and detracts from their inner strengths)*

The Peacefuls
(Phlegmatics)

Family Motto: *Let's not rock the boat*

Family Hymn: *"Leaning on the Everlasting Arms"*

Family Verse: *Blessed are the peacemakers; for they shall be called the children of God.*

Matthew 5:9

The Peaceful babies were every mother's dream. They seldom cried, slept through the night, and didn't care if they were wet or dry. As toddlers they smiled pleasantly, played with anything available, and loved naps. When the Popular children came over, the Peacefuls laughed at all their antics. They could get serious and deep with the Perfects and were motivated into action by the Powerfuls. They were responders to the initiators of life.

The teachers all loved them because they were no trouble in the classroom, although they seldom got excited over any project and couldn't decide whether to go outside for recess.

As teens they got along with everyone. They would laugh with those who laughed and weep with those who wept. They never demanded their own way and were never offensive. Because the Populars had proven to be more talk than action, the Powerfuls had made the rest of the class feel stupid, and the Perfects were sitting back waiting to be coaxed, the Peacefuls were often thrust into leadership. Once in a control position, they were just, fair, unbiased leaders who were not swayed by emotion or the chance of personal gain.

As adults, they liked jobs that didn't demand creative initiative and where advancement was automatic as long as you did your best and didn't cause trouble. They were drawn to education, the military, administration, counseling and personnel, areas where objectivity and compliance were more important than creativity and self-motivation. They became excellent mediators in the problems of other people but avoided personal conflict at any cost. They resisted change.

The Peacefuls didn't intend to go into politics as it appears fraught with difficulties, conflicts and stress, and demands decisions, new ideas, and endless effort. Since they aren't flashy people and tend to resist responsibility, they didn't want to be in charge of anything, but often they won by default, they became the compromise candidate. Their greatest strength was their lack of obvious weaknesses.

As political leaders they tried to keep everyone content, avoided controversial issues, and healed party rifts. Because they didn't have a thirst for Power and didn't need to be Popular or Perfect, they became the comfortable choice in a contentious selection of candidates. Historically speaking, the Peacefuls weren't noted for innovative legislation but for healing the hurts and binding the wounds.

The *Wall Street Journal* summed up ex-President Gerald Ford, an outstanding member of the Peaceful family, in this way:

"We are told that Michigan civic leaders are hesitant to begin raising money for the usual type of commemorative museum for ex-President Gerald R. Ford. One reason, says his old congressional district's Republican chairman, is that the Ford Presidency was 'a passive Presidency rather than an active one. It was extremely important as a time of healing. But how do you make a monument to something that didn't happen?'

"The chairman has a point there. For a while during these years there was a noticeable letup in the grand domestic schemes, the foreign misadventures and the violent partisanship that had provided most of the drama of American politics for more than a decade, which may make Gerald Ford a leading candidate for the best and biggest memorial of all."[1]

As an excellent example of the Peaceful, one who made it to the top, Gerald Ford exemplifies the low-key strengths; easy-going nature, inoffensive, loved by all, and no obvious weaknesses. Like Ford, Peacefuls are passive, with low creativity, a lack of brilliant ideas, and little ability to excite crowds; but they do behave, stay trouble-free, and heal the hurts of others.

The 1988 campaign spawned a series of Peacefuls, including candidates George Bush, Mike Dukakis and Lloyd Bentsen. Columnist David

Shaw suggests that because of the intense media scrutiny of the 80s, we have chosen leaders who are hard-working, conscientious and dull "... increasingly uninteresting people—gray, bland centrists and technocrats unlikely to drift very far from the middle of the road, either stylistically or ideologically." He lists six Peacefuls and then quips, "if you were having a dinner party and wanted witty, lively, charismatic guests—rather than merely famous, powerful guests—to insure an evening of sparkling conversation, it's not likely that any of these gentlemen's names would be on your invitation list."[2]

The Popular wants the FUN WAY.

The Powerful wants MY WAY.

The Perfect wants the RIGHT WAY.

The Peaceful wants the EASY WAY.

The Peacefuls don't often care whether they're in the show, but if they're cast in a supporting role, they'll do their best and not cause any trouble. The Peacefuls have a low-key sense of humor and a dry wit which sometimes produces a Jack Benny, a Will Rogers or a George Burns.

Peaceful Summary
Let's do it the easy way.

Desire:	*Have no conflict, keep peace*
Emotional Needs:	*Sense of respect, feeling of worth, understanding, emotional support*
Key Strengths:	*Balance, even disposition, dry sense of humor, pleasing personality*
Key Weaknesses:	*Lack of decisiveness, enthusiasm, and energy, no obvious flaws but a hidden will of iron*
Gets Depressed When:	*Life is full of conflict, they have to face a personal confrontation, no one wants to help, the buck stops with them*
Is Afraid Of:	*Having to deal with a major personal problem, being left holding the bag, making major changes*
Likes People Who:	*Will make decisions for them, will recognize their strengths, will not ignore them, will give them re-. spect*

Dislikes People Who:	*Are too pushy, too loud and expect too much of them*
Is Valuable In Work:	*Because they cooperate and are a calming influence, keep peace, mediate between contentious people, objectively solve problems*
Could Improve If:	*They set goals and became self-motivated, they were willing to do more and move faster than expected, and could face their own problems as well as they handle other peoples'*
As A Leader They:	*Keep calm, cool and collected, don't make impul:sive decisions, are well-liked and inoffensive, won't cause trouble, but don't often come up with brilliant new ideas*
Tend To Marry:	*Powerfuls because they respect their strength and decisiveness, but later the Peacefuls get tired of being pushed around and looked down upon*
Reaction To Stress:	*Hide from it, watch TV, eat, tune out on life*
Recognized By:	*Calm approach, relaxed posture, sitting or leaning when possible*

Act I —
The Past
1932–1969

— 8 —

Personalities of The Powerful

From the time I was a child, I've had a fascination with the person-alities of Powerful people, especially those in politics. My Popular-Powerful father always wanted to run for some office, but my reticent Peaceful mother wouldn't let him for fear he wouldn't win. "What if you lost? We'd all be humiliated." Father and I were fearless, and we'd often dream of what might have been.

When I was in grammar school, I wore campaign buttons on my blouse and listened to politicians on the radio. Before I got interested in national politics, I often listened to the Mayor of Boston, James Michael Curley, the personification of the Irish politician. He had white hair — I'd seen his picture in the paper — and he had a deep voice like God himself. He quoted Shakespeare and the Bible with equal ease. He was at home on polished platforms or in "poorfarms."

Tip O'Neill writes in *Man of the House,* Curley "was the greatest orator I've ever heard."[1] Although the word *ethnic* had not been in-vented, Curley managed to surround himself with one of every group imaginable. He had his own "Rainbow Coalition" long before Jesse Jackson created his. Curley would always introduce those on the plat-form in such a colorful way that I, as a child listening to the radio, could picture each one clearly.

He would have an Italian talk about his brothers in Sicily, a Greek share the menu from his restaurant, an Armenian recount his flight to freedom, and a Polish factory worker tell a few jokes.

Members of the unions would rise to praise him, widows would weepingly thank him for wandering into their dear departed's wake, and a crippled child would hobble up to tearfully tell of the new crutches he'd received from the mayor for Christmas. A rabbi would give the blessing and a priest the benediction.

Rumor had it that Curley would go into a poor neighborhood each Sunday afternoon and give out silver dollars to the children who would then run screaming into the tenements waving the money and insuring Curley votes from everyone on the street. Curley had the charm and magnetism of the Popular along with the Powerful desire to control and manipulate.

Curley was a politician's politician, one of the last of the machine bosses, who could control cities by quietly robbing the rich and loudly giving to the poor.

O'Neill notes, "On more than one occasion, the mayor spent so much money on public works the city treasury was broke."[2] While in jail for mail fraud, the mayor ran for governor of Massachusetts and won the election. With his Popular-Powerful personality he could sway any crowd, and convince them happily that black was white. My father would frequently say, "Always listen to him, but never vote for him." Curley's motto was: "Do unto others as they wish to do unto you — but do it first."

Throughout my young life, I learned from Curley and our forever president, Franklin Delano Roosevelt, both Popular-Powerfuls, but it was not until I gained knowledge of the personalities that I really understood Roosevelt and all those other fascinating presidents that have followed him. As I share my views of the past Personalities in Power I hope you will enjoy the stories, learn useful and applicable information, and perhaps decide to run for office yourself.

— 9 —

The Fireside Chat

Franklin Delano Roosevelt (1933-45)

Popular-Powerful

Personality Principle: *Accentuate the positives; eliminate, or overcome the negatives.*

The first president in my memory was Franklin Delano Roosevelt, who came to power in 1932 when I was four years old. Without television and its troops of political prognosticators, we had to get our election eve trends by way of flashing light beams against the darkened sky. The process was reminiscent of Revere's "one if by land, two if by sea." Although I can't remember the election code, I recall sitting at the window with my father and counting beams that foretold the 1932 victory for Roosevelt and the loss for Herbert Hoover.

Franklin came from aristocratic stock, and could trace his family back to colonial days. His father was over 50 when Franklin was born, and he became the darling of his Powerful mother, Sara. As a child, who had long blond curls until he was five, he was exceptionally bright, a born leader for his peers, and had a broad scope of interest. Franklin, brought up alone, never attended public school, but was taught by a governess-tutor until he was 14, when he went away to Groton. Even though he had been raised in affluence, at Groton he was required to live in a 6' by 10' cubicle with sparse furnishings and had to rise at dawn and take a cold shower.

Franklin was a dedicated student in such subjects as German, French, Latin, Greek, English and History. Although he was wealthy, he was impressed with Dr. Endicott Peabody's fiery sermons that it was the duty of the privileged to go into public service and raise the standards of the poor. This basic philosophy was the impetus for Franklin's life of political action and care for those less fortunate.

Because he was slight in stature, Franklin never excelled in team sports, but he did immerse himself in books. He not only loved to read books, he loved books. Because he was so frequently alone, he substituted books for people. He would hold a book before him and look at it with the pleasure of someone gazing into the eyes of a friend. Many of the classics became his friends, and in later years he was able to quote from them freely.

As a child he was excited over the sight of ships and dreamed that someday he might be a naval commander. He studied naval history and waged imaginary battles. His mother told him tales of the family's fleet of sailing ships that went to China, and he played with the remnants found in Grandpa Delano's old sea chest in the attic.

He enjoyed possessions that had special meaning and he became a collector of stamps, first-day covers, gadgets, figures of donkeys, dogs and pigs, flags, cigarette lighters, ship models and Christmas cards. In his presidential years he kept many of these items on his desk where he could pick them up and reminisce over their origin. He dabbled in architecture, enjoyed drawing house plans, and designed two wings that were in fact built on the Roosevelt house in Hyde Park.

From these brief comments of his biography, we can see he receives high marks in background, security, self-worth, stability and intelligence. How can we assess his birth personality and see how it influenced his political life? As we could do with any public figure, we can begin a collection of descriptive words from newspapers, magazines, radio-T.V. reports, and biographies. Those who thought highly of him will provide words expressing his strengths, and those opposed will point out his weaknesses. From these words we will be able to piece together a personality profile.

One clue to show that his Powerful personality was evident in childhood is this anecdote from the book *The Boyhood Days of Our Presidents*. Franklin's mother said her little son was becoming bossy. "My boy, don't give orders all the time. Let the others give them too." In the words of a true Powerful child he answered, "Mummie, if I don't give the orders, nothing would ever happen."[1]

Although Franklin's studious nature and collecting craze initially might seem to put him in the Perfect family, a closer look would show that he liked his collections, not to file them away in a systematic order, but to have them on display before him as friends. He loved to hold the figurines, stroke them, and show them to guests.

Some people in Franklin's position in life would not have been drawn to a career in public service, but his Popular personality and Powerful drive for achievement combined with his sanguine love for people and the direct influence of Dr. Peabody made him a natural for political life.

Franklin had all the social skills of a Popular and was described as having a jaunty flirtatiousness, a winning and inspiring personality, a cavalier and regal attitude. Franklin, as a young man, loved laughter, liked to tell stories, and was the life-of-the-party. His secondary Powerful side was his ambition, his self-discipline, his confidence, his sense of fairness and justice, and his boundless energy.

His mother doted on his charm and humor and spent her lifetime controlling his drive and ambition and trying to keep him tied to her side as long as possible. Any girl he married would have had difficulty with Powerful Sara, but she was overwhelming to Eleanor who was shy, insecure and homely.

Cousin Eleanor had lost her mother in her childhood years and was raised by her grandmother because her Popular father was such a roustabout that he was irresponsible and unreliable as a parent. Eleanor worshipped her father for his charisma and wished she could be more like him. Even though he forgot to come home and see her when he said he would and disappointed her frequently, she idolized him and was devastated when he died as a dissipated alcoholic. His letters were magic to her and she carried them with her to read and reread for the remainder of her life.

In 1927 Eleanor wrote an unpublished article "Ethics of Parents" about a child who adored her father. This autobiographical memory spoke of her feelings for herself as a child.

> *She was an ugly little thing, keenly conscious of her deficiencies, and her father, the only person who really cared for her, was away much of the time; but he never criticized her or blamed her, instead he wrote her letters and stories, telling her how he dreamed of her growing up and what they would do together in the future, but she must be truthful, loyal, brave, well-educated, or the woman he dreamed of would not be there when the wonderful day came for them to fare forth together. The child was full of fears and because of them lying was easy; she had no intellectual stimulus at that time and yet she made herself as the years went on into a fairly good copy of the picture he had painted."* [2]

"Father's own little Nell" lived in a dream world of hope that someday gallant, romantic, colorful father might come home, but he never did.

Quiet, moody, sensitive and lonely, Perfect Eleanor was attracted to Franklin as a replica of her father's virtues without his destructive weaknesses. She transferred her sense of worship to Franklin and her insecure nature couldn't believe he would want to marry her. His acceptance of her, as she was, lifted her confidence in spite of Sara's control over where they lived, what they spent, and how they raised the children. Sara was reputed as having let the children know they were "her children" and their mother only gave birth to them. If they stepped out of her prescribed pattern for their behavior, she would threaten them with being disinherited.

As Eleanor tried to placate her mother-in-law and keep up with her husband, she found out he was having an affair with lovely Lucy Mercer, her social secretary. Lucy had everything Eleanor knew she lacked: charm, grace, beauty, ease with people, giggles, magnetic appeal, and a way with men. Poor Eleanor was abandoned by her father whom she worshipped and rejected by her magnetic husband whom she adored.

Even though mother Sara was flattered by Lucy's attention and didn't like Eleanor, she would not allow a divorce to taint the family and Eleanor would not allow the affair to continue. Lucy was sent packing and the marriage was preserved, but Eleanor never got over the feelings of rejection. She made the best of a bad situation and decided to become an independent person on her own, in case such a situation should ever arise again. Little did she know at the time what a quirk of fate would bring this fascinating, attractive man to a paralyzed position, placing him under her control. Leadership was thrust upon a woman who had wanted to stay in the background.

In 1921, Roosevelt, already active in the New York Democratic party, was stricken with infantile paralysis (polio). Suddenly Eleanor was in charge. Franklin couldn't move and he needed her. While Eleanor dedicated herself to helping Franklin recover, Sara took this disaster as a time for her to tighten her hold on the children, even taking some of them to Europe while Franklin was lying in pain.

He emerged from this attack crippled and with the probable prognosis that he would never walk again. Many others who were stricken at that time fulfilled the depressing prediction, but as a Powerful person, he determined to beat the odds. With Eleanor's round-the-clock attention and her physical care, Franklin began to improve. He took therapy in New York and later at a sanitarium. He grew to love the healing waters of Warm Springs, Georgia, a place that was to become a second home in future years and where he succumbed to death in 1945.

Enduring painful therapy that many other victims could not tolerate,

Franklin improved to the point where he could walk with the aid of heavy metal braces on both legs. During this lengthy recovery time Eleanor's secondary Powerful personality that she did not realize she ever had came bursting forth and she became a political personality in her own right. Initially, she got into the New York state Democratic party to keep Franklin's name before the people. She talked about him, expressed his opinions, and brought people to see him. She felt he had presidential possibilities and she was not going to let his paralysis make him a forgotten man. She achieved her goal so perfectly that she became Powerful and soon people were quoting her opinion and not what she reported from recovering Franklin. From that time on Eleanor's stature grew until later she even dared to express views in public that differed from his.

In spite of his physical handicap, Powerful Franklin ran for Governor of New York, forced himself to travel and campaign, and was elected in 1928. He learned to accentuate his positives and overcome his weaknesses. History books and biographies describe him as Popular. He had a winning personality, he loved laughter, and he was a spellbinding storyteller. He was loquacious, gregarious, and hospitable; he was inventive, imaginative, and inspiring. Aided by Eleanor's constant public relations, Franklin's popularity in New York spread to the nation, and in 1932 he was selected as the nominee for president on the Democratic ticket.

This choice was not a gift as the nation was at a disastrous crossroads at that point. The Roaring Twenties had unwound into a depression, and on the day Roosevelt was inaugurated, he closed all the banks nationwide. Who knows what another man might have done in the crisis Franklin met, but he was an overcomer and a creative genius who stood up in his braces and told us all we could make it.

In his 1933 first inaugural address, he gave hope by stating, "All we have to fear is fear itself." This simple sentence reverberated throughout the country, and even we children could repeat it.

Time correspondent, Walter Shapiro, wrote in November 1987, "The Democratic candidate for president during the dark days of 1932 had few firm economic ideas. Buffeted by conflicting advice, he lamely tried to split the difference. His speeches were a study in contradiction, combining hints of bold spending programs with cries for a balanced budget. If Franklin Roosevelt's approach was inconsistent, even intellectually dishonest, it helped produce a landslide victory over Herbert Hoover and ultimately the New Deal."[3]

Popular FDR seemed to make sense. He was Popular enough to win our support and give hope for the future, but he was also Powerful. Once in office, he showed his frightened, hungry nation that he was in charge. He was decisive, straightforward, courageous, adventurous, daring and self-confident, all traits that were sorely needed by a depressed society. He instituted sweeping changes, created a New Deal and cooked up an alphabet soup of initialed agencies such as the CCC (Civilian Conservation Corps), the AAA (Agricultural Adjustment Act), the NIRA (National Industrial Recovery Act), the SSA (Social Security Act), the FHA (Federal Housing Act), the WPA (Works Progress Administration), and the TVA (Tennessee Valley Authority).

In 1936, when FDR was re-elected, I was eight, one brother was four, and the other was a new baby. My father was 60 and my Peaceful, frightened mother was 40. The company my father had worked for and was to retire from had closed in the Depression, and he was left an unemployed older man with no way to support his young family. Roosevelt's WPA created public service jobs, and my father became a timekeeper on a road construction gang. I was the recipient of little WPA-created dresses worn identically by all the "poor girls" at school. I remember going to a charity Christmas party where an elegant lady presented me with two books of Shirley Temple paper dolls. Even as a child I knew I was on the wrong side of the stage. "Someday I'll be on the stage handing out gifts to the poor children," I promised myself.

Just because the New Deal, Roosevelt's recovery reform, was providing employment and clothing to those in dire need did not mean that all of his programs were met with universal enthusiasm. Many recipients, such as my family, who were not used to being charity cases sometimes resented the doles and kept up a murmur of dissent, calling the New Deal a "raw deal." Many believed that Roosevelt's policies prolonged the Depression.

Historian Clarence B. Carson states,

"The New Deal programs did not end the Great Depression; they delayed recovery and prolonged it. Economically, there is but one route to prosperity, and that is through freedom of enterprise, productivity, and competition. The New Deal hampered enterprise and competition. Production was discouraged by such devices as acreage allotments for farmers, shorter hours of work in industry and reducing the number of people in the labor force. Enterprise was hampered by diverting capital from private hands and spending it for public employment and public enterprises. The proof of the pudding came in the period 1937-1939, when in the midst of prolonged depression, the depression deepened. The stock market crashed again in 1937, though not so loudly. Unemployment rose, until in the course of 1938 it reached the highs of 1933, despite such programs as WPA and the CCC. According to some surveys, it reached 11 million in this period. Higher wages resulting from government encouraged unioniza-

tion and wages and hours legislation contributed to the deepening depression." [4]

FDR was passionate in his beliefs that history would prove him right, and he was willing to assume responsibility for the outcome of his programs. In order to keep his Popularity in tact, FDR instituted what became known as his "Fireside Chats," informal types of radio programs where he took his problems straight to the people. He spoke from the Oval Room, and the next day we would see his picture in the paper as he had sat behind the desk laden with his favorite figurines. Even without television we were able to listen to him and picture him in our minds at the same time. These series of frank conversations with the American public gave even his detractors confidence that he really cared.

FDR had a way with words, innate with the Populars, and one of his writers once said, "Franklin Roosevelt is a better phrase-maker than anybody he ever had around him."

In his second inaugural address he stated, "I see one-third of a nation ill-housed, ill-clad, ill-nourished."

In vetoing a tax bill in 1944 he wrote, "It is not a tax bill but a tax relief bill providing relief not for the needy but for the greedy."

FDR's clever use of his communication skills set him above presidents of the past and increased his Popularity to the point that he became our national father. Even those who wouldn't vote for him had to admit his personal appeal.

According to people's differing points of view, he was a brilliant orator or an arrogant leader lacking in humility when he gave speeches such as the one in Madison Square Garden where he claimed eloquently, "I should like to have it said of my first administration that in it the forces of selfishness and of lust for power met its match. I should like to have it said of my second administration that in it these forces met their master." [5]

By 1940, Hitler was marching through Europe and our fear focus had shifted from starvation to war. We were afraid to change horses mid-stream, so we elected FDR to an unprecedented third term. He promised in his campaign that he'd give assistance to the British: "All aid short of war."

No one wanted war; we had hardly pulled out of the Depression. However, on December 7, 1941, Japanese bombers attacked the American naval base at Pearl Harbor without warning. The attack came as a shocking surprise to the American people and showed that our desire to stay neutral had resulted in wishful thinking and willful blindness.

FDR instantly became Commander-in-Chief, and he fit his role well.

I remember the pictures of him sitting regally on the deck of a ship wrapped in his dark navy cape. It wasn't until I studied history in college that I realized his cape was not only for drama but for a convenient cover-up of his wheelchair. He didn't want us to be reminded that he was physically weakened and couldn't bear to wear his heavy braces.

With his keen sense of history and lifetime study of naval operations, FDR became a commanding legend meeting many times with Winston Churchill, a Popular-Powerful himself. Throughout his time as chief executive, FDR maintained his broad interests in life, never succumbed to self-pity, exhibited valiant energy in spite of physical debilitation, and inspired the world to admiration and respect. He was able to withdraw from the crowds, personally inscribe each book he was given as to which library it should ultimately belong, and select some of his major speeches to be bound as gifts for his family and friends.

Although his strength decreased, his mind remained clear, his memory was remarkable, and he continued his amazing powers of concentration. In spite of his exceptional leadership skills, he was denounced as a hypocrite for putting us into war, after he had clearly stated in a campaign speech in Boston on October 30, 1940, "And while I am talking to you mothers and fathers, I give you one more assurance. I have said this before, but I shall say it again and again and again: Your boys are not going to be sent into any foreign wars."

He was impatient when things didn't go his way, and when the party didn't approve of his choice of Henry Wallace for vice-president, he countered, "Well, damn it to hell, they will go for Wallace or I won't run, and you can jolly well tell them so."

He got angry at those who made mistakes or didn't agree with him. When Cactus Jack Garner, his first vice-president, didn't totally support his plans, he left him out of the inner circle after-cabinet meetings and any important decisions. Cactus Jack, a Popular Speaker of the House, said of his position, "I gave up the second most powerful job in the government for one that didn't amount to a hill of beans ... or a bucket of warm spit."

Franklin was considered unconventional in his political approach, and when the conservatives were overruling his programs, he wanted to add six new judges to the Supreme Court, causing him to be accused of "packing the court." He seemed to enjoy controversy, and once said, "There is nothing I love as much as a good fight." Truly, a Powerful statement.

Although he was noted for the intellectual quality of the advisors he chose and the talent he attracted, FDR spent little time in the selection of a vice-president to run with him for his fourth term. While he had better things to do than interview prospective candidates, his advisors pulled an unknown senator, Harry S. Truman, out of the fields of Missouri for political balance.

The two had very different backgrounds, and although they won as a team, they never developed a close relationship and Truman, as Garner, was not included in many of the high-level discussions, leaving him ignorant of important decisions and policies when he suddenly became president.

When it came time for FDR to decide whether to run for an unprecedented fourth term, his health was so poor that in retrospect he shouldn't have even considered another race. The toll of the war and his constant effort to move had so depleted his energy that he hardly ever got out of his wheelchair. Friends who hadn't seen him for a while were shocked at his appearance and begged Eleanor to keep him from running. Instead she encouraged him to go for it as she sincerely believed the country needed him and a new campaign would brighten up his spirits. And it did. He put aside his pain and fatigue and showed us once again he could rise above almost any set of circumstances.

The applause of the crowds gave him renewed vigor and he even regained enough use of his legs to occasionally stand at the rear of his campaign train and speak to the people. Eleanor pushed him and seldom let him rest. When he won his fourth term, Eleanor became almost a second president, instructing him until he had to push her away. She would bring him papers to sign at the end of a long day when all he wanted was a moment of peace and some uplifting words and he soon turned to his daughter, Anna, as a confidant and advisor.

Biographer Joseph P. Lash wrote, "Eleanor was too independent, too strong ethically, too unrelenting to provide him with the kind of relaxed, unjudging company that he wanted. 'The one thing she was not able to bring him,' wrote her son, James, 'was that touch of triviality he needed to lighten his burden ... she was a woman of commanding dignity and of an almost saintly selflessness, whom all admired and some even loved.'"[6]

It was at Warm Springs where FDR spent his last days in the company of pleasant friends, including Lucy. He was posing for a new portrait when he told the artist, "I'll give you exactly 15 minutes." At the end of 15 minutes he grabbed his head and collapsed, dying shortly of a massive cerebral hemorrhage.

The only president in American history to be elected four times left a legacy of warmth, fatherly concern and inspiration. While controversial, he was never boring, and in the face of attack he never lost his sense of humor.

When he was accused during his last campaign of using tax-payers' money to transport his dog, Fala, he countered, "These Republican leaders have not been content with attacks on me, or my wife, or on my sons. No, not content with that, they now include my little dog Fala. Well, of course, I don't resent attacks ... but Fala does resent them ... I think I have a right to resent, to object to libelous statements about my dog ... When Fala heard these stories, his Scotch soul was furious. He has not been the same dog since."[7]

Franklin Delano Roosevelt had the obvious assets of the charming, witty Popular personality combined with the potent strengths of the commanding Powerful, and his unique skill was being able to use his winning ways without letting us see many of his temperamental weaknesses. Few leaders in history have been able to present such a consistent personality over the years.

FDR's personal secretary Grace Tully summed up his sense of mission, "He simply felt that he had been given a grand opportunity to do something about the problems that beset the nation."[8]

I personally remember the day when the news came across the wires and spoke out from our arched Zenith radio in the kitchen, "The president is dead." He'd been the only president I'd known. Whether we agreed with all his programs or not, we loved him as a father. There was security about knowing he was there in times of poverty, in the throes of war.

Of all our modern presidents, Roosevelt was the one who made the very most of his strengths, overcame his physical weaknesses, and rose above handicaps and pain. Eleanor also was able to put the hurts of infidelity behind her, get beyond her lack of physical beauty and bravely march forward to become the most influential first lady we'd ever known.

We can all learn from Eleanor and Franklin to accentuate our positives and eliminate our negatives. As leaders we must learn to make the best of adverse circumstances and rise above our problems.

Franklin D. Roosevelt

Popular (Sanguine)

Strengths

politics of personality
jaunty flirtatiousness
winning personality, inspiring
amusing, life-of-the-party
loved laughter
happy, friendly & warm
loquacious & gregarious
loved to tell stories
good mimic
hospitable
beloved by all
never boring
imaginative
encouraged all
gave hope
articulate

vibrant voice
dramatic & debonair
cavalier attitude
able to attract talent

Weaknesses

too dramatic
played to the audience
pulled out rhetorical stops
practiced storyteller
stretched the truth
deceptive
feather duster
mama's boy

Powerful (Choleric)

Strengths

self-confident
decisive
willing to accept responsibility
straightforward
sense of fairness & justice
courageous
adventurous
passionate in beliefs
active in spite of pain
aggressive
daring and brave
no self-pity
valiant energy
extraordinary political skills
energetic and resilient

Weaknesses

irritated by others
impatient
looked down on dummies
angry
unconventional
enjoyed controversy
insisted on his own way
frank and abrupt

*Words used to describe FDR's and subsequent president's personalities were taken from newspaper articles, magazines and other print media.

10

"Give 'Em Hell!"

Harry S. Truman (1945-53)

Powerful

Personality Principle: *For the Powerful, the impossible just takes a little longer.*

On April 12, 1945, Harry S. Truman became president, and the next day he told reporters, "When they told me yesterday what had happened, I felt like the moon, the stars and all the planets had fallen on me." So did many of us.

Suddenly we found ourselves without the Commander-in-Chief of an entire generation. His obscure substitute was called a "dirt farmer" or the "haberdasher from Kansas City." We had the same feeling of disappointment one might have had in going to see the great Lionel Barrymore and finding out he was being replaced that night by an understudy.

Even the staunchest Democrats were inwardly shaken when they saw what they had on their hands. From the aristocratic, articulate Roosevelt they went to the brash, earthy Truman, who cussed automatically and was ready to "give 'em hell." He had never attended college and was considered to have a chip on his shoulder because of his humble beginnings.

Although Harry had been in the Senate, he was lacking in knowledge or experience in foreign affairs. As Robert Donovan said, "Roosevelt largely ignored him and excluded him from the innermost discussions of strategy and diplomacy as the Second World War was nearing a climax."[1]

Truman was angry that Roosevelt had left him in such a predicament, and he let us all know his feelings. He said of vice-presidents, "They're about as useful as a cow's fifth teat." All they do is sit around "waiting for a funeral."

There is little doubt that Harry started from below zero in a job that was considered far too big for him; however, we didn't realize that Harry came from a long line of Powerfuls who sprint into action when the chips are down and are challenged by the phrase, "It can't be done."

If the Populars heard those words they would respond, "Good, it didn't sound like much fun." The Perfect would say, "Oh, really? I had just figured out how to do it right." The Peaceful would answer, "I'm relieved because it sounded too much like work." Only the Powerful would state, "That's what you think. Just watch me!"

One of the most consistent Powerful traits is the confidence that anything can be solved with the right person in charge. The words "it can't be done" just spur them on to victory. The impossible just takes a little longer. Once at work on the impossible, the Powerfuls will not quit even if the facts show they can't succeed. This trait is a positive in that the Powerfuls can and do accomplish more than others in a shorter time, but it becomes a weakness when they will not listen to advice and insist on fighting to the death.

Harry Truman is a fascinating example of a man with humble beginnings who wouldn't take no for an answer.

Because Harry's father John was a short man nicknamed "Peanuts," he had to exert his Power in feisty ways. He grew up in Missouri in the late 1800s where the family literally fought for its life in border warfare. He became scrappy and defensive at a very early age. He would wheel and deal in anything and at one point he made an exchange that put 500 goats in his backyard. He dabbled in local politics and didn't let anyone push him around. One day when John was a witness at a trial, the lawyer accused him of lying. John jumped out of his seat and chased the big lawyer out of the courthouse ending the case. It is obvious where Harry got his taste of politics and his incendiary nature.

Harry's mother Martha was less controversial but still a hardy soul with a true pioneer spirit. She taught her children that waste and laziness were tools of the devil and that hard work was next to godliness. She called herself a "light-foot Baptist" meaning she was devout but not legalistic and saw nothing wrong in a little dancing if the beat was right, no matter what the deacons thought.

From childhood Harry was extremely nearsighted and his wearing glasses excluded him from athletics in school. Instead he read books about heroes and leaders and by the time he was 12 he had read the Bible through twice.

His mother played the piano, and she began teaching him when he was a child. At age 13 he started with two lessons a week and rose at 5 o'clock each morning to practice for two hours before school. This Powerful family believed strongly in the work ethic, and Harry learned that if you didn't work you didn't eat. Each child had specific jobs, and it never occurred to them not to complete their chores.

Harry's first official job was with L. J. Smith Construction Co., at $35 a month. The tough-talking men made fun of his thick glasses and love of classical music, and it was from this crude group that Harry learned his salty language and became determined to be a winner.

In World War I the Kansas City National Guard was called up and Harry was sent to Germany where he was part of heavy fighting. As a captain, and later as a major, he was in charge of an undisciplined group whom he soon brought under control. Harry learned in the military to strike first before the enemy finds you, and he carried this practice over into politics. Once he became president and emerged from the uncomfortable role as underdog with no control, he came into his own Powerful personality.

Harry decided once again to show us who was boss. Exhilarated by the sense of combat, Harry came out swinging. When the 80th Congress refused to rise to his leadership, he branded them as a "good-for-nothing, do-nothing" group. These words did not inspire them to cheerful support when he ran for re-election, and he found himself in a frequent position of trying to eat up some of his more salty sentences.

Scorned as a "little man" and a "misfit," he had a contempt for his critics that led him into impulsive actions typical of the Powerful personality. His decision to drop the atomic bomb has been debated ever since that time, and it so incensed his stolid Peaceful wife, Bess, that she packed up and went back to Kansas City as a sign of her disapproval. But Harry was buoyant, and he continued to bounce back after defeats. He had remarkable stamina and was determined to do the impossible. Being hit over the head just made him emerge taller.

When it was time to run for re-election, even his own party wasn't consistent in their support. He was disgusted with the lot of them, and determined he would run and win. Governor of New York, Thomas Dewey, previously defeated by Roosevelt, was to be his opponent, and few gave Truman much of a chance.

I remember being on the debate team in college on the Dewey side of the issue and coming up with what I thought were brilliant statements on why Harry couldn't win. Dewey ran a Peaceful, non-confrontational campaign, maintaining the dignity of a sure winner, while Harry, on his 30,000-mile, whistle-stop campaign, got out and "gave 'em hell."

Somehow his vintage American, earthy character quietly caught on, and with the headlines "Dewey wins" already printed, we woke up to find that the country had gone wild about Harry. He let us know, "I told you so," and made it clear he had been vindicated from his critics. The impossible just took more determination and Harry made it happen.

Was there ever a Powerful who laid it on the line so clearly? We never had to worry about what Harry was thinking; he told us. While FDR's Powerful traits were modified by his refined upbringing and lightened by his Popular personality, Harry's lack of finesse and his forthright phrases defined his feisty spirit, and his insecure sense of worth caused him to rattle his cage loudly and sometimes overstep his normal presidential bounds.

Robert Donovan said, "He had a weakness for rushing into action without fully weighing the consequences."[2]

His strong Powerful need for control showed all too clearly when he locked horns with another Powerful, General Douglas MacArthur, who took pleasure in making policy statements without checking them with the president, for whom he had little personal respect.

While the debate of who was right will go on into political history, the way in which Truman chose to dismiss MacArthur for insubordination turned the sympathies toward the general, who had a great sense for theatrics. Afraid that MacArthur would resign before he had a chance to fire him, Harry told an aide that MacArthur wouldn't resign on him, "... I want him fired!" Harry canceled his plans to use the proper military channels and gave out a press release from Washington before informing the general of his decision. A soldier picked up the news on the wire, called the general's wife, who then broke the news to her husband. Even those who sympathized with the president's decision deplored the manner in which it was executed, and Senator Robert Taft called for Truman's impeachment. By the time General MacArthur gave his "old soldiers never die; they just fade away" speech before Congress, the American public was sitting tearfully in the palm of the general's hand.

Harry said of his MacArthur situation, "You have to decide what is right to do and then do it, even if it is unpopular." And of his time in office, "I have tried to give it everything that was in me."

When critic Paul Hume gave daughter Margaret's maiden vocal concert a poor review, Harry sent him an angry, hand-written note, complete with unprintable expletives.

On April 8, 1952, Truman, in a tussle with a lengthy strike by steel workers, seized the steel mills in what he declared a national emergency. Lyndon Johnson, a fellow Democrat with eyes on the White House, declared, "Truman's order showed a trend toward dictatorship."[3]

The press called him a Caesar, an American Hitler, Mussolini, an author of evil, a bully, a usurper, a law breaker, and an architect of a labor dictatorship. The issue went to the Supreme Court, and they declared his order to be unconstitutional. Bombastic Harry had struck out.

While much of the public found Harry's hot tongue and trigger-quick replies to be a humorous relief after FDR's almost god-like image, his own party cooled on his short fuse and spread the word that he would not be supported as a candidate again. Truman, in disbelief and disappointment, knew his days were numbered when his own party, whom he had served faithfully, rejected him, an incumbent president, for Adlai Stevenson.

Although Harry's heart wasn't in it, he agreed to a whistle-stop tour for Stevenson and as the train progressed, Harry's love for declamation warmed him up to such a degree that the people's response to him was more enthusiastic than to the candidate himself. Thousands yelled, "Give 'em hell, Harry," and I wonder if the Democrats wondered whether they had made a mistake in their selection.

After the defeat of Stevenson and the inauguration of General Dwight D. Eisenhower, Truman said in an interview with John Snyder, "Two hours ago I would have said 5 words and been quoted in 15 minutes in every capitol of the world. Now I could talk for two hours and nobody would give a damn."

While Harry's clear words were not considered on a par with Roosevelt's or Churchill's, he was a prolific writer.

Walter Isaacson in *Time* comments on this part of Truman's life: "The last President to leave a cache of candid correspondence was Harry Truman, who wrote more than 1,200 letters just to his wife. Not only do they reveal his delightful personal style, they provide convincing insights on matters ranging from his dealings with Stalin to his decision to drop the atom bomb. There is even a book filled with letters that Truman wrote in moments of pique, then wisely filed away unmailed. His diaries, though intermittent, are no less revealing. In June 1945, as General Douglas MacArthur was closing in on the islands near Japan, Truman's entries foreshadow the bitter personal battles that lay ahead. He describes the general as 'Mr. Prima Donna, Brass Hat Five Star MacArthur' in one entry and adds, 'He's worse than the Cabots and the Lodges—they at least talked to one another before they told God what to do.'"[4]

When Harry looked back on his time as president he said, as a true Powerful, "I never did give anybody hell; I just told the truth and they thought it was hell."

Although Harry left office as a questionable leader, history has been kinder to him than his own party. His words are often quoted today as brilliant and Paul Simon, 1988 candidate for president, called himself a Truman democrat and revived interest in Harry as a folk hero. If Harry were here he'd state proudly, "I told you so."

Harry S. Truman

Powerful (Choleric)

Strengths

frank & outspoken
loyal & honest
bombastic
punctual & decisive
goal-oriented
delightful personal style
hardworker
gutsy
secure and self-confident
theatrical
buoyant
good-natured
remarkable stamina
courageous
strong-willed
earthy
sincere
shrewd
aggressive
excited by challenges
didn't need to be popular

Weaknesses

an American Hitler
architect of labor
dictatorship
seized authority
cussed automatically
impulsive and erratic
outspoken and abrupt
lacking in finesse
bully, usurper
chip on his shoulder
irritated and angry
trigger-quick replies
short-tempered and
   hot-tongued
vindictive
disdainful and brash
ridiculed opponents
wanted revenge

11

"We Like Ike"

Dwight David Eisenhower (1953-61)

Peaceful

Personality Principle: *Everyone gets along with the Peaceful personality.*

After 20 years of Democratic rule led by two Powerful presidents, the country was ready for a change. We'd been disheartened by the Depression and worn down by the war. We wanted to put it all behind us and be normal again. We'd won the war and who better to lead us to national peace-time victory than genial General Dwight D. Eisenhower.

So often at the end of a certain era we look for someone who is totally different in personality from what we've had. We'd lived with the forceful personality of Roosevelt, who had controlled an entire generation, followed by Truman's impulsive need to take charge. We'd had the New Deal followed by the Fair Deal, and Dwight D. Eisenhower offered an Honest Deal.

"Let's drive out the crooks and the cronies." Let's keep it "clean as a hound's tooth." We'd had hot, and we wanted cool. Ike was typical of the Peacefuls who quietly do what is expected of them, walk the middle line of life and manage to offend no one. They smile, nod in agreement, and pacify the contentious. They will agree with either side of an issue if it will keep people happy. Their low-key personality doesn't mean they have nothing intelligent to say; they just reserve their wit for the right time and have no need to add a comment to every conversation. Peacefuls are content to listen to others and give at least token agreement, two traits that make them very popular with the Populars. They are willing to do what pleases others and not buck authority, so they are favorites with the Powerfuls who usually marry one of them. The Peacefuls are able to sit quietly for hours and work on plans, impressing the Perfects. Everyone gets along with the Peaceful Personality and we all liked Ike.

The general had come from humble midwestern beginnings, as Truman had. The Eisenhower family originally came from Germany to Pennsylvania in 1732 to find freedom of worship. Although the word Eisenhower means *Iron Axe,* they were pacifist Quakers who lived by the Golden Rule and felt self-reliance and hard work were the basics of life.

As a child, Ike peddled the family's surplus vegetables, and twice a week he got up at 4:30 A.M. to make the fire and cook the breakfast. In high school, his father got him a job stoking boilers in the creamery where he worked, and in between the shoveling, Ike would read and doze. Even though his parents were Peacefuls and were against war, Ike studied history and was fascinated with military heroes. Much to the family's dismay, he took the examinations for West Point and Annapolis, where his score of 87.7 was the highest. He chose West Point, where his graduating class of 168 men had 56 who ultimately became generals.

He was promoted steadily and recognized for his rational reasoning abilities. He could keep his head while all around him were losing theirs. In typical Peaceful fashion, he had always quietly done the right thing at the right time, pleased his superiors, and not caused any shock waves anywhere along the line. He had a sense of how to get along with others, and he didn't need to have his own way. His easygoing nature, wide grin, and willingness to compromise made him a hit with the hotheads, and Truman even suggested him as a possible Democratic candidate for president. He lunched weekly with Churchill and he personally knew Roosevelt, Stalin, Adenauer, and DeGaulle. He was in a league with Generals Marshall, Bradley, and MacArthur, but Eisenhower alone was considered the peace-loving man of war. As the old Latin saying, Ike was "Gentle in manner, strong in deed."

In the book, *Ike the Soldier,* author Merle Miller compared Ike with General Ulysses S. Grant.

> *"Both Eisenhower and Grant maintained a consistent calmness amid either triumph or adversity; Ike's command of himself is a much-repeated theme among those who recall him. In both Ike and Grant, this quality sprang from a complete self-confidence that underlay an apparent modesty. In both, furthermore, self-*

confidence sprang in turn from a consistency and fixity of purpose that would not let them be diverted from their goals ...

"Throughout the discouraging early phases of the battle, Ike maintained the calmness and underlying confidence that were so characteristic of him, while many other Allied leaders grew nervous and testy." [1]

His grandson David, in his book, *Eisenhower: At War, 1943-1945,* says the General was "known for his affability, his abilities as a negotiator and his talent for reconciling differences among strong personalities." [2] All these traits are typical of the Peacefuls, who are always willing to mediate between people who are at opposite extremes.

Playing upon Truman's inability to end the Korean War that had erupted before the European one had been put to rest, Ike promised in his campaign that he would go to Korea and see firsthand what was going on. We were so tired of war, hardships and scrap drives, that we praised his willingness to make the trip and knew with his experience as a general he would settle the issue of war once and for all time.

Ike in his uniform had the aura of a hero, and we were in need of one. We handed him the country to take care of, and we all settled in for a long winter's nap.

Charles R. Morris said of Eisenhower, "He was a president shrewd enough to know when the country was on a winning streak, and self-disciplined enough to keep his hands out of the machinery." [3]

We all wanted peace, and Ike Peaceful became our "Balm of Gilead." Ruth Montgomery said of Eisenhower that he was "eager to heal the partisan wounds." [4] While we all liked Ike, he was never known for exciting or creative ideas or for many innovative programs. But then we asked little of him but that he leave us alone and let us return to normal.

Eisenhower was an all-purpose, middle-of-the-road president whose greatest strength was his lack of obvious weaknesses. As a typical Peaceful, Ike avoided personal confrontation. When his chief of staff, Sherman Adams, admitted that he had accepted a vicuna coat and some blankets from Bernard Goldfine, Ike looked the other way. Compared to the immoral hi-jinks we have seen in the political arena of late, the gift of a coat and blanket seems trivial, but in the climate of 1958 the headlines made Adams sound like a member of the Mafia.

All Peacefuls resist change and typical Eisenhower was reluctant to part with Adams. When asked why, he answered simply, "I need him." When discipline was demanded by party leaders, Eisenhower sent his aides to do his work, and Adams then resigned.

Later Adams wrote in his memoirs, "Any presidential appointee whose presence in the administration becomes an embarrassment to the president for any reason whatsoever has no choice but to submit his resignation."[5]

Although Ike could plan an invasion, his vision began to dim in time of peace. Nelson Rockefeller, who served under Presidents Roosevelt, Truman and Eisenhower, felt that the Eisenhower administration "was drifting from crisis to crisis, was preparing its plans and managing matters of state on a month-to-month, year-to-year basis, while America's position in the changing world required planning that reached from today over 5 years, over 10 years, into the farthest foreseeable future."[6]

Historian Theodore White found Rockefeller himself to be a Popular-Powerful man of "total security, total confidence, total cheeriness ... one of the sunniest, most expansive and outgoing personalities of American politics."[7]

No wonder Nelson saw Ike as adrift on the ship of state. Other critics murmured that Ike was a remote and detached manager who didn't have any idea what was really going on.

When Lyndon Johnson was Senate Majority Leader, he looked down on Eisenhower's ability and didn't think Ike knew what a bill was or even if he had any. One night after a frustrating visit with Ike, where he couldn't get a definitive answer from him, Johnson roared "that man does not deserve to be president!"[8]

Truman disliked his successor but, according to Tip O'Neill's report, he was very protective of Mrs. Eisenhower and her reported problems with alcohol. In typical, direct style Truman said, "Let me tell you something. Some of the newspapers are making snide remarks about Mrs. Eisenhower, saying she has a drinking problem. Now it wouldn't surprise me if she did, because look what the woman has to put up with."[9]

Referring to the rumor, not confirmed until years later, that Ike had an affair with his chauffeur, Kay Summersby, Truman blew up. "I've got no use for the man and I don't give a damn what you say about him."[10]

Truman also stated, "The General doesn't know any more about politics than a pig knows about Sunday."[11] One thing about Harry, when he opened his mouth you knew he'd be "giving hell" to someone.

The majority of the public looked at Ike's strengths and not his weaknesses. Although he was relaxed, witty and appealing, Ike never had the Popular charisma of FDR. He was able to win the European war, but he was no fighter on the home front. As Gerald Ford was to be in the future, Dwight Eisenhower was a man for his hour: no more and no less.

One of Eisenhower's most winning Peaceful traits was his humility. From his experience in directing the movements of troops in and out of battle, he had been constantly aware of how small a cog he was in the vast wheel of war. In 1945, when being honored in London, Dwight Eisenhower stated, "Humility must always be the portion of any man who receives acclaim earned by the blood of his followers and the sacrifices of his friends."

After years of the ultimate Commander-in-Chief, Franklin Roosevelt, who easily controlled with confidence, and the feisty Harry Truman, who "gave 'em hell," the Peaceful, humble, relaxed and smiling Ike was a welcome and restful change. He became president not because of life-long political ambitions, but as the quiet answer to the call of duty.

Another attribute Ike had was patience. He didn't need it all done yesterday as the Powerful demands. He didn't want to offend, and he was willing to wait until the time was right to move.

In a letter to a friend he wrote, "So all I am trying to say is that the change is gradual. It is not so rapid as to be completely satisfying, even to a person who, I think, is as patient as I am; certainly, I try to be patient."[12]

Had Eisenhower been a Powerful personality instead of a Peaceful one, he might have hastily, upon inauguration, thrown out the "welfare-state psychology" of the New Deal, but instead he applied an objective, businesslike point of view to the transition and refused to be influenced by outside pressures. He possessed persuasive powers typical of the Peaceful phlegmatic person and when he couldn't win a quiet victory, he would resort to the veto.

On one vetoed bill he wrote to Congress, "This kind of legislation, this expectation of something-for-nothing, weakens our national fabric and with each occurrence leaves it more seriously impaired. The spread of this expectation and its reflection in our increase of such legislation are profoundly disturbing for the future of America."

Ike was not influenced by party bosses; he was an outsider and had no future political goals. He just wanted to do a good job and go home. When he was given the use of "Shangri-La," a retreat in the Catoctin Mountains of Maryland, he winced at any place with such a fancy name, and he changed it to "Camp David" in honor of his father. Had Ike not changed the name, President Carter's efforts with Begin and Sadat might not have been the Camp David Agreement but the Shangri-La Settlement!

Even though Eisenhower was noted as a successful general, he never liked war's effects and he turned from personal conflict of any type. In his 1953 inaugural address, he said, "Since this century's beginning a time of tempest has seemed to come upon the continents of the earth."

He wanted to use his strategic skills to calm the times of tempest, not to fight eternal wars. He was willing to give a little here and there to avoid upsetting anyone, and he didn't need the credit for his own ego, a rare trait in a political hero.

He believed strongly in the delegation of authority and he surrounded himself with the ablest team of men he could acquire. He wanted businesslike methods of government and he based his choices on "experience, ability, character, and standing in their own communities." With quiet resolve, Eisenhower and his business associates steered the country away from the welfare state it had become to the free enterprise system we accept as the norm.

Although the benign general did not want involvement in any new wars, conflict around the world kept creeping up before him. The Korean truce talks bogged down, and Eisenhower had to decide whether to push North Korea back to the Yalu River, a venture that would call for more American troops at a time when the country was longing for peace, or accept the divided country.

Thirty-four thousand Americans had already died in Korea, and so Eisenhower signed the Panmunjom Peace Treaty on July 27, 1953. Next, Eisenhower aimed for some cooperative control of the atom bomb and, after much delay, the Russians became part of the International Atomic Energy Agency. They refused, however, to approve Eisenhower's "open skies" plan of mutual inspection of military establishments.

Next came the Vietnam problem, which had been growing more critical with each passing year. The French were tired of battling the Communist invaders, but Eisenhower knew that allowing Vietnam to fall would lead to the demise of Laos and Cambodia, and the spread of Communist control. He was faced with the same type of decision he had made in Korea: either go all the way or accept the division. On July 21, 1954, the Geneva Agreement was signed creating North and South Vietnam. Even though Eisenhower never sent troops to the area, he did all he could to support the Saigon government, including about 1,000 American "advisors."

Hardly had the ink dried on the treaty when the Communists began shelling Quemoy, an island off Formosa where Chiang Kai-shek and two million anti-Communist Chinese had fled in 1949. To preserve a free Formosa, Eisenhower took a hard line, asked Congress to support his stand, and let it be known he might use atomic weapons if provoked. The general's decisions met with severe criticism and verbal attacks from a war-weary country, but the enemy invasion never took place.

The question of whether Eisenhower should run again had been asked repeatedly since he was elected, but his heart attack of September 24, 1955, seemed to provide the answer. He recovered from the attack quickly, reviving hopes that were dashed again when he needed surgery for ileitis. The odds were that he wouldn't run, but his underlying stubborn streak, so typical of the Peaceful, and an OK from Mamie caused him to say, "Why not?" His slogan was "peace, prosperity, and progress," but the campaign was far from peaceful.

In spite of the attacks made on him, Eisenhower stayed above the fray and won the day. He surpassed his own previous landslide.

We still liked Ike.

Eisenhower had yet to face the Suez Canal Crisis, the defense of Lebanon, the Sputnik scare, the U-2 incident, Castro's control of Cuba, Khrushchev's shoe banging, and the criticism for sending troops into Little Rock. He always did what he felt was right, whether or not it was popular. As the old soldier he marched straight ahead, played according to the rules, and always responded to the call of duty.

Contrary to Roosevelt and Truman, who were both Powerful and who kept their vice-presidents at a long arm's length, Eisenhower was not concerned with power for its own sake, and he gave Richard Nixon authority in many areas. Ike asked his opinion and seated him across from him at meetings of the Cabinet and National Security Council. He sent him on international missions, and historians feel that Nixon was the best-utilized vice-president of this century.

When Nixon campaigned against Kennedy, a young Democratic Catholic, logic made Nixon the winner. Eisenhower gave him his low-key blessing, and even did some campaign appearances, but many feel it was too little too late.

The American public loved the genial general, but when his time was up, they were ready to replace age with youth, wisdom with vigor, Peace with Popularity and Power.

Dwight D. Eisenhower

Peaceful (Phlegmatic)

Strengths
humble & modest
courageous
will of iron
nerves of steel
calm & casual
honest
good listener
spoke cautiously
persuasive
open to other opinions
straightforward
compromising
willing to delegate
candid yet tactful
able to accept criticism
engaging grin
self-disciplined
mantle of popularity
affable
aura of a hero
negotiator
reconcilor
soldier-statesman
million-volt personality
instinctive good will
fundamental
middle-of-the-roader
consistent calmness
quiet self-confidence
apparent modesty
fixity of purpose

Weaknesses
indecisive
hesitant
detached and inattentive
content to reign not rule
drifting & dreaming
avoided confrontations
weak
remote
unsure & confused
deceptive
unyielding
a waif with a winning
  smile

— 12 —

Nature vs. Nurture

For years there has been a debate over whether we inherit our personality or whether we are born as blank pages waiting for our circumstances to write our script. Heredity vs. environment has been an enigma equal to the chicken and the egg. Recently scientists have come up with impressive evidence that "heredity has a greater influence on one's personality and behavior than either one's upbringing or the most crushing social pressure. The debate over what has been called 'nature vs. nurture' seems to be taking a decisive turn."[1]

In a scholarly report published in the *Journal of Personality and Social Psychology*, researchers for the Minnesota Center for Twin and Adoption Research have concluded that our personality is determined by our genes and that our environment influences and molds our inborn traits. Although the study does not use the four basic personality patterns, the characteristics they tested fit our terms. As reported in the *Journal*, the evaluations were made on:

- Leadership, dominance, dedication to hard work, achievement, taste for revenge — all traits of the Powerful Personality.
- Social potency, cheerful and optimistic, capacity for being caught up in imaginative experiences, propensity to talk to strangers, liking to be the center of attention — all traits of the Popular Personality.
- Cautiousness, avoiding conflict, risks and dangers, conformity, respecting tradition and authority, following the rules — all traits of the Peaceful Personality.
- Perfectionism, orderliness, careful planning, rational decisions,

tendency to become lost in thought and abstractions — all traits of the Perfect Personality.

In proving that we inherit our basic personality, the University brought together 348 sets of twins, including 44 pairs of identical twins, reared apart. After six days of testing and more than 15,000 questions, the study showed amazing similarities in the identical twins, even though they had not seen each other since infancy and were raised in different environments.

One set of identical twins who had been separated four weeks after birth in 1940 were both named Tim, both drove the same model blue Chevrolet, chain-smoked Salems, chewed their fingernails, owned dogs named Toy and vacationed on the same strip of beach in Florida.

Psychologist David Lykken of the Minnesota project stated, "the evidence is so compelling that it is hard to understand how people could *not* believe in the strong influence of genetics on behavior."[2]

Applying this theory personally to my adopted son, we could conclude that when I received him at three months of age, he already had within him the deep, serious melancholy nature he has today. His case worker told me he had never smiled and would lie in the crib and stare at the people around as if he were analyzing them. He had a Perfect personality from the start, and he has never changed.

As adoptive parents, Fred and I have influenced him in becoming business-minded, in giving him basic manners, and in instilling spiritual truth, self-confidence and bearing. His inborn personality had nothing to do with us, but in providing a nurturing environment, we have influenced the finished product.

As we review the past presidents, we can see verification of the inherited personality, plus the direction given by the parents and the childhood circumstances. Franklin Roosevelt and John Kennedy had similar birth personalities. From the earliest of reports they were both born leaders with Powerful potential. They also had the natural charm of the Popular, and a way with words. People were attracted to them because of their obvious magnetism, their optimistic approach to life, and their colorful ability to make every occasion an event.

Their differences came in how they were raised. Even though both were wealthy, FDR was an only child, groomed as a gentleman, educated in the classics, with no great need to go out into the world and make a living. Had Roosevelt been born a Peaceful, he might have gratefully settled into Hyde Park and become a country squire. Had he been a Perfect, he might easily have lost himself in his books and become a scholar. Because he had the Powerful urge to lead and the Popular personality to make people want to follow him, he left the family comfort zone and ventured out to find purpose in helping those less fortunate.

Kennedy's environmental difference, as we will see in the following chapter, came from the driving family force to achieve both money and status and show those Back Bay Brahmins that an Irishman could get to the top. The family demands for winners and Jack's anointing for the presidency by his father amplified his controlling nature and put him into a perpetual overdrive.

Both FDR and JFK had the same temperament pattern, but the intensity of Jack's upbringing caused him to be more eager and impulsive. He *had* to be the winner. Where FDR was drawn to politics to serve the people, JFK was programmed into leadership to serve his father's interests. He seemed to have little choice.

Truman and Eisenhower had similar midwest, down-on-the-farm backgrounds where the work ethic was a religion, but their birth personalities were diametrically opposite. Harry's Powerful drive, not tempered by any Popular, light-hearted nature like Roosevelt and Kennedy, made him a president who *had* to be in control and who wasn't going to let people and pressures change his mind. Because he and MacArthur had the same stubborn nature, neither of them would budge an inch. Truman won the victory but MacArthur had the last word.

Eisenhower was opposite in personality. He was born a Peaceful and wanted to avoid personal conflict if at all possible. He quietly compromised instead of insisting upon his own way, and he fought, not to win wars, but to establish Peace.

As we look at John Kennedy's life, we will see both his inherited personality and the influence his upbringing and circumstances made upon it.

Camelot

John F. Kennedy (1961-63)

Popular-Powerful

Personality Principle: *We inherit our personality and our environment modifies our behavior.*

The obvious heir to the Eisenhower throne was Richard Nixon, his dutiful vice-president. However, Ike never appeared comfortable with him, and couldn't bring himself to wholeheartedly endorse him. Although he included him in governmental strategy meetings much more than Roosevelt did with Truman, he seemed to leave him stranded on the front step of sociability.

At the beginning of the 1956 campaign, a friend remembers journeying with Nixon to the Eisenhower farm at Gettysburg for a major press conference kicking off the campaign. According to historian Theodore White, "When the ceremony was over, President Eisenhower jovially beckoned to two of his cronies and invited them into the farmhouse with him. Nixon, standing beside his friend on the lawn, watched the little group enter the farmhouse, then turned to his friend and remarked bitterly, as the friend remembers, 'Do you know he's never asked me into that house yet.'"[1]

Because Nixon saw himself as being left out on the lawn alone, he wanted desperately to win the presidential plum on his own. As a Perfect-Powerful, he was going to do it right and show them he didn't need to ride on anyone's coattails.

Running against the vice-president with his years of governmental experience was an unlikely opponent: John Fitzgerald Kennedy. White reports, "He and his men had planned them a campaign that seemed utterly preposterous — to take the youngest Democratic candidate to offer himself in this century, of the minority Catholic faith, a man burdened by wealth and controversial family, relying on lieutenants scarcely more than boys, and make him president, one that would sweep out of the decade of the sixties America's past prejudices, the sediment of yesterday's politics, and make a new politics of the future."[2]

Indeed a preposterous plan! Yet in Eisenhower's last years we'd seen him age through heart and stomach problems and a small stroke. He was no longer quite the *macho* hero he had been after the war we were trying to forget. He was a general no longer in command of the troops. It was time for the old soldier and all he stood for to fade away.

We were excited by youth and we loved the way Kennedy ran up the stairs to any waiting plane and turned at the top to wave a personal farewell to each one of us. We felt part of the family football games, and we all wanted to have fun and feel young again.

Charles Morris in *Time of Passion* explains:

> *"Kennedy offered an attitude, a sense of omnicompetence that had been missing during the Eisenhower years, a style of problem solving — cool, pragmatic, non-ideological to be sure, but brimming with confidence that the world could be made a much better place than it was. ...*
>
> *"Kennedy was acutely aware that he was the adventurous alternative, and he and his entourage self-consciously adopted a coolly heroic mien."[3]*

The 1960 Kennedy-Nixon debate gave a national platform on television to the challenger. He was able to exude charm and vigor, youth and vitality. Although the debate was short on significant substance, it was long on Irish style and wit.

In the wake of Peaceful Eisenhower, we were happy to hear the Kennedy war cry, "I will get the country moving again," and just enough of America fell into line.

With the close victory of Kennedy over Nixon, we were transported into Fairyland. Pack up the Depression and the Wars in an old kit bag and smile, smile, smile. Jack always smiled. Not only did we have a Popular-Powerful president, but we had a Perfect princess. Following Eleanor, Bess and Mamie, hardly a beauty pageant line-up, we had elegant, charming, classy Jackie. We watched everything she wore with covetous attention, and we all ran out to buy pill-box hats.

Jackie had an air of mystery about her as every fairy princess must have, and she seemed so secure in social situations. We stood with her next to the queen, the wives of assorted European prime-ministers, and we were so proud when she put them all to shame. We didn't even blame her when she took one look at the White House and knew it had to be done over before she could feel at home. Jackie dressed perfectly, charmed dignitaries perfectly, decorated perfectly and entertained perfectly. Jackie was Perfect, and we could understand why she didn't want to play football with the family. No one thought of asking how much she spent on clothes or whether she borrowed her gowns from French designers.

The White House became Camelot as it was the setting for lavish state dinners and the stage for a continuous stream of Hollywood celebrities. The front door was always open and there was new style, elegance and zest for life — or better said, *joie de vivre*, as Jackie preferred French.

When our princess tired of entertaining, she would vacation on the yacht of Greek shipping tycoon, Aristotle Onassis, and we would pretend we were with her. In retrospect those little trips may not have been so innocent as we assumed they were, but we weren't looking for trouble; we just wanted to live happily ever after.

Jack's presenting personality was Popular. He was fun-loving, charming, even intoxicating. He exuded sex-appeal, whether in a T-shirt or in a tuxedo. He had a sense of humor, was a spontaneous storyteller, and was always the center of attention. He was able to look presidential without being pompous, and could shine brightly while standing next to superstars.

Nancy Dickerson, Washington reporter, said Jack took "unabashed delight at being at the summit."[4] Jack's whole life had been spent in preparation for "the summit," even though his family had humble beginnings.

Great-grandfather Patrick Kennedy emigrated from Ireland in 1848 during the potato famine and arrived in Boston penniless. He took a job as a barrel-maker and let his children know they had to work hard to overcome their immigrant background. In those days, Boston was a bastion of Back Bay Brahmins, and the new poor Irish were looked down upon as slaves. They could find only menial tasks and it soon became fashionable to have an Irish maid or two.

Patrick's second generation son, P.J., couldn't accept his non-acceptance, and he determined to rise above his lowly status. He quit high school to go to work, first as a stevedore, and later as a bartender. By hard work and with a good personality, he soon owned a saloon and later went into the wholesale whiskey business. He raised his family with the iron hand fathers exerted in those days, and no one dared buck his authority.

The fastest way for an Irishman to raise his community status was to enter politics. P.J., who was assumedly a Popular-Powerful, got into ward politics in East Boston, and soon people knew if you needed a favor, go see P.J. He was on the rising crest of Ward Boss politics, and he was a natural.

He was elected to the state House of Representatives at the age of 28, and later became a state senator. With these positions came a certain amount of local power and the chance to be respected as a leader.

P.J. never lost any opportunities to move up the Irish social ladder, and he taught his only son Joseph how to manipulate people and control cash. Joe went the rounds with his father, and often saw how the one man-one vote rule meant little in Boston. He would attend the celebration parties for the victors and cheer for the citizen who had been able to vote the most times in one election.

The Irish felt because they were the underdogs that any tactic was ethical and any opponent fair game in order that they might win. P.J. often said, "There's only room for one at the top."

Young Joe grew up with an insatiable thirst to be that one on the top. He wasn't content to be a hero only to the Irish, he wanted to move into the mainline society, a daring thought way beyond the dreams of immigrant Patrick. Joe embraced his father's willingness to work and inherited his zeal for making money. As a child he sold the pigeons he captured in the park and peddled candy on sightseeing boats.

The last major step up the social ladder was Joe's acceptance into Harvard. He was not only the first Kennedy to go to college, but it was to Harvard. Nothing less would have done for him or his ambitious father. P.J. got Joe part of a sight-seeing bus franchise in Boston to help with the money needed to finance his education.

After graduation, with no experience, young Joe was appointed as a state bank examiner. As a Powerful blend like his father, he grabbed this opportunity and became an immediate expert in Massachusetts banking. Where his father had the additional engaging Popular Irish personality, Joe was a Perfect who devoured facts and figures and who didn't care as much about charm as about cash.

At age 25 he saved his father's own bank from devastating losses, took over and became the youngest bank president in Massachusetts. Joe's single-minded devotion to wealth and power brought him both, plus the attention of the mayor's daughter, Rose. "HoneyFitz" Fitzgerald, a true Popular, was the epitome of the typical Irish politician, an extrovert who loved to sing, dance, give speeches, and attend wakes. Rose was socially above Joe and he was aware of the advantages he would receive as the mayor's son-in-law.

While Rose raised the children, Joe learned more about banking, business and the stock market. His keen sense for finance and his political contacts moved him ahead rapidly.

According to biographer Nancy Clinch, "Joe Kennedy amassed a personal fortune, and Boston became too small an arena for his monetary and social ambitions. Realizing that he could never crack the social snobbery of the New England aristocracy no matter how brilliant his business successes, he packed the family aboard a private railroad car in 1926 and moved to New York, where the Irish *nouveau riche* family might be more acceptable. Perhaps, too, he wished to succeed on his own away from his father's native city."[5]

Once settled into New York, Joe headed for the excitement of Wall Street and soon learned how to move the Market to his advantage. Conscience was never a deterrent to Joe's lust for success. When the Stock Market crashed in 1929, no one who knew Joseph Kennedy was surprised to find that he had cashed out a few weeks before. While others were jumping out of windows, Joe was counting his money. He bought into Hollywood film companies, owned a chain of theatres and began his real estate business.

Through his political contacts and support of FDR, he became friends with James Roosevelt, and while on a trip with him to England just happened to pick up liquor franchises that appeared to be useless because of Prohibition. Months later Prohibition was repealed and he was instantly in a very lucrative business. What took him $100,000 to set up in 1933, he sold for $8 million.

Along with Joe's material successes came the deep desire for his children to achieve and receive the social acceptance that had eluded him. He taught them maxims such as "Don't play unless you can be captain," "Win at all costs," and "Second place is failure." When Father Joe said, "If you don't win, don't come home," he meant it.

With Joseph's success in the financial world and in Hollywood came his own allowance to himself to have relationships with women outside of marriage and to pass this permission on to his sons.

Pearl Buck wrote in *The Kennedy Women,* "Rose Kennedy showed for years a steadfast loyalty to her husband while he continued a long relationship with a beautiful film actress (supposedly Gloria Swanson). Outwardly she maintained a proud silence. But the inner struggle must have left its mark on the children. ... The Kennedy men were never celebrated for their faithfulness to their wives, but their wives found it worthwhile to continue as wives and mothers."[6]

Whatever it took to keep up the Kennedy climb, looking the other way, tampering with the system, manipulating others, Joe was all for it.

Since winning was all, he had to make his sons winners. After a lackluster term as Ambassador to the Court of St. James, Joseph knew he'd gone as far as he could go in the political world, and he turned all of his single-minded attention to his sons.

He chose Joe, Jr. to become his alter-ego, and he personally groomed him to be president. He was set up as a model for his younger brothers and he was allowed to discipline them if he felt the need. He actually was a junior version of Joe, Sr., and Joe looked to the future in excited expectation of the time when he could live the presidency vicariously through young Joe. In August of 1944 the dream came to a drastic end when Joe, Jr. was killed on a dangerous mission in the war. "The son he had molded in his own image and on whom he had lavished the greatest care was dead. The news was like a sword thrust deep into Joseph Kennedy's heart, an agony from which he never fully recovered."[7]

As with royalty, the mantle fell on Jack, the next in line, and his father quickly groomed him as the replacement, insisting he run for the House of Representatives from Massachusetts. Jack had looks, charisma and style, so with Joe's strategy, money and influence, they made a winning team. Within two years of young Joe's death, Jack had been elected to national office.

Six years later Joe got the taste of sweet revenge when he pitted his son against Henry Cabot Lodge, the incumbent, aristocratic Senator, and won. Joe managed every detail superbly and the campaign went down in Massachusetts history as the most methodical and scientific. Joe's Perfect mind moved meticulously, and he managed a campaign that defied the odds and paved the way for Jack's road to the presidency.

About Jack's win over Lodge, Joe said proudly, "When you've beaten him you've beaten the best. ... At last we've evened the score."

Father Joe's Perfect personality believed the world was a jungle where only the fittest could survive, and his Powerful side determined that the Kennedys would be the fittest, and they would not only survive, but be the big winners.

In the book *Man of the House* by Tip O'Neill the former Democratic speaker tells that Old Joe Kennedy handed out cash-filled briefcases to politicians who would do his bidding and kept a careful watch on the progress of his sons. "The old man," Tip says, "even had a maid in Jack's Washington house who reported to him."[8]

The family backgrounds of the Trumans and the Eisenhowers while they were basic, godly, and hard-working people, had little to do with their political achievements. Neither set of parents would have projected such lofty ambitions upon their sons, but the Kennedys were a breed unto themselves. They aimed and they achieved, and Jack, second best in his father's eyes, became President of the United States.

Nancy Clinch concludes, "In effect, the boys became what Dad wanted them to become. No amount of rhapsodizing over Kennedy successes can hide the fact that the chief life task of each son, especially the older sons, was to attain the peaks of social success, acceptability and prominence that eluded the father."[9]

Although there was little similarity with the Trumans and Eisenhowers, there were some parallels with the Roosevelts. While the Kennedys were considered *nouveau riche* versus the long heritage of the Roosevelts, both Franklin and Jack were aristocratic, well-educated, affirmed by their parents, financially secure, and able to fit into any strata of society. They were each rich men who were noted for their compassion for the poor. They both felt anything was possible once they were in control. They were both Popular and Powerful.

Jack's Powerful nature made him a fast mover, and a highly competitive opponent. When he walked into a room he had instant control, and he used his ability to manipulate skillfully and without effort. His father had put an emphasis on ability and the pursuit of excellence, and he endorsed these principles wholeheartedly.

Theodore White writes: "John F. Kennedy, in his 14 years in politics has had many servants, many aides, many helpers. As he has outgrown each level of operation, he has gently stripped off his earlier helpers and retained only those who could go on with him effectively to the next level. ... In the personal Kennedy lexicon, no phrase is more damning than, 'He's a very common man,' or 'That's a very ordinary type.' Kennedy, elegant in dress, in phrase, in manner, has always required quality work."[10] Although this statement was made before Jack's election, it was also to prove true while he was in office.

Jack was Popular and Powerful: he wanted it done his way — immediately. His demand for excellence was often carried to the extreme. Nancy Dickerson said of his competitive nature that his motto should state, "Be tough and have trophies to prove it."[11]

His quest for the best caused him to be impatient with those not meeting his standards, to be irritated by those who didn't move quickly, and to be annoyed by the "dummies of life" with whom he occasionally had to deal. His desire for action covered a fear of boredom, and he was uncomfortable whenever he was not in control. He had an ability to look in disdain at those who did not see it his way, and he could make anyone feel guilty if he caught them at a time when they were not doing anything. His *machismo* attitude might today be looked upon as chauvinistic, but then we women saw it as virility and strength.

How did Jack's personality pattern and his family background affect his limited time as president? When we look at the Popular part of his personality we see the inborn traits of making life fun, looking through rose-colored glasses, desiring the adulations of the crowd, and wanting everyone to love him. With these strengths came his overemphasis on illusions vs. reality and his deceptive way of making us think he was accomplishing more than was actually going on. Indeed, many political pundits recognize that Kennedy's popularity is rooted more in fiction than reality. Author and political observer George Will comments "John Kennedy ... became a permeating presence in the nation's imagination only after, and because of his death."[12]

His Powerful side gave him the innate drive for success so easily harnessed by both father and mother, the need to be a winner and not a runner-up, and the obsession with masculine strength and control. When we add these personality patterns together and stuff them into a handsome, dynamic man with an abundance of charisma, we can see what a product old Joe had to package and sell to the American public.

Jack came into power like a king and in his efforts to get us moving again, he set aside his "first thousand days" to effect long-lasting results.

As with most politicians, Jack found that exciting change looks easier from the outside than it becomes when faced with the reality of compromise and Congress. Since he came into office as a hero, Jack wanted to act like one, and when it was suggested that he help a group of Cuban exiles invade their homeland, he had to give the idea serious consideration. The CIA had made the plans and the Joint Chiefs of Staff were willing to act. The quick invasion of an apparently Communist country, manned by their own native exiles seeking to be restored, sounded like movie stuff and appeared to have few risks. If, in spite of careful planning, the operation failed, it would not be a major defeat. Kennedy rationalized optimistically, "If we have to get rid of these 800 men it is much better to dump them in Cuba than in the United States."

The invasion failed miserably and Castro's forces rounded up not 800 men but approximately 1,200 to 1,500 exiled Cubans. "Kennedy had been indecisive, neither intervening to call off the attempt nor providing the support that would have been necessary for success."[13]

"Cyrus Sulzberger, the New York *Times* columnist, lamented that the United States 'looked like fools to our friends, rascals to our enemies, and incompetents to the rest.' It was hardly an auspicious way for the new president to demonstrate his mastery of foreign policy."[14]

Columnist Pat Buchanan expressed the opinion of many Americans,

"... the Bay of Pigs disaster had shown a hesitancy, a timidity, and a confusion on the part of President Kennedy, in the use of military power, that were ominous. Strike hard, or not at all, was among the oldest of military maxims. That is the way Americans had fought and won World War II. ... "[15]

Kennedy seemed better at winning elections than at winning wars. His Irish luck had failed, and he needed to turn over a whole new four-leaf clover. New adventure came in response to the first manned flight of Gagarin launched by the Russians the same week as the Bay of Pigs fiasco. Kennedy sent a memo to Lyndon Johnson, head of the National Space Council, and asked could we go to the moon and how much would it cost. The answer of cost didn't seem to matter, and Kennedy announced his all-out Space Program in May of 1961. "Fly me to the moon!" We had little time to mourn the Bay of Pigs as we were in a flurry of activity to reach the moon.

Nancy Clinch said, "The importance of reaching the moon was never spelled out. Instead, Kennedy tried to carry his audience along on a vicarious and allegedly exciting experience."[16]

Over a year after the Bay of Pigs it appeared that Kennedy's honeymoon was beginning to wane. " ... Khrushchev posed another challenge, this time not on the exposed periphery of American power but near its heart, ninety miles off the coast of Florida. Kennedy's unwillingness to commit the forces necessary to overthrow Castro and his acquiescence in the Berlin Wall seemed to signify a failure of will, and the Russians apparently reasoned that they could install missiles in Cuba with relative impunity. ..."[17]

This time Kruschev underestimated Kennedy. Our president, determined to be Powerful, insisted that the Soviets remove their missiles. Khrushchev agreed and entered into an agreement to remove the missiles in return for an American commitment not to invade Cuba. Castro is still in power; we have never invaded Cuba; Kennedy is dead.

On March 5, 1987, 25 years after the crisis, a group of Kennedy advisors met for a class reunion, to relive the two weeks of crises. Sponsored by Harvard University's John F. Kennedy School of Government, the gathering included former Secretary of Defense Robert McNamara, presidential aides Theodore Sorenson and Arthur Schlesinger, former Under Secretary of State George Ball, and many others whose purpose was to discuss the events in retrospect and see how they might bear upon current crises. The *New York Times* review of this meeting stated about the missile crises, "For perhaps no event since World War II so preoccupies the makers and critics of foreign policy as those '13 days' when the world seemed to tremble on the brink of nuclear apocalypse."[18]

Kennedy seemed crisis-prone as he went from the Bay of Pigs to Berlin, to Moon Plans, to missiles in less than two years. Behind these upfront decisions was the boiling question of Vietnam. Presidents Roosevelt and Truman had been involved in the determination of whether France should be in control of this misbegotten country. From 1946-54, the United States had poured some $2 billion into French support, only to have the Communists defeat them in May of 1954.

Peaceful Eisenhower, with support from Congress and then Senator John Kennedy, refused to intervene, and a line was drawn between South and North Vietnam. We were willing to aid the South and we sent Ngo Dinh Diem from this country to be the temporary leader. He must have been a Powerful person because he loved power and he took over for good. He had no interest in elections and his regime became as repressive as Ho Chi Minh's in the North.

Even though our support was conditional on fair democratic elections which never happened, we looked the other way and continued contributing to the Diem government while increasing pockets of guerrillas were opposing the regime.

Kennedy first had to get a supposed truce in Laos: He sent troops into Thailand, and then he had to look at Vietnam. Had no action been taken, the same North Vietnamese that are now in control probably would have won, only sooner and without our losses. But at the time, "counterinsurgency" or limited intervention seemed to be the direction. From 1961-63, our involvement grew from 2,000 men to 15,500. On November 1, Diem was captured and shot by a military *junta* who seized control of Saigon. Three weeks later Kennedy was assassinated.

We will never know whether the future of Vietnam would have been different if Kennedy had lived, but the seemingly endless war became the burden and ultimately the downfall of the next president, Lyndon Johnson.

Historian Clarence B. Carson summed up the general belief about his administration, "Kennedy had not been a very effective president during his first two-and-a-half years or so. He had not been able to get what he reckoned to be his major legislation through a Democratic [friendly] Congress. His administration had in general been crisis-ridden. Foreign action, if any, tended to be decided in the midst of crisis, which might not have occurred if his policy had been known in advance. ... "[19]

In retrospect, every president could have done better, but surely Kennedy, young, Popular and Powerful, was faced with a series of crises that confounded him and kept him from establishing a sound legacy. But we liked his looks, his charm, and his aura of leadership.

As he tried to put out fires around the world, we watched the parties and the glamour of the family.

As a country we let him pull us to happy-ever-after-land, because we wanted to believe. When we found he didn't know the way and hadn't counted the cost, we were surprised. We didn't realize he had no serious destination in mind and that he agreed with the ad, "getting there is half the fun," but we were willing to overlook his mistakes because he'd given us a vicarious vision of royalty, and we wanted to live happily ever after in a castle.

Suddenly it was over, our hero was gone, reality hit hard. We all cried as we watched John-John at the funeral; we admired Jackie's presence and composure; we said good-bye to our version of a king.

Shortly after Kennedy's death Jacquelyn Kennedy, speaking to a reporter about their life, said, "At night we would play records, and the song he loved most came from a current Broadway hit *Camelot,* based on the legends of King Arthur: 'Don't let it be forgot, that once there was a spot, for one brief shining moment, that was known as Camelot' — and then she concluded wistfully, 'and it will never be that way again.'"[20]

John F. Kennedy

Popular (Sanguine)

Strengths

fairy-tale image
optimistic & outgoing
charming & regal
storyteller extraordinary
center of attention
intoxicating like champagne
liked superstars
open & hospitable
surprising & innovative
captivating to women
aura of glamour
dramatic
too good to be true

Weaknesses

aching for greatness
needs to be a hero
afraid of boredom
shows-off
womanizer
pseudo-hero

Powerful (Choleric)

Strengths

competitive
winning is everything
be tough & win trophies
fast-moving
quick & active
used power to control
everything is possible
emphasis on ability
courageous
youthful vigor & vitality

Weaknesses

made unreasonable demands
overwhelming ambition
drive to heroic gratification
indifferent to danger
impatient
manipulated by money
uncomfortable when not in control
irritable
male chauvinist
made everyone keep moving
instilled guilt
reckless
domineering

— 14 —

"All The Way With LBJ"

Lyndon Baines Johnson (1963-69)

Popular-Powerful

Personality Principle: *Strengths carried to extremes become weaknesses.*

There was never any doubt that Lyndon Johnson wanted to be president, but he had not expected to receive the title in such a tragic way. A young Popular-Powerful president had been assassinated, and Lyndon was called to fill his shoes. He had been preparing for this role for years, he'd done his homework, he was ready. He'd been an effective Senate majority leader and he was confident that when he got in control of any situation he could make things happen. He always had.

Like Kennedy, LBJ was also a Popular-Powerful man, but there was a difference in the manifestation of his personality in his childhood background and in his concept of self-worth. Both Roosevelt and Kennedy had come from wealthy parents, had classical educations, and were comfortable with prince or pauper. Truman and Johnson had not been so privileged; their roots were in the soil. In spite of their brash behavior, they were both insecure underneath. Johnson was sensitive when people made fun of his Texas background, called him a cowboy, or ridiculed his accent. Kennedy and Roosevelt always seemed to hide their temperament weaknesses from public view by covering their impatience and intolerance for incompetence with a cloak of charisma.

Johnson couldn't find a place big enough in all of Texas to encase his enormous ego or hold down his anger when things didn't go his way.

In 1948 when he ran for the Senate, he daringly broadcast to the people while whirling around in a helicopter. Because of his known love for dramatic oratory plus the circling blades of the helicopter, his machine was dubbed the "Johnson City Windmill."

LBJ was his own Horatio Alger story. From the time he was a child he wanted to be in charge, and he was constantly convincing others that his way was the right way. He could see early on that politics was the step-ladder to Power, and he wanted to spend as little time as possible on each rung.

He married his Lady Bird from a well-feathered nest, and she became a Perfect counter-balance for his volatile Powerful personality. Lady Bird was genuinely gracious in a more homespun way than Jackie's regal style of entertaining. For years at the ranch Lady Bird had been hospitable to any number of people at any time, with or without advance notice, for when Lyndon said, "Y'all come," he really meant "you all."

As he was flamboyant, she was disciplined and controlled, organized and efficient. As he was Popular, she was willing to give him center stage. As he needed to monologue a message and be the life of the party, she was willing to listen attentively and act as if she'd never heard that line before. As he was prone to exaggeration and had a habitual disregard for the truth, she did her homework, knew her facts, and talked intelligently.

When LBJ was chosen to be Kennedy's vice-president, he knew it was not that Jack liked him, but because he provided balance. Jack was young and new to national politics, Lyndon had been around forever and had immeasurable influence in Congress. Jack was Eastern Establishment; Lyndon was Texas Southern complete with drawl.

Even though LBJ had not wanted to be second place, he was so eager for increased power that he was willing to accept the vice-presidency. He felt he would have a strong influence on the new Democratic team and he often said, "Power is where power goes."

Once Lyndon tried to exert power with the young Kennedys and their friends, he found they didn't care for his suggestions, and he soon had to admit to himself that he just didn't fit in. Disappointed but undaunted, he set out to design his office in a way to denote power. His choice was a spacious suite so lavishly decorated that it was soon nicknamed the Taj Mahal. The youth team made sport of him behind his broad back and they took lightly his list of demanding prerogatives he sent to the president. He was always seeking moments when he could be in front and he desperately wanted to be Popular and Powerful. He grabbed onto the authority that came with being head of the Space Agency, and he was his true flamboyant self when riding in an open car down Broadway with Astronaut John Glenn.

Because his opinion was not asked for by the young president, LBJ set up his own fiefdom in the Taj Mahal and was not allowed to be closely in tune with the inner circle. This separation of power kept him from knowing what was really going on, and when Kennedy was shot LBJ was shocked, sympathetic, and released.

After an appropriate time of mourning, Lyndon dared to come into his own bigger-than-life image. He was a born politician who knew how to twist arms quietly and give people "the Johnson treatment."

"You are a very important person to me and I need your help now." He was a born power-broker; he knew how to use his personal contacts for gain and when to call in his markers. He had used this skill with uncanny results in the Senate, but he soon learned that he had a different cast in the White House. He was a born storyteller, had a legendary charm and wit, and was exhilarated into brilliance by adoring crowds.

He would give a lecture on anything to anyone, at any place at the drop of a ten-gallon hat.

Nancy Dickerson, who knew Lyndon well, praised him for his speaking skills. She watched him become "a full-blown orator," the "image of a messianic preacher." She said he, above all, made "talk an art." How every Popular person wishes these words could be said of them!

In their early days in the White House, the Johnsons entertained Texas style until the press made fun of their ranch beans and quipped that the rose garden had been turned into a barbecue pit. While LBJ liked to kid with others, he had a thin skin when anyone made fun of him.

Popular people have a desperate need to be loved by all, and they can't bear to think there's anyone who doesn't like them. Powerful people try to stay in control strongly enough that no one will dare turn against them. Johnson, being a bountiful blend of the two, resented any negative comments. He would become like a little hurt boy when the press took him on, and he'd say sadly, "I'm the only president they've got."

For all of Johnson's apparent confidence in himself, and his formidable ego, he was always insecure with his Texas origins and his lack of prestigious credentials. He covered his concerns with his outgoing Popular personality, and because he was uncomfortable when not in control, he seized every opportunity to be in charge and to exert his energetic and sometimes exhausting power.

Jimmy Carter once said of Lyndon: "Johnson never felt secure inside, especially around the Eastern Establishment — the professors, experts, writers and media people — and that's why they got him in the end."

Nancy Dickerson reports that LBJ felt any rejection of him or his policies by anyone denoted a lack of patriotism. Everything was black or white. You were either for him or against him. As a correspondent assigned to the White House, Nancy said Lyndon made three mistakes with the press that came to haunt him.

1. He showered the reporters with gifts as a manner of control. They took it to mean that if they'd play the game by his rules, they'd get along just fine. However, "LBJ's lack of subtlety backfired. His blatant attempts to influence sometimes forced reporters into being overly critical just to preserve their independence."[1]

2. He toyed with the press by not telling the whole truth, a lifetime habit that he did not see as dishonesty. He twisted words to imply meaning that wasn't correct and then was relieved when the press drew their own wrong conclusions.

3. He tried to manipulate press conferences by planting questions and when the reporters didn't come through with the topics he wanted, he would berate them.

This combination of press control by the president was sufficiently upsetting to the correspondents to cause them to ridicule his background, his lack of style and his Texas accent, infuriating him. For a man who dearly wished to be loved, he turned the most vocal force in the country against him.

Lyndon loved to have his picture taken and his craving for attention sometimes caused his better judgment to go astray. In 1964 he allowed himself to be photographed while yanking his pet Beagle "Her" off the ground by her ears, causing animal lovers across the land to protest loudly. In 1963, after a gall bladder and kidney stone operation, he happily showed off his scar by lifting his shirt for the photographers. The resulting picture was so offensive as it was spread across the nation's pages that it produced a cry of outrage.

LBJ laid himself out for further ridicule when he offered his excised gall stones to the Smithsonian Institute and they refused to display them.

When it was time for Lyndon to choose a vice-president to run with him in 1964, he stalled and teased many potential candidates to draw out the procedure and to keep the country in suspense. He believed in any tactic that would keep him on the front page.

Ultimately, he selected Horatio Hubert Humphrey, who felt he deserved to be president, but in lieu of that option, he was willing to accept second place as Johnson himself had done. Humphrey was a true Popular and whatever came in his ears went out his mouth without staying around long enough to ferment. He always looked wide-eyed and innocent, and he had a quick answer for every question — not necessarily based on fact. Neither HHH nor LBJ ever let the truth stand in the way of a good story.

Once, when asked about his exuberance in talking endlessly on any topic, Humphrey replied, "I do — I like every subject. I can't help it — it's just glands."

And so it was with both him and his boss. This constant chatter annoyed LBJ, who no doubt missed their similarities, and he said hopefully of Hubert, "If I could only breed him to Calvin Coolidge."

Although Lyndon had resented the Kennedy exclusion of him when he was vice-president, he evidently didn't learn much from his neglect, because he kept gregarious and garrulous Hubert at arm's length. Before the president would accept Humphrey, he had to pledge absolute loyalty and agree never to disagree. He was to try to keep his mouth shut, never upstage Lyndon, and avoid making headlines. "No deviation from administration policy would be tolerated."[2] When he later dared oppose the bombing of Vietnam, he was excluded from the inner circle as punishment.

Isn't it amazing that the cloak of authority we consider unacceptable when someone else is wearing it, we put on quickly when we get to sit in their chair!

During the 1964 campaign, opponent Powerful Barry Goldwater, viewing the war of attrition in Vietnam, called for us to go in there and finish them all off. His tough talk branded him as an incendiary warmonger, and LBJ, with his political instincts, capitalized on this view of Goldwater and appeared to be the peace candidate. The last thing anyone wanted was a real war.

In the midst of the campaigning on August 4, 1964, North Vietnam was reported as attacking U.S. warships in the Gulf of Tonkin, and Johnson made his most famous speech calling for retaliation. This moving message led to the Gulf of Tonkin Resolution granting Johnson freedom of action in South Vietnam. His lust for power grabbed hold of this aggressive attack and used it as reason to accelerate the non-war.

Imagine Goldwater's emotions as he was defeated in a landslide election while being labeled trigger-happy by a president who was sending troops to an undeclared war and bombing the enemy.

As the situation in Vietnam worsened, civil rights issues boiled, and the hippies and flower children experimented with drugs, Johnson found himself in a no-win position after an overwhelming win. His Powerful nature recoiled at anything he couldn't control, and his Popular personality was infuriated by any kind of criticism. He wanted obedience and adoration, and he was getting neither.

Political writer Doris Kearns Goodwin said of this situation, "Even though one could not have predicted the disaster of Vietnam, it would have been possible to foresee LBJ's difficulty in dealing with any situation that would not yield to his enormous talents for persuasion and compromise."[3]

By March 1968, President Johnson finally had to admit to himself that he couldn't get out of Vietnam. He tried his Popular best to get the people with him, but his most pleading exhortations fell on deaf ears and he lost face with the friends who had re-elected him in faith that he would put out the fires. His natural optimism faded away and his craving for positive attention went unfed. He felt deserted and unloved.

Nancy Dickerson wrote: "He went into the White House thinking that he could do better than anyone else; he left knowing that only another president could end the war." He meant well and "No man could have tried harder."[4]

LBJ believed anything is possible if you just work hard enough. When he couldn't end the Vietnam War, his life-long "work ethic" fell apart. He was so proud of the Great Society he was creating out of the fragments of the New Frontier, and he couldn't believe his people wouldn't accept his strengths and overlook his weaknesses.

Bob Pierpoint of CBS wrote: "Johnson was probably the most qualified president I've covered. He really understood how the American system should work. He was colorful and unpredictable. He had experience and background, knew all the inside angles. But he couldn't work himself out of the Vietnam war. He had three different press secretaries — George Reedy, Bill Moyers, George Christian — all good, but they couldn't prevent Johnson from putting his foot in it."[5]

When a Powerful has no power and a Popular is no longer popular, he becomes depressed. The photographers showed him despondent. One captioned a downhearted picture, "You love me or I'll leave."

Although he wanted another term, Lyndon couldn't stand the thought of a possible defeat, so he decided not to run. He accepted the typical Powerful theory, "If you're not sure you'll win the game, it's better not to play."

Lyndon was a man whose strengths when carried to extremes become weaknesses.

Because of his underlying insecurity, he forced himself to be more than charming, more than dynamic, more than successful. He became somewhat of an exaggeration of himself. FDR and JFK each functioned about 50 percent Popular and 50 percent Powerful, but LBJ came across as 100 percent of each. His overwhelming personality made him a 200 percent man. There was a lot of Lyndon!

With each personality there is the possibility that the strengths can go too far and become weaknesses.

As with Johnson, the Populars' greatest strength is their ability to talk anywhere at anytime on any subject with or without information. Carried to an extreme, they talk all the time, interrupting others, on subjects of which they know little, bearing a distant relationship to the truth.

Also as with LBJ, the Powerfuls are born leaders, can take charge of any group without having read the by-laws, can make instant decisions without research, and can correct the mistakes of the inept without asking them. These excellent abilities, when carried to extremes, make the Powerfuls appear bossy and arrogant, make others feel indecisive and weak, and cause them to take control of situations that are none of their business, leaving a trail of wounded victims in their wake.

The Perfects are just the opposite in that they are addicted to the facts. Their greatest strength is that they delve deeply into every subject, analyze every alternative, and deliberate every decision. Carried to an extreme they become dulled by details, too deep to be understood, and easily depressed.

The Peacefuls like Eisenhower wouldn't hurt a soul. Where the Powerfuls easily cut the insecure into pieces, one of the Peacefuls' greatest strengths is their natural ability to heal the wounded and bring hope to the downtrodden. They avoid any kind of trouble and will withdraw rather than take a chance of stepping on anybody's toes. Carried to an extreme, they become so passive as to be colorless, so indecisive as to appear weak.

As we look next at the life of Richard Nixon, we will see another example of a man whose greatest strengths ultimately became his weaknesses.

Lyndon B. Johnson

Popular (Sanguine)

Strengths

grandiose style
running monologue
legendary charm
open, friendly, generous
natural host
loved uniforms and costumes
full of surprises
made talk an art
messianic preacher
optimistic
exhilarated by crowds
constantly lecturing
gabbing vigorously
liked picture taken
loved attention

Weaknesses

enormous ego
blatant demonstrations
largest press badge
disregard for truth
prone to exaggeration
needed an audience
insecure with Texas
   background
loud and garrulous
twisted words to suit
exasperated by
   interruptions
desperate need for love

Powerful (Choleric)

Weaknesses

insisted on total
   commitment
irritated by delays
crude wheeler-dealer
two-faced
demanding of others
exhausting to be with
bossy and bragging
had temper tantrums
infuriated by critics
formidable foe
restless volcano
manipulative
impulsive

Strengths

gave "Johnson treatment"
always in charge
stood tall in the saddle
wanted to run everything
power-balancer
constantly convincing others
went first class
liked to exhort the masses
just like a fox

Act II —
The Past
1969–1988

— 15 —

"Knowledge Is Power"

Richard Nixon (1969-74)

Perfect-Powerful

Personality Principle: *We come in on our strengths and leave on our weaknesses.*

At the moment of this writing we have several past presidents who are still alive and very active. Each one has a different personality, yet their backgrounds have some similarity; each one had humble beginnings and had to work hard to become somebody. As we look at their terms in office, we can clearly see that they all came into the presidency on their strengths and left on their weaknesses.

Richard Nixon, a Perfect-Powerful, is an exceptional example of the deep, analytical perfectionist with a strong need for control whose strengths and weaknesses are both exaggerated because of a frustrating childhood of insecurity. His father, Frank Nixon, was a man who wanted to succeed but never could pull all of life together at one time. He struggled with various occupations as diverse as carpentry, storekeeping, and operating a trolley car. He also struggled with the mental image he had of himself as the typical male head of the household. Father Frank was no more successful in shepherding a family than in running a business, and his failure factor frustrated him into bursts of anger and violence. He learned that a temper tantrum taught all those around to toe the line, and he controlled by intimidation.

Because he could not deal consciously with his occasional feelings of childhood rebellion, young Richard buried his emotions. This repression satisfied his Perfect nature that did not want to face the facts that he was surrounded by imperfection, legalism, uncertainties, rejection and the death of two brothers. His Powerful personality rose to take control of his life. He suppressed grief and guilt and determined to succeed. His strong aggressive impulses were unacceptable to his domineering religious mother, Hannah Milhous, to his pacifist Quaker grandmother, who spoke in "thee's" and "thou's," and his insecure yet authoritarian father.

Dr. Eli Chesen, who analyzed Nixon and wrote a *Psychiatric Profile*, said that young Richard "functioned in this rigidly controlled emotional straight-jacket."[1]

Psychologists tell us that when our real feelings are repressed, they come out somewhere at some time. Nixon's melancholy mind remembered every hurt and rejection, and he could burst out like a lion and pounce upon those who had triggered his hidden anger.

His brother Donald remembers: "He couldn't argue much with me but once, where he had just about as much of me as he could take he cut loose and kept at it for a half hour. He went back a year listing things I had done. He didn't leave out a thing. I've had a lot of respect ever since for the way he can keep things on his mind."[2]

Young Richard learned early in life that he was not Popular or particularly handsome, so he opted to develop his mind. He became obsessed with the mastery of details and needed to know everything about every subject. He found that Perfect knowledge is power and when you have Perfect control of facts you can soon control people and situations and have power.

Nixon's childhood was not a happy one. His brother Harold's fatal illness occupied much of his mother's time and he was relegated to what he considered female tasks to help her out. When he did the dishes he was so afraid someone would see him that he pulled the shades. He had an intense fear of being thought a sissy or weak in any way, and this concern kept him from allowing any friends to get to know him. He stayed remote and emotionally uninvolved with people, and was nicknamed, "Gloomy Gus." His desire to hide his true self from others as a youth stayed with him as an adult, where he kept his emotional shades pulled much of the time.

Young Richard had ambivalent feelings about his parents. He wanted to be masculine like his father, but Frank was a failure, and his son was obsessed with the vision of success. He related more with his domineering mother, who was ambitious, but he feared her female influence.

When Richard was 12 his mother left him in charge of the household for two years while she took Harold to Arizona in search of a cure for his TB. Richard felt abandoned, rejected, and unloved. He also felt as if he were the "woman of the house," and when both brothers, Harold and Arthur, died, he somehow thought it must be his fault. If only he'd known what to do. He determined never to let anything get beyond his control again.

His combination of guilt for his brothers' deaths, fear of not being masculine or strong, anxiety over insecurity and rejection and need to keep people from knowing who he was or how he felt, drove him into an inferiority complex and a lifelong fear of failure. A little resident black cloud hovered over him. Eli Chesen calls Nixon's anxieties "a feeling of vague impending doom ... While all of us experience anxiety in a multitude of forms, few people have been able to harness this energy as effectively and as efficiently as Richard Nixon. This accounts for much of this man's greatness as well as weakness."[3]

Nixon has been a clear example of the principle that a strength carried to extreme becomes a weakness. The strengths of his anxieties led him to study deeply, memorize facts, train his brilliant mind, win debates and get a scholarship to law school. The weaknesses manifested later caused him to have a compulsive need to win, even if he had to bend the rules to do so.

Richard's youthful insecurities grew along with him for a lifetime, and Charles Morris says of him, "The constant pricking of his inferiority was like picking off a scab."[4] His emotional wounds have never healed, but he has successfully covered them with a large Band-Aid of knowledge and control. These childhood problems, when not dealt with in a healthy way, sometimes lead to what is called the "obsessive-compulsive personality."

The American Psychiatric Association Diagnostic and Statistical Manual defines the obsessive-compulsive personality as follows: "This behavior pattern is characterized by excessive concern with conformity and adherence to standards of conscience. Consequently, individuals in this group may be rigid, over-inhibited, over-conscientious, over-dutiful and unable to relax easily."[5]

Chesen says, "This definition, while accurate, is incomplete. The outward characteristics of this personality (overinhibition, compulsivity, overconscientiousness, and striving for perfection) are all mechanisms used by the obsessive-compulsive. These mechanisms are used by such a person to gain control over himself and his environment. In this way, he will not lose control of himself — and his environment will not be able to control him."[6]

Richard Nixon wanted to be in control and be Powerful; he had a passion for facts, a need to know it all, an ability to take advantage of others, and an obsession to be Perfect. With the Perfect-Powerful personality, he decided to go into politics.

Time writes of him, "An unliklier politician would be hard to concoct. Reserved, secretive, glowering, as awkward at backslapping and gladhanding as an android at a stag party."[7] Later when questioned on his tactics, Nixon answered, "I had to win. That's the thing you don't understand. The important thing is to win."[8]

And win he did! As junior congressman from California, Nixon arrived in Washington during a brief period of Republican control and was put on the House Un-American Activities Committee at a time when Joe McCarthy was bent on purging the country of communists.

Nixon's biographer, Stephen Ambrose, writes, "McCarthy's charges were so extreme, his inability to back them up so obvious, that he made Nixon look like a scholar and statesman in comparison."[9]

Nixon's compulsion to get the facts put him in a positive position when in pursuit of Alger Hiss. His attention to detail and persistence led to conviction and he suddenly became a new young star for the Republican Party. When Dwight Eisenhower was convinced to run for President, the old general needed a young lawyer to do his dirty work. Richard Nixon fit the prescription and he freed Ike up to be presidential and fatherly. While Ike grinned, Nixon glowered.

For Nixon, success often turned into a crisis. Some of his California friends raised $18,000 for him and when the *New York Post* caught wind of it, they headlined "Secret Nixon Fund." At that time, the thought of any improprieties in Perfect-Powerful Nixon shocked us all, and I remember listening as he came on TV to explain emotionally how poor and humble he really was. He told us how his wife, Peaceful Pat, wore a "respectable Republican cloth coat" and hoped we'd all let him keep the gift of a little cocker spaniel named Checkers. He had us all in tears with him as he concluded his plea followed by Ike giving his blessing of "you're my boy."

We were all convinced "Tricky Dick" had been picked on and were grateful for Ike's paternal support. As time went on, Peaceful Ike became less enchanted with Nixon's penchant for controversy and conflict and by the time Nixon was ready to face Kennedy for president, Ike suggested that he wasn't "presidential timber."

When a reporter asked Ike what Nixon's major vice-presidential decisions had been he answered, "If you give me a week, I might think of one."[10] Perhaps this was Ike's Peaceful, low-key sense of humor, for biographer Ambrose says that Nixon, "became the most visible vice-president of the 20th century, and the most successful."[11] He inferred that life with Ike in his sunset years was confusing and indecisive.

"After ordering Nixon to take the low road while he stayed on the high road, Eisenhower would admonish Nixon that he had gone too far — and then once again order Nixon to go after the Democrats."[12]

The frosty relationship between these two was a natural personality clash. The Peaceful Ike held down the Powerful Richard and let him know that he wasn't yet Perfect.

Nixon went from vice-president to an unexpected loss to Jack Kennedy followed by a defeat for governor of California, a job that seemed a natural win for such a national figure. The anger he had repressed since his teen years refused to stay under control, and he told the press off in another moving moment by saying, "You won't have Nixon to kick around any more."

And we didn't, at least for a while. It was in this interim period that I met Nixon at a party honoring him in Milford, Connecticut. My husband had the food service contract at the Schick headquarters, and when they asked Fred to put on a spread for their top executives, Richard Nixon, Barron Hilton, and their president, Patrick Frawley, I volunteered to be the hostess. The pictures I'd seen of Nixon made me feel he only came in black and white, but when I met him I was surprised to see a well-tanned, attractive man in living color. He greeted me most cordially, considering he wasn't running for office at the time, and he seemed at ease with his business peers.

By the time Nixon announced he was available to be president and salvage Johnson's unpopular war, the country was ready for a change. We'd had enough of brash promises and exaggerated stories. We'd been a little embarrassed when LBJ, on a whim, invited the camel driver from Pakistan to visit the White House and he'd come.

We were sick of flower children, druggies, and criminals who had more rights than the victims. We'd given up on the New Frontier that had become old, and we were disenchanted with the Great Society that hadn't gotten better.

Nixon promised to end the war and he took a tough stand on Law and Order, expressing that the Warren Court had gone too far in favor of the criminal. As President, Nixon was at his best. His whole life had been a rehearsal for such a time as this, and he faced the nation with confidence. His personality patterns shone in their strengths and he put his weaknesses to bed for a season.

Nancy Dickerson said of Washington at that time, "The city gamely tried to discover virtues in Richard Nixon that had never been perceived before."[13]

In *Nixon's Psychiatric Profile,* Eli Chesen states, "His tendency to over prepare has made him a master of political capability and diplomatic awareness. He is almost always well-researched and exhibits an impressive ability to recall detail. ... he tends to be a genius of interpersonal diplomacy and expert in his forte — foreign affairs."[14]

Charles Morris wrote that Nixon had "daring and imaginative pragmatism," "unusual sweep and clarity of mind," "bold courage for the brilliant stroke."[15]

From these words of praise and his landslide reelection, we could assume that Nixon would go down in history as one of the greats, a genius, a foreign policy expert. What happened? Where was the fatal flaw?

When we understand the basic personalities, we can see how little it takes to move a person from his strengths to his weaknesses. Nixon's underlying fear of ever losing again and his consistent need to gather every possible fact led to the creation of the Plumbers, a unit of special investigators designed to stop leaks. Daniel Ellsberg had infuriated Nixon with his publication of secret Pentagon papers, so the Plumbers entered his psychiatrist's office to find damaging evidence. Tapping telephones of newsmen gave Nixon advance information to fortify any weakness before things got out of control. Investigating Ted Kennedy's Chappaquiddick fiasco gave Nixon an unused stockpile of information for the future. Nixon's need for omniscience allowed his Plumbers to eagerly apply wrenches to any dripping pipeline they saw. Nixon would have won without any subterfuge, but he wanted to win big.

In retrospect, he says of himself and of the Watergate break-in of the Democratic headquarters: "There was no way McGovern was going to win the election. So we should have faced up to [Watergate] very early and said, 'Look, who did this thing, and so forth and so on, we're sorry that it happened.' When you try to compare the deed itself [the break in], rather than the cover-up of the deed — the deed itself was a nonsense thing. It didn't produce anything.

"Without the Watergate episode I would be rated, I should think, rather high. Without it. But with it, it depends on who's doing the rating."[16]

Yes, without Watergate Nixon would have ranked as one of the most brilliant and successful presidents. He will still be remembered as those Shakespearean heroes, a great man with a tragic flaw. His childhood insecurities and inferiorities taught him that knowledge was power and that he needed all he could get. Experience showed him that even with a mastery of the details he could still lose and so he took no chances.

From his childhood on, his fear of people knowing his inner thoughts and his pulling down the shades on life grew into a fetish in his presidential years. He was so afraid someone would tap his wires while he was taping their words that he had nine separate private offices all with full communications equipment: The Oval Office, one in the Executive Office Building, the Lincoln Study, two at Camp David, one at Key Biscayne, one on Grand Cayman and two in San Clemente.

His obsessive need to know all caused him to install eavesdropping equipment and his sense of his place in history added to his preoccupation with detail. He wanted to leave nothing out of his memoirs and be sure his words were preserved for history. When he talked with an unsuspecting person, he could weigh his words while the guest said what came to him naturally.

This deception created somewhat of a Candid Camera event. He always had to have the upper hand, to know more than the enemy. He was a man whose fearful childhood emotions never grew up with his body.

Nancy Dickerson said, "He was a prisoner not so much of his position as of his own personality."[17]

Doris Kearns Goodwin added, "The administration of Richard Nixon demonstrated most dramatically of all that the greatest powers are vulnerable to the most sordid defects of personal character and understanding."[18]

David Willis McCullough, in his review of the book *Nixon*, sums up the mystery of the man: "Richard Nixon, whose story always remains political, seems well on his way to becoming a perpetually reexamined man. Tales of his rise and fall will be continually retold and reanalyzed as successive waves of historians and political scientists — not to mention psychiatrists with and without diplomas — try to figure out what went wrong. In a curious way, Nixon has become a scab no one can quite leave alone."[19]

After 10 years of reclusive life interspersed with occasional forays into the political arena, Ex-President Nixon began his well-planned emergence into public life. He has made himself available as a consultant wherever his vast knowledge is useful and he is still considered as the top foreign relations expert in either party.

Nixon has accepted that he will probably never be officially selected for a government position, but he has carefully promoted himself as an elder statesman who is well-received in other countries. Without public knowledge, Nixon has quietly mediated between Gorbachev and Reagan, and in July 1986, he presented Reagan with a 26-page document expressing his views of Gorbachev, "a velvet glove with a steel fist," giving suggestions on future relationships and diplomatic accommodations.

Because of his forced resignation and the confiscation of 44 million pages of presidential material and 4,000 hours of tape, Nixon has been unable to establish a library or museum to house what he does have available.

Gerald Ford has a presidential library in Ann Arbor, Michigan, the Carters are turning Plains, Georgia, into an historic town, and Ronald Reagan is already building his memorial in Ventura County, near his ranch in California.

After waiting for the city of San Clemente to debate for four years over whether to build a Nixon library, Nixon gave up and moved his request to Yorba Linda, his birthplace. Assuming they proceed with the proposal, Yorba Linda will own the distinction of having the only Presidential library without Presidential papers.

Richard Nixon still has unprecedented comprehension of government intricacies and foreign policy, but now his vast knowledge can produce only limited power. He is a brilliant man, a tragic hero with a near-fatal flaw.

Richard Nixon came in on his strengths and left on his weaknesses.

Richard M. Nixon

Perfect (Melancholy)

Weaknesses	Strengths
devoid of charm	brilliant mind, a genius
reserved, secretive,	amazing ability to judge others
glowering	master of details
split-personality	efficient & analytical
male Greta Garbo	sobering influence on others
paranoid about press	programmed body movements
uncomfortable host	introspective to the extreme
reclusive & remote	idealistic & perfectionistic
mercurial mood changes	premeditated responses
mentally erratic	publicly pious
mean streak underneath	memory for details
brooding & depressed	passion for facts
cut off from reality	scholar & statesman
suspicious & untrusting	well-researched
deceptive	guarded, self-contained
search for solitude	

Powerful (Choleric)

Weaknesses	Strengths
	conveyed image of being in charge
	penchant for notable firsts
	admired General DeGaulle
	daring & imaginative pragmatist
monarchical vision	unusual sweep & clarity of mind
grandiose stance	bold courage for the brilliant stroke
couldn't say "I'm sorry"	extraordinary
volatile, quick-tempered	harnessed energy
refused counsel	confident
critical of opposition	loyal (yet ruthless)
self-conscious	didn't need friends
pretensions to greatness	goal-oriented
desperate need to win	law & order
vulgar language	all-powerful
above the rules	all-knowing

16

"...A Time Of War And A Time Of Peace" *Ecclesiastes 3:8*

Gerald Ford (1974–77)

Peaceful

Personality Principle: *The Peaceful is a team player and has no enemies.*

If there ever was a president whose personality fit the need of the hour it was Gerald Ford. Having just said farewell to a Perfect-Powerful whose motto "Knowledge is Power" had been carried to extremes, we wanted Peace. Just leave us alone and let us recover from Watergate. We didn't want any New Frontiers or Great Societies, we just wanted to tune out for a while. We didn't need a person of great vision and expanded horizons, we just wanted a decent, honest man whom we could trust.

And there was Gerald Ford with his Peaceful personality. Not since the election of Dwight Eisenhower at the end of the war had we been looking for a man of Peace who would take us in his arms and rock us to sleep. When Ford was inaugurated as the 38th president, he even had the Bible open to an appropriate verse from Ecclesiastes: "There is a time to love and a time to hate; a time of war and a time of peace." He told us our "long national nightmare" was over, and he was ready to give us "conciliation, compromise, and cooperation," all words that express the virtues of the Peaceful personality.

Gerald Ford came in on his strengths: quiet, low-key nature, non-controversial, well-liked by all, calm, cool and collected, totally inoffensive. He came in as the All-Purpose President, a Man for All Seasons, a team player.

He didn't have the impulsive nature of Kennedy, keeping us on the edge of our seats with a combination of fear and excitement. He didn't have the compulsive nature of Nixon, desperately needing to know and tape every thought. He didn't have an ego that cried to be stroked like Johnson. He was just happily surprised to be president after all those years of steady performance in the House of Representatives.

Gerald Ford was almost too good to be true. He surely strolled in on his strengths.

Ford grew up in the Depression days and didn't find out until he was in high school that he had originally been named Leslie King, Jr. His parents were divorced when he was two, and his stepfather adopted him and changed his name to Gerald Ford, Jr.

One day while Jerry was working in a restaurant as a busboy, a stranger came in and identified himself as his real father. He obviously had more money than the Ford family, but after a lunch out with Jerry, he disappeared and only showed up one more time when Jerry was in Yale Law School. He brought along his son by his new marriage, and we can imagine the hurts that these rejections put upon the young Ford.

Because of his Peaceful nature, Jerry was able to accept his situation and not let adverse circumstances bring him down. Jerry worked hard to get through law school and then settled into law practice in Grand Rapids, Michigan. As is often the case, we marry opposites, and Jerry chose Powerful Betty who was strong, decisive, brave, dramatic, talented, attractive, forthright and fearless.

In 1948, Senator Arthur Vandenberg was looking for a young, likeable lawyer to run for Congress on the Republican ticket, and Jerry fit the profile. He had no enemies, he carried no negative baggage, and he won. In 1965 he became the minority leader for the same reasons.

Author Doris Kearns Goodwin sums up his political pattern this way: "At each significant advance in his career Ford's primary qualification was not that he demonstrated superior leadership ability or oratorical skill but that because he was well-liked and had very few enemies, he suited the purpose of others."[1]

When Nixon announced before the assembled Congress that his choice for vice-president was "a man who had served for 25 years on the Hill with great distinction," the audience knew who it was and was thrilled with his selection. People from both parties applauded the choice. Gerald Ford was a team player whether in football or in politics. He never tried to be the star or do flashy footwork, he just wanted to do his best and be well liked.

Ford was the ideal vice-president. He was willing to go from being leader in the House to being in Nixon's long dark shadow.

We saw many pictures of the Ford family, all beautiful and camera ready. We read biographies of the new vice-president, all warm and glowing. Hardly had we adjusted to the demise of Spiro Agnew and the acceptance of the "fairhaired boy" as a replacement, when the rumors increased that Nixon was going to be forced to resign and *Voila!* we had an instant president. Truman, Johnson and Ford all were instant presidents. Like instant rice, they were all dropped into a pot of boiling water and had to expand to fill their roles. We the consumers poured all-American catsup on Truman's rice, Texas barbecue sauce on Johnson's, and ate Ford's rice just plain.

No one would choose to become president under adverse circumstances, but Ford was ready. His public life had been a preparation for such a time as this. Reporters searched for new depths and found little information. Some looked for skeletons in old closets and found none.

Ford was nick-named "Mr. Clean" and "Goody-Two-Shoes" because no one knew of anything he'd done wrong. His ability to mediate opposing forces and to smooth down any ruffled feathers was an asset as he headed into the most crucial political position in the country.

No one doubted his obvious decency, although some wondered about his leadership qualifications. "Is he big enough for the job?" "Can he carry the ball?"

Some questioned his intelligence. NBC-TV correspondent Tom Brokaw asked Ford if he felt smart enough to handle the position. As others gasped, Ford calmly answered with no touch of anger, "I was in the upper third of my class when at Yale Law School."[2]

When reporters could find little color in Ford's life to write about, in desperation they resurrected Lyndon Johnson's old quip, "Gerald Ford is so dumb he can't walk and chew gum at the same time."[3] When Ford would bump his head on a door or trip on a stair, some wag would quote Lyndon again.

Ford's honeymoon lasted from August 9, 1974, when he was sworn in, until September 8, 1974, when he surprised the press and the nation by granting Nixon a "full, free and absolute pardon." Acting out of his forgiving spirit and wanting to avoid investigations which might be damaging to his administration, he cut off any further disclosure of Nixon's involvement in Watergate. At the same time, Ford dropped 16 points in the popularity polls.

Many political writers feel his early pardon of Nixon was a mistake from which he never recovered, but Ford felt it was something he had to do in good conscience, and the sooner the better.

When the Cambodians seized the merchant ship Mayaguez, Ford acted swiftly by directing a naval task force to the area. They saved the ship and 39 men, and Ford was hailed as a "decisive" leader, a term that had not previously been applied to him.

After the proper and formal entertaining of the Nixons, the casual open warmth of the Ford family was a welcome change. They loved people and parties, and Betty, a former dance instructor, looked radiant as her husband would twirl her around on the dance floor while the band played on.

Betty was a refreshing alternative to her more guarded predecessors, and women related to her as a real person. Some applauded her frank stand on women's rights, although many were shocked when she said she assumed her children had tried marijuana. She let it be known that she did not intend to sleep in a separate bedroom from the president, and when interviewed for *McCall's* and asked how often she slept with her husband, she quickly quipped, "as often as possible."

Her public rallied to her support when she had to undergo breast removal because of cancer. Ironically, Happy Rockefeller, wife of Vice-President Nelson, had a double mastectomy within a few months of Betty's surgery, opening up the subject for free discussion, articles and TV reports. This attention to the topic of breast cancer brought on public awareness of the need for preventive examinations and testing, revived again in 1987 when Nancy Reagan had a "modified radical mastectomy."

Gerald Ford's dignified and compassionate response to Betty's surgery encouraged other women facing similar situations and belied the myth that once you've had this surgery your husband won't love you any more.

In later years when Betty admitted she had alcohol and drug problems and checked into a rehabilitation center, she again showed her open frankness and encouraged others to get help. After her successful treatment, she founded the Betty Ford Clinic near Palm Springs, California. Those of us who live in the area are kept informed in the daily paper of each celebrity who enters, news gathered, I assume, by some eager reporter in a palm tree with a telescopic lens.

As Betty sparkled and the children were shining examples, the president kept a soft, steady glow. His low wattage never ignited any fires in his people, and he became somewhat of a baby-sitter, a temporary parent.

As Eisenhower, a fellow Peaceful, was the direct opposite of Truman, so Ford was totally different from the preceding presidents. Where Johnson was larger than life, entertaining, hugging, laughing, manipulating, controlling, Ford was reserved, open-minded, unpretentious, and sympathetic. Where Lyndon was brash, Jerry was soft-spoken; where Lyndon was hilarious with humor that often made fun of someone, Jerry had a dry wit, a pleasant smile, and a totally inoffensive nature.

Ford was opposite from Nixon in that the latter had a total control of facts on every important subject, and Ford was often caught short on the details. Ford didn't have Roosevelt's classical background, and was considered an intellectual lightweight. Since the press could find little substantial criticism to make, they grabbed onto mis-statements such as his reference to Paul Revere's "one if by day and two if by night."

Ford was different from Kennedy in that he did not *need* to win. He liked being president, but he wasn't threatened by Powerful people around him. He was not an initiator in Congress or as president, and his campaign to Whip Inflation Now, ironically dubbed WIN never quite WON. Ford was more manager than innovator, and he gave us a feeling of quiet contentment rather than of dynamic leadership.

When it was time for Ford to run on his own for reelection, the public accepted the prospect that he would be voted in. He had done nothing wrong although little that could be considered inspirational. He had been inoffensive and had no enemies, however he'd never succeeded in getting us to march to his drum-beat, mainly because he wasn't beating any drums.

Ford's Peaceful strengths became weaknesses as he limped through a lackluster campaign with little commanding oratory. His detachment from the facts was brought to our attention when in the debate with Jimmy Carter he stated that in his eyes the Soviet Union most certainly did not control the nations of Eastern Europe.

The campaign coasted downhill from Eastern Europe to Ford's defeat at the polls by an upstart peanut farmer who had organized his bid for national attention Perfectly.

Gerald Ford came in on his Peaceful strengths and left after 895 days on his weaknesses. He just never got out of the chair and ran. He took his defeat calmly, gave no negative condemnations to any of his staff, blamed no one but himself, graciously turned his position of power over to his successor, packed his bags and retired to Rancho Mirage, near Palm Springs.

As an ex-president, Ford had no goals and no wealth so when agent Norman Brokaw offered to make a few financial contacts for him, he accepted. Suddenly Ford became a hot property. As the calls came in, Ford was amazed, "I never had that experience before, so it was quite surprising."[4]

NBC paid Ford about $1 million to appear in documentaries. Harper and Row with Reader's Digest produced another $1 million for memoirs of Jerry and Betty. She got a half-million for two NBC specials, and suddenly their financial picture took on a brighter look. Offers for consulting on different businesses and for board of directors positions came flooding in, and Ford found himself in a whole new line of work.

Ronald Brownstein of the *National Journal* says that Ford, "was reared on the pieties of free enterprise; long ago he absorbed them, and now they have absorbed him. He sees nothing in his business career that requires great soul-searching or introspection. No, he says, it doesn't bother him that the other living former presidents have refused the business opportunities offered them. 'Each one of us has our interests.' No, he's never asked the companies he works for why they want him around. 'I assumed they had good reasons.' Ford's weary voice makes it apparent that he doesn't quite see what all the fuss is about. His conscience is clear."[5]

At the Republican National Convention in New Orleans, both Betty and Jerry were honored and he gave the most dynamic speech of his life, saying that he would not stand by and let somebody pick on his friend George Bush. There was a new confidence and assurance about Gerald Ford, the successful businessman, the director of boards, the consultant in demand.

Gerald Ford came into office as an unelected president on his Peaceful strengths and left on his few weaknesses. Since then he has entered a new stream of life and like Ole Man River, Ford just keeps rolling Peacefully along.

Gerald Ford

Peaceful (Phlegmatic)

Strengths

quiet and peaceful
perennial good guy
refreshing, natural
genuine, honest and true
obviously decent
reservoir of goodwill
all-American boy made good
Eagle Scout in the White House
well-liked
no enemies
aimed for long-term solutions
didn't want to be in control
talked simple sense
comfortable and relaxed
naturally sensitive
friendly, courteous & polite
skilled at negotiations and
    compromise
inspired affection and trust
uncomplaining and forgiving
unbiased
avoids conflict
affable and of good cheer
not naughty or proud
clear conscience
cool under fire
team-player
non-controversial
content
available
unassuming
normal
well-balanced
easygoing

Weaknesses

didn't understand
    urgencies
slow in decisions
avoided problems
didn't seem to take charge
couldn't face
    confrontations
had a do-nothing aura
didn't get up and run
indecisive
dull speaker
plodding
pedestrian
inarticulate

17

"Jimmy Who?"

James Earl Carter (1977-81)

Perfect

Personality Principle: *The Perfect person has deep strengths and deep depressions.*

James Earl Carter came into office somewhat like a school teacher bringing the class back to order after recess. As a nation we'd been somewhat out to lunch, and it was time to get organized again. We'd dealt with the crises of Kennedy, the Vietnam escalation with Johnson, and the Watergate scandal with Nixon. We'd needed a rest time with Ford to regroup our thoughts, and now we were after a restoration of order and ethics. No wonder we were intrigued by Jimmy's obvious morality and his serious-minded desire to get us organized and on the move again.

The political insiders had disappointed us, and the idea of a new, intelligent and spiritual outsider seemed to refresh us. When Carter first emerged in the Democratic caucuses, few of us had ever heard of him. "JIMMY WHO?" the headlines asked. Could anything good come out of Plains, Georgia?

Jimmy had indeed come out of little, unknown Plains, a town of only 600 people. His personality fit the Perfect profile right from the beginning as he was an excellent student, loved to read, and was fascinated by engineering. Admiral Hyman Rickover took him as a protegé and trained him on nuclear submarines. Carter had intended to make the Navy his career until his father died and he had to return to Plains to save the family peanut business.

Rosalyn had also grown up in Plains and was a friend of Jimmy's sister Ruth. She felt too poor and insecure as a teenager, but she set high standards for herself, got all A's, and became the valedictorian of his class. She had the drive of a Powerful personality and she remembers that she always wanted to win. She had always looked up to Jimmy in awe, but had not dared approach him.

When she saw a picture of Jimmy in his naval officer's uniform, she fell in love with his image and set a goal — unrealistic at the time — to marry him. She held her emotions inside and didn't tell anyone her thoughts. When Jimmy came home on leave, Ruth invited Rosalyn over and a romance started that quickly blossomed into a lifetime love affair.

After moving frequently with the Navy, the couple settled back in Plains, against Rosalyn's wishes. As Jimmy fit into his home community again, he became director of the County Chamber of Commerce, a member of the Library Board and County School Board, a scoutmaster, a deacon in the Baptist church, state president of the Georgia Crop Improvement Association, state chairman of the March of Dimes and district governor of Lions International. What was there left to do?

Jimmy was well known in Plains and had already built a reputation for fair leadership across the state through his civic positions, so he ran for state senator and won. During the early '60s the integration problems hit the South, and Jimmy began to work on behalf of civil rights for the blacks.

Jimmy's stand was immediately unpopular with Southern whites and led to a confrontation in his own church. A black man wished to attend and the deacons made a ruling, hardly a spiritual decision, that no blacks could come to their church. When the vote came before the church body, Jimmy stood up and spoke against the measure. His moral sense of justice would allow him no other choice; the vote passed and his fellow church members were angry with him for his stand.

Even though the state had been predominantly Democratic, the party loyalty split in 1964. The Georgians were so anti-integration that they couldn't even find a chairman for Lyndon Johnson's campaign, and so Jimmy's widowed mother, fondly known as Miss Lillian, took the position. Threats were made against the Carter family if they didn't pull away from their "liberal integration stand." Georgia was one of the few states that Barry Goldwater carried in 1964 against Johnson.

The Carters did not retreat from what they knew to be a fair and just freedom for the blacks, and this strong stand caused Jimmy the loss of many votes in the future. In 1966 he ran for governor of Georgia against then-Governor Lester Maddox, a staunch segregationist who owned a restaurant. He had already chased blacks out of his establishment and had been pictured wielding an axe handle at his front door.

The Carter family campaigned day and night, crossing the state and speaking at every possible stop. Rosalyn worked days in the peanut warehouse, did Jimmy's Senate correspondence at night, kept files on every voter who helped Jimmy, and did the housework in between campaign trips. Powerful Rosalyn, nick-named the Iron Magnolia, gave Jimmy's bid for nomination all she had while he plotted out every move systematically on paper. When the votes were tallied, Jimmy had lost. The state of Georgia in 1966 preferred an axe-swinging governor to an integrationist.

In an interview with Doris Kearns Goodwin, Jimmy said, "I've always had superb confidence in myself, but since 1966 it's been different. I was always thinking of myself. I had to prove myself to others. I had to win every battle, which meant when I lost the race for governor of Georgia in 1966, it was horrible. ... When I had failures it was very upsetting. Even the smallest failures seemed like calamities to me. Life had no purpose."[1]

During this time of Jimmy's deep depression, typical of the Perfect personality, his sister, Ruth Carter Stapleton, shared with him how the Lord had healed her of depression. Jimmy made a spiritual commitment to Christ, which changed his attitudes of pessimism in defeat to the peaceful acceptance that God had a plan for his life.

The next time Jimmy ran for governor he was even more organized than he had been before. He blocked the state out in zones, noted everyone he knew in that area, and systematically went out to win friends and votes. Rosalyn wrote personal notes to each individual who had responded to Jimmy's messages each day, and Jimmy started a file of coded speeches and usable jokes by number. Jimmy knew he didn't have a ready sense of humor like the Popular politicians, so he wrote down funny stories and filed them. If he spoke in your town today and told jokes 1, 14 and 110, when he returned he would check his card on you and be sure not to repeat his stories.

Can't you imagine Jimmy and Rosalyn driving toward a motel after a long day of campaigning. To lighten the load and save energy he'd say to her, "Number 8." She'd laugh heartily and counter with "Number 62!" Such great fun with such little effort!

As Nixon believed "knowledge is power," so Carter knew his potential was in the Perfect assimilation of details. He constantly studied the issues so he would know every possible fact, and he consulted experts on each current topic.

Perfect Jimmy made perfect plans, kept perfect files, and won. When Rosalyn moved into the governor's mansion she felt all her dreams had come true. She'd gone from being a plain little girl in Plains, to marrying her Prince Charming, to living in a mansion and being the governor's wife. Surely she would live happily ever after. Although she had been brought up in a poor family with no emphasis on the social graces, Rosalyn made a quick study of protocol and became a confident and gracious hostess. She even trained inmates from the penitentiary to be waiters at her formal dinners. She planted new roses and enjoyed working in the yard. Jimmy even did some gardening and planted a row of peanuts to frame the rose garden and remind them constantly of their humble beginnings.

Jimmy scheduled every day ahead, including time for a bathroom break, and he usually kept to within five minutes of his detailed plan. In 1972 he began working on his organizational charts for his presidential bid in 1976. While few knew what he was planning, he had it all mapped out.

According to Doris Kearns Goodwin, he had "a strategy that called for 250 days of campaigning with visits to 40 states and 200 cities. Carefully allotting a precise amount of time to each state, Carter worked six days a week from 6 a.m. to midnight. And when it all worked out exactly as he had calculated, even down to the number of delegates he had estimated he was likely to win from each state, most of us — but not Carter — were taken by surprise."[2]

Once "Jimmy who?" had won the election in 1976, he began to study all the inaugural addresses of the past presidents in order that he might compose his from a wealth of background. He had no pretensions of grandeur, and he wanted his message to be simple and his demeanor to be humble. He wanted to be a leader on the level with the people, not a lofty king above the crowds. To demonstrate his servant's attitude, he chose to walk in the inaugural parade instead of ride in an open limousine as was the usual custom. He had read where Thomas Jefferson had walked to his inauguration, and he felt this change would symbolize an open and accessible atmosphere for his new administration. As another touch of basic humility, the parade featured a huge helium-filled balloon shaped like a peanut. Carter never strayed far from his peanuts.

Jimmy Carter came into office partly because of America's longing for morality in government. Columnist William A. Rusher wrote, "America in the last decade has been shaken to its roots by the most divisive war in over a century, then shocked by revelations of corruption and lawbreaking at the highest levels of government and in both major parties.

"It is not only unsurprising but downright healthy that, at such a time, the American people should seek fresh contact with the bedrock of religious faith, and look for leaders who are doing the same."

Carter's strong beliefs and his open willingness to talk about God made him different from the passively religious presidents before him, some of whom would well have blushed if asked to give the blessing at a banquet.

Episcopal rector Frederick Rapp of Port Washington, New York, stated in 1976, "There is a yearning for spiritual and moral leadership in high places, a yearning to be able to trust our government and not have our trust misplaced."[3]

Carter came into the Oval Office on his morality, his firm confidence, his amazing self-discipline, his studied knowledge of major issues, his refusal to compromise his standards, and his appeal as an honest outsider.

Although his morality was never seriously questioned, his lack of guile once caused him to open his mouth without thinking of how his statement could be used to ridicule his virtue. In an interview with Playboy, hardly a religious experience, Carter was asked about his fidelity with Rosalyn. Not wishing to seem prudish to the Playboy readers, he said he had not committed adultery, but he had looked upon women with lust in his heart. Had Jack Kennedy made such a statement, it would have been taken lightly and with no surprise, but coming from the mouth of Moses, it provided the reporters with a rare opportunity to make fun of the president's morals.

Jimmy was actually quoting from Matthew 5:28 where Jesus said, "I say unto you that whosoever looketh on a woman to lust after her hath committed adultery with her already in his heart." But since the Playboy reporter didn't know Matthew from Mark, Luke or John, the concept and comment were attributed to Jimmy and provided humor from then until this very day.

On May 7, 1983, the *Los Angeles Times'* Ross Baker wrote about the appetite of the press for scandalous tidbits. "The dutiful watchdog, however, has lately been transformed into a snarling attack dog — or at least a dyspeptic bloodhound — that can be found rooting around in everything from Henry Kissinger's trash can to Gary Hart's driveway. ... Politicians, foolishly, invite such probing. Jimmy Carter, with his smirking sanctimony, virtually dared the press to pick a hole in his coat, and then gave it the tool to accomplish that with his 'lust in the heart' statement."[4]

Old stories never die.

Carter's confidence gradually eroded as he found that not everyone had his Perfect principles or wished to follow his sincere directions. Inflation wouldn't listen to him, recession continued even when he said stop, and the fuel shortage got worse and worse in spite of his threats. He proposed what he called "the most massive peacetime commitment of funds and resources in our nation's history" to develop new sources of energy, but lines kept forming at the filling stations, and they were honking their horns at him.

Carter's superhuman discipline didn't seem to work on others and his detailed 12-point program appealed to few. *Newsweek* said of him, "Jimmy Carter appears to have been a hard man to work for — demanding, highly critical of inadequate staff work, yet rarely complimentary of a good job."[5] Carter put so much effort into plotting out his schedules that soon critics said he had become a manager instead of a leader. He had to give up some of his noble, idealistic visions so typical of the Perfect personality, and these losses of great plans began to depress him.

His study of crucial issues became so overwhelming that he had to retreat to Camp David to think, causing him to be considered a loner, a mystic, or a sick man. He hadn't expected the seizure of our embassy in Iran, he didn't know the Ayatollah Khomeini, and he had no idea of what to do with a deposed, sick Shah who didn't have a place to stay. No one told him the hottest issues of his administration would be burning in Iran and that his inability to release the hostages would bring his reign to a dismal close.

His refusal to compromise sounded brave and noble until Congress disagreed with his plans, and he had to back off in what he felt was defeat. "All the legislation in the world can't fix what's wrong with America," he said in defense of himself. "It's a crisis of confidence. It is a crisis that strikes at the very heart, soul, and spirit of our national will. ... [and] is threatening to destroy the social and political fabric of America." He called for a "rebirth of the American spirit,"[6] which depressed those of us who didn't know it had died.

Carter's appeal as an honest outsider didn't wear well either. Though no one doubted his basic integrity, his "outside" mentality caused him trouble as he did not have the usual, old-line political cronies to call upon in time of need, and soon he referred to Washington as "poison" to him.

By his third year in power, Perfect Carter's strengths had turned into weaknesses, and the press began to use words like: aimless, drifting, remote, losing touch, depressed, dismal, frightening. Carter created a memorable phrase when he told us with the heavy heart of the Perfect nature that we were in a "national malaise." What a melancholy word, malaise! The dictionary says malaise is "an indefinite feeling of bodily uneasiness or discomfort." As Jimmy lost his comfort, we all became uneasy.

By the time in July 1979, when his Presidency had dropped to its lowest ebb in public esteem, Carter did what Perfects do when life becomes imperfect, he retreated to Camp David, where he spent two weeks on the mountaintop communing with God and a steady stream of advisors. His discouraging conclusion was that we had, according to *Newsweek*, "a sickness of the national spirit — a crisis of faith that makes effective governance nearly impossible for him or anyone else."[7]

What does any religious man do after two weeks on a mountaintop? Come down and make a speech. The comparison of Jimmy with Moses was so obvious that many cartoonists drew a white-robed Moses with Jimmy's face and teeth, descending the Catoctin Mountain, stone tablets in hand. In order to give the president television time to report, CBS- TV ironically had to cancel the episode in their series, "Moses the Lawgiver," in which Moses descended from Mt. Sinai with the Ten Commandments.

One of his staff, worried about Carter's unexciting delivery, suggested he hire Charleton Heston to present his message, but Carter didn't need Charleton that night as he presented his material on the crisis of the American spirit "with an urgency, a passion and an eloquence rare in his or any other recent Presidency."[8] He admitted his failures and said we were standing "at a turning point in our history." He looked straight at us and said, "I need your help."[9]

Newsweek reported, "Carter had approached the speech full of melancholy at America's psychic landscape and misgivings about his own hitherto small powers to alter it. ... But he felt he had to do something to shake the nation free of its malaise."[10]

Charles Morris in his book *A Time of Passion* sums up how Carter came in on his strengths and left on his weaknesses.

"Carter's sudden slippage in the last weeks of the presidential race reflected growing doubts about his capacity for office, a concern that turned out to be well-founded. His informality and lack of pomp in his first days in office — his walk to the inaugural, his relaxed official dinners, his jeans and cardigan — were a pleasant contrast to the imperial trappings that had grown up around the White House. But he never succeeded in establishing control over the political process and was from the outset engulfed by events.

"With the exception of the peace agreement he wrung from Israel and Egypt at Camp David, his administration was a failure in virtually every respect. ... The failure of the helicopter mission to rescue the Iranian hostages was the knell for Carter's administration; from that point, he had no chance to win re-election. Intelligence, goodwill, and simple decency were not enough for a successful presidency."[11]

Meg Greenfield says that we who put them there are at least partly responsible for the change of attitude about each president. "Those who compose the epitaphs for departed administrations are invariably inconsistent and unfair. The same public that hailed Ford for his down-to-earth good-heartedness and simplicity after the byzantine Nixon years derided him and his works as 'dumb' by the time he left; it embraced Carter's walk down Pennsylvania Avenue and his homely insistence on reforming the 'imperial presidency' by toting his own suitcase and the like and then decided it hated and was demeaned by all these hokey gestures."[12]

Although Jimmy's sincere humility was shown in his walking to the Inaugural and not wearing a tall silk hat, this "just-one-of-the-guys" attitude was interpreted to denote a lack of strong leadership skills. I'm sure Jimmy meant well, but he misread the public's concept of what constitutes a leader. This country has inherited from England a penchant for royalty, even though we wouldn't verbalize it.

Because of this desire we created the Kennedy myth with the Perfect Queen and the Popular King living in Camelot. We trooped vicariously through the White House and watched film clips of the galas on the nightly news. We studied the Royal Children as they grew, and expected the Dynasty to be carried on through Bobby, Ted and, ultimately, John-John.

While the Carter family was basic, we missed the pageantry. Humorous articles on the meaning of leadership were published, and somehow humility wasn't one of the characteristics mentioned. The press ridiculed Jimmy and they seemed to select pictures of him where he looked depressed. Here we had an honest man who sincerely thought that he could straighten out the problems of the country. He'd done his best, he'd run the race, but he didn't win the prize on his second try.

In the book the Carter's wrote together, *Everything to Gain — Making the Most of the Rest of Your Life,* they expressed their reaction to their unexpected loss to Ronald Reagan. Jimmy, with his deep strengths and faith, tells of how disappointed he was, how he bottled up his hurts, and how he meditated on what he could have done differently. Rosalyn was in turn "angry, sad, anxious, and worried."

Although they don't designate their personality types in the book, Perfect Jimmy kept calm and reflected deeply on what might have been. Powerful Rosalyn was distraught and upset and was determined they would run again and win. Rosalyn wrote, "There was no way I could understand our defeat. It didn't seem fair that everything we had hoped for, all our plans and dreams for the country could have been gone when the votes were counted on Election Day. We had done all we could, and somehow it had not been enough. Events had mocked us. Jimmy said he had always heard that it was harder for a loving wife to accept anything that hurt her husband than it was for the husband to accept it, and I believe that to be true. I agreed that we had been given opportunities and achievements granted to very few, but I had to grieve over our loss before I could look into the future. Where could our lives possibly be as meaningful as they might have been in the White House?"

As Rosalyn grieved, Jimmy pondered and analyzed. "Once I was convinced, correctly or not, that we had done our best, then it was easier to accept the judgment of the voters and move on to other things. Rosalyn was not able to do this. She went about her official duties with her chin up, but she found it impossible to accept the result of the election. Over and over she would raise the same questions: 'How could the press have been so bad?' 'Why didn't the people understand our goals and accomplishments?' 'How could God have let this happen?' Although some of the same questions pressed on me, I did not — or could not — express them, and spent a lot of our private time attempting to reassure her. My arguments and explanations didn't help much. The only thing that sustained her was the hope and expectation that I would run again for president and be elected. She found very little support for this from me or the rest of the family.

"I have to admit to a lot of somewhat artificial cheerfulness during those early weeks. The more Rosalyn was upset, the more I tried to find ways to comfort her. I never admitted how deeply I was hurt and I still find it hard to do so. We had a few strained and unpleasant moments between us in those early weeks, and now I realize that with my calm and reassuring attitude it seemed to Rosalyn that I didn't recognize her pain."

How difficult it is for people who don't understand the personalities to see why we don't all grieve in the same way. Marilyn Heavilin, in her excellent book, *Roses in December,* has a chapter on how each personality grieves differently.

Jimmy and Rosalyn have put their grief behind them and moved on. Jimmy was honored as an elder statesman at the Democratic Convention in Atlanta and in August 1988 Bantam published his new book *An Outdoor Journal, Adventures and Reflections.* Jimmy tells of his childhood and of his desire for his father's attention. "He seemed to love me more and treated me as something of an equal when we were in the dove field, walking behind a bird dog, or on a stream."[13]

LA Times reviewer Frank Levering summed up his feelings about Carter and his *Outdoor Journal.* "As president, Jimmy Carter became ensnared in a web of public and media perception —that he was weak, ineffective, too slight a man for the job. But the Carter of this book — the man he wants us to know — is a man's man, tough, durable, courageous. ... 'Carter is setting the record straight, combating the lingering image of weakness and salvaging his pride in an imposing exhibition of manly arts. ...

"Carter the outdoorsman wants us to see him as he wanted us to see him walking down Pennsylvania Avenue at his inauguration; not larger than life but as an ordinary man called to perform extraordinary feats."[14]

James (Jimmy) E. Carter

Perfect (Melancholy)

Strengths

analytical mind
sense of mission
strong spiritual values
high moral standards
self disciplined
complex personality
tightly scheduled
engineer's mind
essential loner
missionary zeal
inner-directed
empathy with the poor
highly organized
intelligent
deeply informed
impressive credentials
immersed in issues
humble
dedicated to family
compassionate to needy

Weaknesses

saw national malaise
full of melancholy
depressed over failures
no sense of humor
secretive and mysterious
withdrawn
rarely complimentary
lost touch with people
bogged down in details
doom-crier
vague and touchy
brooded on the mountain
somber and grave
compared to Moses
    in meditation

— 18 —

Let Reagan Be Reagan

Personality Principle: *Keep people functioning in their strengths and not their weaknesses.*

We all have such an urge to make people over into what we think
they ought to be. We'd love to play amateur psychologist or fairy
godmother. By using the personalities in our everyday life, we soon see
that everyone functions better when they're natural. When we play God
with other people's personalities, especially our children's and our mates',
we may change the original behavior, but what do we have on our
hands? We have a mongrel, a phony personality, one that is forced to
function in weaknesses and not in strengths. It's like breeding a Schnau-
zer with a poodle. It's a cute little thing, but what is it?

In our business life we would never advertise for a typist and an
artist and then place them in the opposite positions and expect them to
excel. We would hire them for their strengths and then keep them where
they would function to their peak efficiency.

Unfortunately, in love, in politics and in the church, we often make
the wrong choices and instead of finding where the person's talent lies
and placing them in it, we try to make them over in hopes we might
produce what we wanted in the first place.

In marriage counseling I find this problem frequently. The Perfect
man, for example, marries the Popular fluffy wife, takes her home and
tries to make her Perfect. She does the best she can, functioning in her
weaknesses and sublimating her original fun-loving nature. One day Mr.

Perfect comes home and says, "You're not the same girl I married. You're not the fun you used to be."

Is there any wonder she's not the same girl he married? Then he adds, "but I've found someone who is." The next one is a Popular like she used to be before he stripped her of her strengths and made her move into her weaknesses.

After I used this example speaking at a medical convention, a doctor came up and thanked me for my explanation. "Now I see what I've done. I'm just divorcing my fourth wife and each one has started out as a Popular personality and ended up broken and sad. I had no idea it was my fault. I just thought I had bad luck."

What a shame that we can't see what we're doing to one another.

In the political theatre we are often guilty of trying to make our candidates fit the image we have in mind. If we've cast them in the wrong roles we just change them, turn them into robots or vote them out.

When we choose a pastor, without the understanding of the four personalities, we expect him to be an all-purpose person. We want him to have the charisma of the Popular Pastor in the pulpit, the command and control of the Powerful Pastor in leadership, the spiritual depth, dedication, and attention to details of the Perfect Pastor and the ability to keep everyone functioning in harmony like the Peaceful Pastor.

What we all need to remember is that each personality has positives and negatives and our job is to keep our children, mates, employees, and leaders functioning in their strengths and not their weaknesses.

Do you remember the Carter-Reagan debate, the pivotal point of the 1980 campaign? Perfect President Carter had been laboring through his "national malaise" for four years. He'd planned and charted it all out, but somehow it had never all come together at one time. He'd pulled Begin and Sadat to Camp David and had gotten them on speaking terms, but he couldn't get the hostages home. He'd become increasingly depressed and even changed the part in his hair to cheer himself up.

He had seriously approached the presidency, had only begun on his list of goals, and sincerely wanted another four years to work the whole thing through.

His opponent, Ronald Reagan, it was suggested, by the media, was a lightweight. He proved otherwise.

Carter prepared for the debate with an obvious edge. He was the incumbent and he hadn't made what he felt were any serious mistakes. He was an honest and moral man, no one doubted that, even though many felt his religion got in the way of his good sense. He had worn the presidential mantle with humility, he was one of the ordinary people, just plain folks from Plains. He wore sweaters, put his feet up with the boys, and most down-home of all, he grew peanuts.

Opposing President Perfect was Candidate Popular. It was assumed that because Carter as president had access to many facts that Reagan didn't he would have the edge. On the other hand Reagan was charming, sincere and had down-to-earth anecdotes of the past that we all remembered with nostalgia. He stood up for traditional values, the family and church. It seemed America was ready to get back to her roots. Even though he was far older than his Perfect opponent, Reagan appeared far younger than his years, and had the vigor of youth.

As long as Carter could keep Reagan groping for the facts that he as president already knew, he would come out ahead. It all seemed so logical.   Both candidates had prepared and practiced. Just before they went out, Reagan was handed his instructions from James Baker. It was a small piece of paper with one word of advice: "Chuckle."

Carter answered his questions Perfectly while throwing negative innuendos toward Reagan, who appeared to be the underdog. People who were watching perceived Carter to be picking on his opponent, and at one point he pushed too far. Reagan looked up, tilted his head like a little boy, and with a slight youthful grin and a shrug he said, "There he goes again."

With that one masterful stroke of his media brush, he painted himself a winner. The next day reporters quoted that one sentence as the turning point in the debate. "There he goes again" will not go down in history with the Gettysburg Address, but it did provide a Popular man with a push on the presidential path.

Many of us thought back on that first televised debate in 1960 when Nixon, after eight years of vice-presidential experience where he had even governed during Eisenhower's recovery from a heart attack, looked as if he hadn't shaved.

T. H. White observed that Nixon's wretched appearance was the result of "his transparent skin that shows the tiniest hair growing in the skin follicles beneath the surface."[1] Standing next to handsome, tanned, athletic, All-American boy Popular-Powerful Kennedy, Perfect-Powerful Nixon lost the beauty contest and later the election.

By the time Reagan was to debate Walter Mondale in 1984, the president's popularity was high, he knew the facts through four years of daily experience, and his confidence level was at its peak. I tuned in that night, assured that Reagan would tell a few stories, answer the questions adequately, and come out a clear winner. Mondale, a Perfect vice-president, had cataloged dates, figures, and places, but he had little charm or appeal. When you consider Nixon's loss on looks and Reagan's win on "There he goes again," you know anything can happen. And it did.

We all expected Mondale to attack Reagan and run with his "lawnmower approach" which he had used to cut up Gary Hart, but he came on kindly and even tried to tell a joke. He gave uncharacteristic smiles and looked strangely at ease. He didn't yell, accuse or fight; he wasn't himself.

What about the Great Communicator, the one who was a natural before the cameras, who had been on the stage forever, who never failed to answer difficult questions with an appropriate anecdote? He came on without his usual confidence, he floundered around for answers, and he seemed to have left his omnipresent mental joke book at home.

Newsweek later called Reagan's blanks as sounds of silence "those painful spaces in which Reagan appeared to be searching in his mind and coming up empty." He was "groping for words and numbers, struggling to order his syntax and his thoughts, showing — or seeming to show — every last one of his 73 years."[2] Overnight comments went from, "Isn't he adorable?" to "Is he senile?"

How quickly one view on television can shift opinion. What went wrong? Why did neither candidate seem to be himself? My personal assumption was that by some fluke each one of them had been trained to be like the other. I thought to myself: Someone must have said to Mondale, "You come across too heavy, you've got those dark circles, your neck tenses up, you have no sense of humor. Why don't you act cute like Ronnie, tell a few stories, smile a lot, relax. Don't be yourself, be like him."

Conversely, I assumed someone told the president, "The media says you come across like a lightweight. You've been president now almost four years and they expect you to know everything to the most intricate detail. We've prepared briefing books for you. In them is every fact you need to know from the days of Eisenhower on to the present. The ones printed in black are all-purpose information, the ones in red are hot issues. Don't discuss these topics under any provocation. The blue printing means cool issues. Take credit for them, look down in humility and tilt your head. You should not be yourself; you should be like Mondale."

I pictured Mondale practicing jokes and trying to change his personality while Reagan was locked alone in a closet memorizing details. The Perfect presidential candidate was trying to put on a Popular mask, which didn't fit and made him artificial, while the Popular President was being told to throw away what had made him Popular and put on a Perfect mask of mastery.

If my picture were anywhere close, no wonder neither one looked natural. Reagan hadn't suddenly gone senile. He was a man who was overloaded with facts and figures. When a question was asked he couldn't just answer it in his anecdotal, adorable style. He had to think about it, and grope for it. He wasn't being the Ronald Reagan that America loved.

By the time the debate was finished the press was crying "Senile!"

I used this little scenario that week in my seminars as a humorous example of how phony we appear to others when we are masquerading as someone we weren't meant to be.

Within a week, it all came true. The news magazines told of the intensive training each man had been put through and as I hungrily ate each article, I was delighted to see how close to the facts my suppositions had been. It wasn't that I had inside information but that I knew their basic personalities and could tell they were not themselves that night.

The facts were that Mondale's coaches blocked out eight full days for preparation and presented him with two large, appropriately black, ring binders. One had summaries of 45 major issues and the other gave answers to 22 questions that might be posed. His writers had put in what Reagan would probably say and what he should say that would, of course, be better.

When Patrick Caddell read the material, he felt that Reagan's hypothetical weak responses as written by the Mondale men sounded better than the right answers from Mondale. He then developed a new procedure for a different Mondale who would plot a sneak attack along the lines of least expectation. Caddell devised the "gold-watch approach." Instead of beating Reagan down with his abundance of facts and risking a backlash in Reagan's favor, Mondale was to treat him like a kindly old gentleman who had served the nation well and who, for his own good, ought to retire — "sort of embracing a grandfather and gently pushing him aside."

Newsweek wrote of this, "The president would be scripted to respond to Fighting Fritz and would find himself face to face with Gentleman Fritz instead — a deferential soul who praised him for his sincerity, credited him with honorable intentions and stipulated his achievements in reviving the economy and the national spirit."[3]

Lacking a better approach, the trainers went along with Caddell's suggestions. Mondale was to look strong and masculine and hope Reagan would look elderly and confused. A reflective piece of white paper was to be placed on the podium, brightening Mondale's countenance and lightening his circles. One other tactic Caddell created was for Mondale to speak softly and turn his head away from Reagan so people would be aware of how deaf the president had become. Gratefully, Mondale, a decent man, refused to play this game.

No one was to know of the new Fritz, for the element of surprise was what would make it work. Caddell suggested "a pantomime of deception ... the strategy must be protected by a bodyguard of lies."[4]

While Fritz was working on his Popular mask, what was happening in the Reagan camp? His aids were not willing to let well enough alone; they weren't going to let Ronnie go in there and wing it. One melancholy aide wrote a message creating a hypothetical scenario on how Mondale could win if Reagan didn't shape up and get serious about this whole debate. Obviously, this person had no understanding of the Popular personality that can get devastated by defeating facts. Even as children, the Popular, fun-loving, light-hearted nature is the one that can not be disciplined by negative threats. While others may respond, the Popular at any age is motivated by positives — "Won't it be fun if. ..." "You will win when. ... " "You look younger than you did four years ago."

Compliments are food for the Populars; confidence from their troops makes them great leaders and the roar of the crowds exhilarates them. Remember how Roosevelt, sick and actually not far from death, revived and improved when he went out to the hustings on his fourth presidential campaign. Populars and Powerfuls receive strength from people, while the Peacefuls and Perfects are drained by the crowds.

Conversely, the questioning of his command of facts, being told the worst that could possibly happen, and being instructed to become something he wasn't, discouraged Reagan and made him dread the debate that he had looked forward to with optimism in light of his past success, his exceptional debating skills, and his innate feel for the camera.

William Buckley, the quintessential debater, had this to say about Reagan's ability. "Those who doubt that Ronald Reagan is an effective debater should try debating with him. I once did —subject: The Panama Canal Treaty. He was resourceful, humorous, cunning and eloquent." Left to his own ability Reagan can be a masterful debater. His aids almost made a fatal mistake.

Naturally, the men trying to train him to be perfect were Perfects. *Newsweek* calls them "high-IQ sorts and unbashful about it." Reagan, as with all Popular/Powerful personalities, was "uncomfortable in the company of intellectuals — those, in any case, whom he felt to be flaunting their own qualities of mind or belittling his. ... they had intimidated Reagan by their bearing alone."[5]

This group felt Reagan had gone soft and had no killer instinct, so they set up mock debates where David Stockman was Mondale. *Newsweek* said, "Stockman totaled him — pummeled him with facts, figures and accusations to a point where the president lost his patience, his temper and finally, some thought, his confidence in himself."[6]

His trainers, not understanding the differences in personalities, tried to make a Popular into a Perfect, like themselves. By doing this, they stripped him of his natural strengths, made him put on a foreign mask, and sent him out to function in his weaknesses.

How many of us are doing that to others? How many of us expect everyone else to function as we do and, when they don't, try to make them over? We force them to put on a mask and to tread water in a sea of weaknesses.

When we saw that debate, we viewed a Mondale trying to be funny and a truly humorous man groping for facts. Neither one was natural, we were all uneasy as viewers, and now we know why.

As Paul Laxalt said, "Let Reagan be Reagan."

19

The Great Communicator

Ronald Reagan (1981-89)

Popular

Personality Principle: *No one can be all things to all people.*

One of the major reasons why we, as the American public, become disillusioned with our leaders is that we feel, way down inside, that there is a perfect president, a perfect pastor, a perfect person. The most practical-minded businessman still has fairy-tale ideas about the possibility that the next president will have the "right stuff."

We practice this wish-fulfillment theory in our choice of mates, friends, business associates, and pastors, and carry it over to our expectations of our children. We want them all to exhibit every strength we have projected on them and no matter how intelligent we may be, we are still shocked when our choice, or our flesh and blood, fails us.

"How could you do this to me?"

"I expected more of you than this!"

"My son, looking like that!"

Until we have a concept of the four basic personalities, we are constantly open to disappointment in others; but once we understand that each person comes pre-packaged, with sets of strengths and weaknesses, we can anticipate both their victories and their failures and not be surprised. We have a measuring stick we can use that may be able to predict some future reactions and behavior patterns. Of course all of us have a free will and can minimize our weaknesses and enhance our strengths.

If we had realized Perfect-Powerful Nixon's need for absolute, unquestioning control and his fanatical search for every last detail, we would not have been so shocked with his abuse of power and willingness to cheat to get the facts. Had we sensed the soft, gentle spirit of Peaceful Ford, we would not have been surprised when he came up with no significant visions for our future and we would have been grateful he was quietly helping us lick our wounds. Had we observed how deeply Perfect Carter felt about morality, justice, peace, order, and humility, we would have understood why he got depressed when the Ayatollah didn't play by the rules, when his own staff fell out of order, and the public mocked his "just one of the folks" philosophy.

No one can be all things to all people and the sooner we learn to accept those others as they were created, not as we wish they were, the happier we will be.

Ronald Reagan, a Popular President, has many of the obvious leadership strengths that people wanted, but leaders of both parties put impossible expectations upon him and then were stunned when he faltered.

No one can be all things to all people!

We tried Powerful Nixon, Peaceful Ford, and Perfect Carter and when they failed, we reached for President Popular to star in *Good Morning America.*

Ronald Reagan appeared on the national stage on call. We had been viewing the *Tragedy of Watergate* with the Shakespearean hero, King Richard, a brilliant brooding man with a tragic flaw, and we had been placated by the plotless pantomime at the Ford Theatre. We had become depressed over the deep drama of Mr. Everyman, carrying his own suitcase and retreating to Camp David and we were sick of those bags of peanuts at intermission. We were ready for a star who knew he could lead us and had been trained for it. We wanted a Popular President to take charge and let us smile again.

George Will commented that, "The nation needed what he delivered — confidence and a sense that government could act decisively. ... "[1]

In the beginning, no one expected his show to run for eight years, but in spite of conflicts inserted to heighten suspense, Ronald Reagan has played to an exhilarated audience and sustained applause. Recession turned into recovery, the Federal Deficit roamed around like a toothless dragon never quite scaring the public psyche. Iran and Nicaragua seemed too distant to be real and if there was a problem, new actor, Col. Oliver North with his courage and engaging smile would surely get it all under control. Even perennial Soviet villains were driven to lay aside their cloaks and daggers by Reagan's policies of peace through strength. The national media didn't believe it would work, but it did. The Soviets finally sent Gregarious Gorbachev and his well-costumed wife, Raisa, to play the role of International Man of Peace and *Time's* Man of the Year, but it was Reagan who brought it about.

Not only has the plot progressed, according to Reagan's plan, but he and Nancy have worn their costumes well and have moved Hollywood glitter and glamour to the grey stages of Washington. They have placed themselves against a variety of sparkling backdrops, have kept fireworks blazing, flags waving, and balloons bursting forth. They have marched to colorfully costumed bands, cried to the tune of funeral dirges, and waltzed to Lester Lanin and his society orchestra.

Francis X. Clives, in the New York *Times,* commends Reagan's ability to place himself in attractive settings. "He has used his Oval Office desk and the world beyond, such dramatic sites as the invasion beaches of Normandy, as a stage for presentations of a presidential image that is carefully groomed by his managers but instinctively acted by Mr. Reagan himself. ... "

Like FDR, Reagan was Popular enough to win our hearts and give us hope for the future, but he was also Powerful. And "Now, Mr. Reagan, is again playing from his patented strength; his ability to appeal to the nation's idealism and simplicity in the face of the government's complexities."[2]

William Rusher, publisher of *National Review* commenting on Reagan's ability, said, "Like a skillful club boxer, Reagan moved into the attack, landed his punches, backed off, shifted his weight, parried, and attacked again. I came to feel that I was watching a protagonist who knew precisely what he wanted, enjoyed battling for it, and firmly intended to get it in the long run. Conservatism, it seemed to me, not only had never had a finer champion in the White House but, in the light of the odds in politics, could rarely if ever expect to be quite so lucky again."[3]

As a military leader, our president marched soldiers into a Marxist dominated country named Grenada, slew evil men, set the captives free, and emerged a hero.

After sitting through the "Perils of Presidents Powerful, Peaceful, and Perfect," the public was ready for the Marlboro man to come in on his horse, tell a few tall tales and turn into President Popular right before our eyes.

As with all Populars, President Reagan loves the spotlight and can take even an ordinary script and sanctify it into a moving soliloquy.

When he was running against Walter Mondale, a meticulous Perfect whose hair never blew in the wind, Reagan played the engaging Prince to Walter's Pauper.

Murray Kempton, New York columnist, wrote of these two: "Mondale's candle emits a faint glow, to be sure, but even if it took flame, the blaze of Ronald Reagan's light would still obscure it. For Reagan is an artist and Mondale is no more than the rest of us. ... "[4]

As we have sat happily in the audience, what roles has our president played? In tribute to his leadership ability, the oldest president ever comes across as the "All-American Boy." *Newsweek* says, "There is a good deal of crinkly-eyed, apple-cheeked, next-door-neighborly warmth as well, a quality of likability that typecast Reagan as a nice guy in 53 of his 54 movies, and has disarmed his enemies ever since. His public persona is less Superman than Clark Kent, a decent, down-to-earth and occasionally tangle-footed mortal. Even his advanced age seems to work for him, placing him somehow beyond ambition. 'He has a high Q-factor,' one of his managers says. 'People like and trust him, and everything else is irrelevant. Clint Eastwood and Walter Cronkite have it, and John Wayne had it. So does Ronald Reagan.'"[5]

The article also calls him "an unabashed period piece—an American-hurrah throwback to the can-do spirit and the black-and-white simplicities of the past, a revival of 'Mr. Smith Goes to Washington.'

" ... They showcase his warmth, his sentiment, his cookie-jar grin and his genius for plain speech. 'He isn't Churchill,' his polltaker Richard Wirthlin says, 'but in terms of knowing the precise words that will convey an emotion, he is superb.'

"He has had a free ride in the politics of 1984 thus far, bobbing above the political marketplace like a balloon in a Thanksgiving Day parade while a pallid lot of Democrats scratch and claw one another in the streets below."[6]

President Popular turns his American boy image into the aura of a hero and makes everyone watching feel "tall in the saddle." As Lance Morrow says, "He gives America heroes — heroes in the gallery when he delivers a State of the Union address, heroes from the Olympics, heroes from old movies, John Wayne and Gary Cooper quotations in the middle of political speeches. His amiable being — the sheer niceness and normality of the man —seems to transcend his policies, to immunize him from the poisonous implications of some of his own opinions. Americans respond to the strength and clarity of his character, the predictability of his resolve.

" ... He has made a brilliant career out of being underestimated. Critics have rather superciliously thought that an actor coming into politics was somehow getting in over his head, working in deeper professional waters than he should try. To a politician, an actor was a lightweight, which may say something about the limited self-awareness of politicians. If they had thought more carefully, or taken Reagan more seriously, they might have recognized that the actor's gift, applied to politics, has profound implications. ...

"But then Reagan has always been attended by an aura of amiable averageness."[7]

Our Popular President is not only the All-American boy of "amiable averageness" floating above the mundane problems of life, he is also a magician. The term, "the Reagan magic," has been used from the beginning to mean two things. One, he has such charisma that he draws people to him like a magnet and, two, he can get involved in sticky situations, face adverse circumstances that would have overwhelmed Ford and put Carter on valium, and he waves his magic wand and comes out smelling like the proverbial rose.

Morrow writes, "The business of magic is sleight of hand; now you see it, now you don't. Ronald Reagan is a sort of masterpiece of American magic — apparently one of the simplest, most uncomplicated creatures alive, and yet a character of rich meanings, of complexities that connect him with the myths and powers of his country in an unprecedented way."[8]

Even when critics have proclaimed Reagan to be down and on his way out, his magic touch has transformed his public image. Hugh Sidey calls him "the great Houdini of American politics ... looking for the rainbow just beyond the thunderheads that always threaten but have not yet driven him down."[9]

After *Time* had raised the question of whether Reagan could recover from the Iran inquisition, Madhuri Talibuddin from Bombay, India, wrote a letter to the editors: "In spite of his grave folly, President Reagan is well on his way to regaining public confidence. He is a survivor par excellence. A head of state can have all the requisites for leadership, but without charisma he will not make a dent. Even Reagan's worst critics must concede that it does not matter what attributes he has or lacks; he has that essential magnetic spell."[10]

With his magnetic spell, his magic touch, Reagan has been able to create an aura of leadership, a combination, at the best, of FDR and JFK, without the negatively aggressive traits that sometimes tainted their charm.

In addition to being Popular, Reagan has a touch of both the Powerful in decisions and the Peaceful that keeps him from appearing too eager or too tense. Former White House Communications Director and writer Pat Buchanan said "Ronald Reagan was, and is, among the most decent and gracious human beings ever to serve in high office, a delight to work for and with, a genuinely lovable man. ... "[11]

Another commentator said, "He's the least neurotic president we've ever had." Some have seen him as so laid back and relaxed that he appears to be "disengaged." Because the media have apparently spent no time learning the concepts of Hippocrates' four basic temperaments, they never seem to grasp why a political leader succeeds or fails in any certain direction.

For those of us who do understand the different personalities, we don't have to grope for explanations. We know the Popular will have charm, style and humor, and be weak on details, memory and facts. The Peaceful part gives him an unruffled calm and amiability detracted by a stubborn streak and remote attitude when the subject is dull and dreary. The Powerful part gives him that ability to make hard commanding decisions seemingly at will and to succeed almost effortlessly.

Because we know the strengths and weaknesses of each personality, we are not as surprised by Reagan's magnetism as others seem to be. *Newsweek* praised, "Although it may be too much to say that Ronald Reagan has reinvented the presidency during his first 45 months in office, he has unquestionably revitalized it.

"The aura of leadership may be the most significant accomplishment of Reagan's first term ... He has demonstrated a master of the bully pulpit that is equaled only by FDR in modern times."[12]

Again, *Newsweek* says, "He is a genius in the master of the functions of the office — its ceremonial role in the national psyche, the president as a father figure, cheerleader, commander-in-chief. Reagan's own amiable personality and even his practiced command of television are only part of that leadership style. ...

"Reagan has undeniably brought about a revival of patriotism, confidence and national purpose. ...

"Reagan personifies an idealized image of what America would like to be."[13]

" ... he brought skills as a public speaker and experienced television performer which served him well in presenting his views to the American people, and that, unlike the three previous presidents, he refused to compromise his basic outlook on what ailed the economy or what America's role in the world should be. Drift and equivocation were replaced with confident leadership that even some liberal critics admired. ...

"Reagan's economic proposals were pure full-strength conservative medicine for the decade-long stagflation. His 'supply-side' economics, soon dubbed 'Reaganomics,' presumed that the economic problems were a result of government intrusions into the marketplace and excessive taxes on workers and business. ... "[14]

Yes, he's the all-American boy, the hero, the balloon floating serenely overhead, the magician, the leader with unexplained appeal. Even though he makes mistakes, the people love him enough to forgive him. "That immunity from all the usual laws of politics — the teflon factor — is the ultimate mystery of Ronald Reagan's success."[15]

Another role Reagan plays with ease is the Lucky Irishman. Tom Morganthau attributes part of Reagan's luck to being in the right place at the right time and catching the sense of "the nation's deep-seated need to believe in itself again. Reagan was fortunate to take office after four failed presidencies and 16 years of national humiliation — Vietnam, Watergate, the Arab oil embargo, Iran. America had a colossal case of the jitters, a historic case of self-doubt; Jimmy Carter was right about the 'national malaise,' but woefully mistaken about its remedy. Reagan has found the tonic for America. He has wrapped himself in the symbols of patriotism, reasserted traditional values and re-evoked the slumbering sense of national destiny. It smacks of jingoistic nostalgia to some in his audience and strikes others as wholly synthetic — but the polls suggest that it plays wonderfully well with the majority."[16]

Yes, Reagan's Irish Luck plays well with the audience who so desperately want a leader they can admire. Even though we won the Revolutionary War and emerged from the yoke of royal rule, for two centuries we've missed the pomp and circumstance of a monarchy and that settled feeling of a destiny determined by some divine appointment. I've always wanted to be a queen myself, and in my years of studying presidential personalities, aside from the brief spot of Camelot, no one has compared our democratically elected leaders with royalty until the reign of the Reagans. At the time of Reagan's second nomination, Richard Moose, Secretary of State for African Affairs in the Carter Administration, wrote from London that the Republicans should nominate Ronald Reagan to be king of the United States.

"Mr. Reagan obviously possesses many of the attributes of the modern constitutional monarch. He can play virtually any role. ...

"Think, too, of the kingly duties that Mr. Reagan already handles so well. There could be no more appropriate figure in our United States to open the Olympics, to congratulate the Astronaut of the Week or to perform other non-controversial but meaningful national rituals. In sum, Mr. Reagan is a genuinely unifying figure. ... "[17]

The most obvious strength of the Popular is their sense of humor, their ability to turn any trivial happening of life into a comedy routine, and humor has served Reagan well.

Sam Donaldson in his book *Hold on, Mr. President* gives Reagan credit for being funny. "In 1984 I told him, '(Walter Mondale) says you're intellectually lazy and you're forgetful. He says you're providing leadership by amnesia.' Reagan rose to the moment. 'I'm surprised he knew what the word meant.'"

Donaldson's favorite Reagan line on Mondale came when NBC's Andrea Mitchell yelled, "What about Mondale's charges?"

"'He ought to pay them,' said the president."[18]

Columnist James Reston, in writing of the '84 election, said the only fun was that nobody knew what was going on. He felt campaigning was a "goofy way" to pick a president but it gives the people something to think about after the world series. He felt Mondale and Hart, two serious Perfects, were too heavy handed and said of Reagan, "He's the only guy in this presidential race with a sense of humor. He turns all his defects to advantage, and even laughs at his old age...

"The other day, addressing a convention of old geezers, he told them he had been around for quite awhile himself — now the oldest president in the history of the republic — but he insisted that he was still so active that he proposed this year 'to campaign in all 13 states'."[19]

On Reagan's 76th birthday, he was heard to say, "I've been around for a while. I can remember when a hot story broke and the reporters would run in yelling, 'Stop the chisels!'"

At the 150th birthday party for the state of Texas, he quipped, "I'm always happy to be any place that's twice as old as I am."

When speaking in Florida, he opened with, "Ponce de Leon looked for the fountain of youth. And just in case he found it, I've got a Thermos jug."

When he was shot and being wheeled into surgery with a bullet near his heart, he looked up and said, "I hope the surgeon is a Republican."

Reagan uses his humor to entertain, to defuse tension, and to help himself relax. Once he has the first laughing response in a speech, he is at ease. He will often stray from the text to insert a story. Speaking on the shores of Lake Michigan, he ad libbed, "Being here along the lake reminds me of a story — when you're my age, everything reminds you of a story."

Whenever he thinks of a story he tells it even if he's at a serious meeting. Some feel he rambles on to avoid confrontations and distract the opposition. A new hobby for the president is the collecting and telling of Russian jokes. One favorite is, "The man goes to the official agency, puts down his money and is told that he can take delivery of his automobile in exactly 10 years.

"'Morning or afternoon?' the purchaser asks. 'Ten years from now, what difference does it make?' replies the clerk.

"'Well,' says the car-buyer, 'the plumber's coming in the morning.'"

Here are two more from his current collection:

"What are the four things wrong with Soviet agriculture? Spring, summer, winter and fall."

"What is the definition of a Communist? Someone who has read the works of Marx and Lenin. What is the definition of an anti-Communist? Someone who understands the works of Marx and Lenin."[20]

Along with Reagan's sense of humor comes his unique ability to personalize politics. He can take a complex issue and bring it into focus by making a personal analogy that the public can understand. Roger Rosenblatt explains it this way, "In forests of complex issues, Reagan likes to point to the trees, to individuals.

" ... Think back to all you know of Ronald Reagan, and there is almost always some other person in the picture. Originally, that person was you, the individual tree he addressed with startling success when he posed the question in the 1980 presidential debates, 'Are you better off than you were four years ago?' In the six years since, you have remained pre-eminent in the president's view. It still is you he addresses in weekly radio broadcasts and in television appearances, establishing an intimacy by look and voice that television, for all its domestic directness, usually denies. ...

"Britain is America's ally, but that abstract agreement is brought to life by personification, by the friendship and ideological comradeship of Reagan and Margaret Thatcher. Libya is America's enemy, but that enmity glowers as a private hostility between Reagan and Muammar Gaddafi. If the values of American initiative need commending, Reagan will shed his spotlight on a Mother Hale of Harlem, as he did in the 1985 State of the Union message, and elevate one woman to emblemize an entire economic and social theory. If heroism in war is to be honored, a single veteran will stand beside the president on the White House steps, creating a tableau that speaks, if imprecisely, for itself. ...

" ... Reagan wholeheartedly seems to believe that individuals and stories about individuals are the keys to general truths."[21]

Whatever Reagan says and does, the press looks upon it as part of an eight-act play. I assume if he'd been a doctor they'd have described him in medical terms or, had he been a general, like Ike, they'd have used military expressions. But Reagan was an actor and the media loves to write reviews of his roles.

When Reagan performed well with Gorbachev at the Geneva Summit,

Thomas Griffith wrote, "The press has long treated Reagan's acting career as a poor qualification for office, but one valuable lesson Reagan surely learned in Hollywood: how to fit himself into a role and stay consistent in the part, even when a film is being shot over a period of weeks."[22]

In March 1987, the president "put on a performance" for the press at a news conference and gave "well-rehearsed answers." George Church wrote in *Time*, "As theatre it was an effective show, calculated to convey the impression of a president physically and mentally recovered from his Iranscam doldrums and back in charge. ... "[23]

Hugh Sidey wrote of the presidential trips as a sideshow, "The spring henbit touched the pastures of Missouri with a delicate lavender, and the 'Kewpie' cheerleaders were deep into Ivory soap when Ronald Reagan arrived in Columbia last week in search of himself. He's playing America again after months as a captive inside the Washington Beltway, where always is heard a discouraging word and the skies are cloudy most days."[24]

Sidey later wrote about Reagan's message of explanation in theatrical terms. "The curtain is down on the summer's Iran-Contra drama ... It was a speech that satisfied neither friends nor enemies. But it was one that was inside the president as simple and pure as a diamond and had to come out, audience acceptance or not."

Typical of his personality, Reagan remained " ... stubborn and unbowed and believing and upbeat; he refuses to hold a grudge ... Reagan is calling for the nation to forget and move into the future. ... And Reagan has read the American audience better than any other politician of this decade."[25]

Much to the dismay of his opponents, Reagan can hold an audience better than anyone else. His years of acting experience, his natural humor and quick wit, his sincere confidence in his ability all add up to his designation as the Great Communicator. He is able to bring people over to his side in such a charming way that they don't realize they've moved until they hear themselves saying "I do." Suddenly, they're married to an idea they may not have understood before because the walk up the aisle was so convincing.

In a *Times Mirror* report, the electorate was divided into 11 categories, with colorful names such as Moralists, Upbeats, Disaffecteds, and Passive Poor. One of the report's major conclusions is that Ronald Reagan has cut across all previous segments of society to unite people behind him, but not necessarily to the Republican party. His personal magnetism has been the attraction. ... He has broadened his base of appeal, but the report wonders how these disparate segments will vote when there is no Ronald Reagan at the head of the party. In a conclusion, the report states, "Reagan surely earned his 'Great Communicator' fame by conquering four distinct appeals to four distinct groups without turning one against the other. It will be a difficult feat to match."[26]

And so it will!

Newsweek calls Reagan "the Master of the Media," and tells of his trip to Ireland, where he " ... played his part like a pro, hoisting a glass with the villagers in John and Mary O'Farrell's pub in Ballyporeen and noting his authentically humble origins in the authentically Irish town. Landing earlier at Shannon airport, he said he came to find not only his own roots, but America's roots as well — a bit of hyperbole that must have rung true to at least some of the 40 million Irish-Americans at home. It was boffo, solid gold at the political box office, and it left his aides wishing for more."[27]

And there was more. "In November of 1985, we had gone to Geneva for the president's first encounter with Secretary Gorbachev, with the press warning the summit would blow up if we refused to compromise on SDI. The president refused, and we came home in triumph.

"In October of 1986, we had gone to Reykjavik, where the president played that wild Sunday afternoon poker game on nuclear weapons; and when the president angrily walked out of the first-floor room at Hofdi House, rather than yield up SDI to Mikhail Gorbachev, he escaped the Russian bear trap and returned home to another triumphant welcome — to the puzzlement, again, of a press corps that had already laid at Ronald Reagan's feet blame for the summit's collapse.

"From an approval rating in the mid-50s in February of 1985, Ronald Reagan, by the fall of 1986, was in the mid-70s — an unprecedented register of national esteem for a second-term president."[28]

As with every set of strengths, there are accompanying weaknesses. The Powerfuls have strong, loud assets with equally noticeable weaknesses. The Peacefuls have quiet, low-key strengths and weaknesses that aren't obvious. The Perfects have deep intellectual analytical, strengths, which, when thwarted, turn into depression. Primary Populars, like Reagan, have appealing, obviously optimistic strengths that show. They feel it's what's up front that counts. Those who criticize, claim the Populars have no depth, no goals, no concern for facts, and an utter disregard for the harsh realities of life. But Reagan has minimized his weaknesses and they are balanced by his Powerful decisiveness and Peaceful amiability.

His Powerful nature and Popular charm enabled him to force his policies through a hostile Congress that resulted in the great reduction in interest rates and eventually unemployment. In foreign policy we saw him free Grenada and punish Libya for its terrorists acts against Americans. However, because of his Peaceful tendencies Reagan often delegated responsibilities to others and was not as aware as he should have been of what they actually were doing.

Throughout the Iranscam investigations, there have been numerous explanations of Reagan's involvement and detachment from the arms for hostages negotiations. Political pundits have asked, "What did the president forget and when did he choose to forget it?"

The thinking public has been shocked at Reagan's lack of knowledge about what was going on and Chuck Colson, who certainly has experience in cover-up operations, has said, "In the Nixon White House, you couldn't make any foreign-policy decision, I don't care how insignificant, without the president. The fact that foreign policy could be conducted out of the basement of the White House without the president knowing about it — I slept less well at night."[29]

In all the copy I've read from different political perspectives, no one has connected Reagan's supposed failures with his inborn personality especially as it fits into a typical Popular pattern so perfectly.

Brent Scowcroft of the Tower Commission explained that the president's concept of what was going on "was not accurately reflected in the reality of the operation." Even after Reagan had the truth laid out clearly before him, not couched in journalistic jargon, he couldn't see that he'd done anything wrong. His classic explanation given on television could well go down in history books written for Populars. "A few months ago, I told the American people I didn't trade arms for hostages. My heart and my best intentions still tell me that is true, but the facts and the evidence tell me it is not."

Despite the fact that for months the press has tried to present President Reagan as a liar to the American people, three major investigations of the Iran-Contra affair have found him innocent of wrongdoing, and as a typical sanguine he has once again landed on his feet.

As the press wondered why the president often left details to subordinates, no one came up with a better rationale than "that's his management style." He was born optimistic and his "can do" approach put him in the presidency. He is not a peculiar, one-of-a-kind person, as the press might make him appear. He is not "out to lunch," he is "out to win." He has known since childhood that there is a desire in each one of us to live happily ever after and he's going to keep that little flickering flame alive in the hearts of the American people.

Reagan knows we, the public, like silver linings better than dark clouds and he correctly estimated that the majority of Americans saw Oliver North as patriotic. He sensed we weren't up to another Watergate investigated by sanctimonious senators and puritanical prosecutors, many of whom wouldn't have made it to the top if they hadn't compromised many standards along the way.

Reagan has a sixth-sense of what the public wants, that is typical of the Popular. He's not acting; for him, "all the world's a stage."

In Washington, the Perfect pundits assume the president is plotting all night, coming up with carefully phrased reasons, but he's sleeping soundly knowing that, when he opens his mouth, creative reasons will flow forth effortlessly. They always have. He lives what he says.

The press didn't realize that Ronald Reagan was a man of high ideals and convictions. He had been proclaiming and living his ideology since before Goldwater. Says George Will, "Reagan was, from the start, a 'conviction politician,' working for an ideological movement before he began seeking an office."[30]

When the stock market crash produced Black Monday, and he had difficulty getting his Supreme Court nominees through the Judiciary Committee, and Nancy had breast cancer surgery, even ebullient Ronnie had difficulty in bouncing back. As a Popular, he couldn't face life when it wasn't fun and his Peaceful touch refused to deal with confrontation. While the people waited for a sign from "Daddy" that all's well with the world, he stayed in his room. The Great Communicator refused to communicate.

Populars usually marry Perfects who prepare a way for them and pick up the pieces behind them. This arrangement has worked well for the Reagans. He smiled, she worried. When he had surgery, she cared for him. Then the scene changed, Nancy was in the hospital. The steady one was unsteady. The roles were reversed. President Popular had his props pulled out from under him and the press attacked.

Nancy said, "We've hit bottom. It can't get any lower than this." But Ronnie, after reviewing reality, packed up his troubles in an old kit bag and regained his usual optimism. He turned his back on his critics and invited Gorbachev to a summit. The king's not dead, he just took a nap.

Reagan's reign will be remembered for the depth of its characters, the intricacies of its plot, the many policy successes, the brilliance of its setting, the humor of its script, the resiliency of its cast, the charisma of its leading man and the conclusion we all wanted to see: "They lived happily ever after."

No one can be all things to all people, but Ronald Reagan has used his strengths to their fullest and not let his weaknesses slow him down.

President Ronald Reagan, a legend in his own time, received the standing ovation of his life at the Superdome in New Orleans. As I had the exciting privilege to be among the chanting and footstomping thousands at the Republican convention, I was able to personally experience the magnetic attraction that Reagan's appearance created by his merely standing at the podium without saying a word. Here was the all-American boy with his winning smile looking down from the huge TV monitors high above the convention floor. Here was the hero we all desperately wanted, tall in the saddle, an average person who had fulfilled the American dream of becoming president. Here was the magician who took words that appeared ordinary on paper and turned them into a moving message so full of conviction, so rich in rosy images, so touching as to bring tears to thousands. Here was the master showman who with a sweep of his hand or a choke in his throat could cause chanting and applause to interrupt his 44-minute message 60 times. Here was the king with the passionate desire to please his subjects, waving to the beat of "Hail to the Chief," as the delegates erupted into screams and cheers while holding placards saying "Ron for King." Here was the eternal optimist lifting the hopes of his people.

"When I pack up my bags in Washington, don't expect me to be happy to hear all this talk about the twilight of my life," he said. "Twilight? Not in America. Here, it's a sunrise every day. Fresh new opportunities. Dreams to build."

Here was the movie star encouraging his cast. "So George," he said, "I'm in your corner. I'm ready to volunteer a little advice now and then, and offer a pointer or two on strategy if asked. I'll help keep the facts straight or just stand back and cheer. But George, just one personal request: Go out there and win one for the Gipper."

By the time Ronald Reagan told George to win one for the Gipper, I was in tears and couldn't imagine our country without the Popular personality of this president. No matter what anyone might think of his credentials, his creeds or his accomplishments, one would have to be moved by his magnetic presence and wonder who could possibly fill his shoes. As the crowd exploded in cheers and tears, thousands of red, white and blue balloons dropped from the Superdome ceiling, confetti floated through the air and a costumed marching band played "The Stars and Stripes Forever."

It was the last act of an eight-part play as Ronnie kissed Nancy tenderly, took her hand in his, waved a last good-by and walked off the stage to the song "Proud to be an American."

This was the swan song, a classic moment, the last hurrah of a Popular President.

Reagan will remain forever as a true representative of the Popular Personality. No matter what criticism he received he could turn it into humor, gently making fun of himself. No matter how serious his mistakes or how forgetful his mind, he could shrug his shoulders and smile and we'd be on his side.

Ronald Reagan knew how to win friends and influence people; he could keep the public's eye focusing on his strengths and quickly forgiving his weaknesses. The teflon president closed his era of peace and prosperity with the extraordinary approval rating of 60 percent. The Great Communicator came in on his strengths and with minor dips in his ratings he maintained his popularity at a remarkable level.

In the final days of the 1988 campaign, he challenged us to go out and vote. With a farewell choke in his voice, he said softly, "Help George win one for the Gipper." And he did!

Ronald Reagan

Popular (Sanguine)

Strengths

master of the media
magnetic storyteller
totes a magic wand
has that essential magic spell
refuses to hold a grudge
fairy tale of American power
makes reality conform with
  his desires
looks through lens of best
  intentions
afternoon family theatre
people like him & trust him
the old master
the great communicator
looking for the rainbow
accentuates the positive
waxes eloquent
able to stage the news

stands tall in the saddle
upbeat spirit
patriotic vitality
the great disarmer

Weaknesses

sometimes disengaged
drifts into oft-repeated
  anecdotes
unfounded optimism
erratic & selective
  memory
gives salesmen speeches
slides around the question
tends to delegate too much
  authority

Ronald Reagan

Powerful (Choleric)

Strengths
audaciously enterprising
bucks the tide
excels in emergencies
inspires loyalty from his
   subordinates
self-assured in his plan
   of action
decisive and unwavering
keen in discernment
evokes praise even from
   his enemies
born leader and organizer
persuasive and eloquent
able to induce hostile
   democrats into supporting
   his legislation

Weaknesses
manipulative
overbearing
impatient
intolerant
impetuous
unduly confident
recklessly bold

Peaceful (Phlegmatic)

Weaknesses
does not like to confront
monumental indiffer-
   ence
can be passive in the face
   of problems
sometimes delegates
   without proper
   supervision

Strengths
simple & pure as a diamond
least neurotic of all
avoids confrontations at all
   costs
refuses to get upset
sheer serenity

Act III—
The Campaign
of 1988

20

Searching For A Superman In 1988

Personality Principle: *We want a leader with all strengths and no weaknesses.*

History has shown that every campaign has its own brand of humor but who would have created the concept of calling the candidates the Seven Dwarfs unless there was some resemblance. Once the thought was triggered, the idea caught on and suddenly the Seven Dwarfs were everywhere. In the Fall of 1987, the seven appeared on television so frequently that an inexperienced viewer might have thought they came together as some sort of a package deal. Instead of voting for one Giant, you cast your ballot for the Seven Dwarfs, seven presidents rolled up into one.

Time writer Walter Shapiro called them the "Somber Seven" and the "Not-Ready-for-Prime-Time-Players." In his hilarious review of William F. Buckley taunting the seven on his TV show, *Firing Line,* Shapiro said, "Painfully earnest and briefing-book glib," the somber septet seemed like participants in a video dating service for Democrats. "Jesse Jackson and Delaware Senator Joseph Biden, the orators of the group, seemed to believe that flights of rhetoric would be unseemly at such a high-tone forum. Two of the technocratic moderates in the race, Missouri Congressman Richard Gephardt and Tennessee Senator Albert Gore, Jr., were largely content to enhance their images of quiet competence. That void left Massachusetts Governor Michael Dukakis, Illinois Senator Paul Simon and former Arizona Governor Bruce Babbitt in charge of providing charisma, a task akin to asking Comedian Jay Leno to dance *Swan Lake*."[1]

Republican consultant Roger Ailes more aptly described the group when he said, "If these guys were on 'The Dating Game' nobody would get picked."[2]

In a line-up of Democratic dwarfs and Republican robots, the American people of 1988 were searching for a Superman. We wanted to create a new type of hero with all strengths and no weaknesses. Laurence Barrett wrote, "The active contenders will be searching for growth hormones. ... "[3] The Democratic six survivors and the Republican six-pack tried desperately to become the dozen dynamos. With Biden self-destructing and searching for a new script, the other candidates were looking for some mythical beanstalk to climb that would transform one of them into a giant when he reached the top.

Humorous suggestions were made on selecting a sure winner.

GOP National Committee Chairman Frank Fahrenkopf suggested the Democrats run Ronald McDonald. "Finally, the Democrats will have a presidential candidate with positive name recognition," he said.

Harper's Index reported that in 1985 44 percent of Americans did not recognize George Bush while only seven percent did not recognize Mr. Clean. With a 93 percent recognition factor Mr. Clean could make a clean sweep, clean up our problems, and not take us to the cleaners.

SPY magazine, reaching into the realm of the absurd, reported their survey of a fitting replacement for Ronald Reagan. First choice was Charleton Heston, who surely has dignity, authority and the voice of God Himself. Second was Paul Newman, who might give out free salad dressing as a campaign gimmick. Third was Bill Cosby who would definitely edge out Jesse Jackson.

In sixth place was Johnny Carson, who would add a needed sense of humor to the campaign. If elected he could be introduced at press conferences by Ed McMahon, White House Chief of Staff, with the familiar "Here's Johnny," giving us all a comfortable and secure feeling. He could even change wives once or twice during his term to give us fresh first ladies as replacements for the ones wearing down from the routines and regimens of public life.

The *SPY* survey showed that four percent of the American public was excited about Paul Simon for president, believing he is the popular singer and not the bow-tied Senator.

Could we create the perfect candidate? One who looks like Paul Newman, speaks like Charleton Heston, promotes family values like Bill Cosby, is morally spotless like Mr. Clean, is a TV natural like Johnny Carson, sings like Paul Simon, and is revered internationally like Ronald McDonald?

Is there such a person? Can we ever find a Superman sitting on a pot of gold at the end of our romantic rainbow?

George Will, tongue in cheek, has already filled the U.N. Ambassador post with Barbara Streisand: "She is left and loud, so she would fit right in,"[4] and suggested Joe Biden as the first Supreme Court nominee. He deserves to go through the intensive investigation he gave Judge Robert Bork.

We want our Superman to perform with the charm of Reagan, but shed all of his weaknesses. We want him both the same and different. We want the Shakespearean hero without the tragic flaw.

Norman J. Ornstein, resident scholar at the American Enterprise Institute, wrote, "There are things about Ronald Reagan people have liked and things about Ronald Reagan people have disliked. They liked the bold president, who could move with broad brushstrokes and define problems and act on them, that they saw in 1981. They liked the president who could come in, knock some heads together and against all the odds make Washington work as he did in 1981. They liked the president who seemed strong and self-assured and willing to get out there and do tough things. They liked the president who was optimistic. And finally they liked the president who was very secure in himself, did not have, it seemed, a dark side.

"But people did not like the inattention to detail. They didn't like the administrative botch-ups. ... And I think what we're looking for here is somebody who embodies those positive characteristics of leadership that Reagan represented while rather joyfully rejecting the negatives."[5]

In an article entitled "Ordinary Isn't Bad for a President," Lewis Lapham, editor of *Harper's* said we shouldn't be searching for a superman. Talking of "political dwarfs" he refreshed our memory, "that most American presidents have proved themselves as resolutely second-rate as Benjamin Harrison, James Buchanan, Rutherford B. Hayes, William McKinley and Millard Fillmore. Nor, apparently, do the critics know, or wish to know, that in the music halls of American Politics mediocrity is the norm, not the exception.

"How could it be otherwise? Mediocrity is the common clay of the human condition."[6]

In the campaign of 1988 the musical halls were full of mediocrity as the people were searching for a star.

When the people don't understand the basic personality patterns they assume that there really is a leader who has all strengths and no weaknesses. The week before the election *Newsweek* wrote, "The dream persists of a candidate who will one day cast off the handlers, ignore the polls and focus groups, sound genuine notes of leadership and rouse the country to a new sense of purpose."[7]

Until we awake from the dream and accept our leaders as fallible human beings, we'll keep searching for a Superman.

21

Hart Attack

Gary Hart

Perfect

Personality Principle: *The Perfect person may be mystical, remote and out of touch with reality.*

In the good old days presidential campaigns didn't get revved up until after the two political conventions when the nominees were chosen, but in these days it seems as though the new president is hardly able to sit down in the Oval Office before speculation begins on who will try to unseat him. There was something exciting about the conventions when you didn't know who would be chosen by his party.

I can remember as a child sitting with my father by the radio and listening to each state cast its votes for nomination. We would keep a tally on a little chart and add on as each number was announced. Somehow it made us feel a part of the selection process and gave us a special evening of suspense.

But things have changed now with the Iowa caucus and Super Tuesday. Someone seems to be running for president all the time. Gary Hart had hardly given up to Mondale in 1984 when he announced he would run again. He must have met himself coming and going. Because of his name identification and a ready organization, he got the early start and was labeled the front-runner before there really was a pack to be in front of.

Gary had never been a typical candidate as there was something strange and mysterious about him. He was apparently intellectual and focused on idealistic issues, but Washington worried about why he'd changed his name from Gary Hartpence and why he seemed to be uncertain about his own age.

He grew up in Ottawa, Kansas, with a Peaceful father, Carl, who delivered heating oil and spent the rest of his time fishing. His mother was a Perfect: neat, orderly, fastidious, religious, moralistic and directive. She believed that to be a good church member you couldn't do anything that might be considered fun. Frivolity was a sin. Nina wore no make-up or jewelry and forbade Gary from smoking, drinking, dancing and going to the movies.

This didn't leave him many options but studying and going to church. He stayed by himself and read books. In the 5th grade he set a goal to read 100 books, and he did. He was obviously looked upon as a bookworm, and seemed a little remote, somewhat out of the mainstream of life, small though the social stream was in Ottawa, Kansas.

Mother Nina doted on her only son, helped him with his homework, and picked out his clothes. She kept him in church as much as possible and at age 14 he preached his first sermon. Living in a town of about 11,000, with all the restrictions he had upon him, depressed him, and he aimed to get out of town and make something of himself. His mother had high hopes for Gary that did not include his driving fast cars, and bleaching his hair, his two teen-age tokens of rebellion.

At Bethany Nazarene College he fell in love with the most Popular girl on campus, Lee Ludwig, whose father was a Nazarene pastor. While at Yale Divinity School, he began to question his faith, his marriage and his purpose in life. It was at this point that he first saw John F. Kennedy and caught the vision of a new venue in politics, which led him to the McGovern campaign and later a position in the Senate. He changed from Yale Divinity School to Yale Law School, dropped the idea of ministry and changed his name.

No one has cared that he changed it except for the fact that he hid the transfer and when pressed on it denied it was his idea. Later he recanted, causing us to wonder why he would be deceptive on such a minor matter.

He has always had organizational skills, he carefully outlines his messages, and he has written spy novels; yet he finds it difficult to be real with people and to show warmth and affection. He seems to be playing a part, rehearsing for the lead.

Newsweek said of him in the April 13, 1987 edition before any of his escapades had been made public, "There is something defiantly unfinished about him — enigmatic is the currently fashionable word ... he must in the months ahead reveal himself — something he has been loath to do. Hart has always preferred the role of the insurgent, a crusader. That way it was the movement not the man that mattered. ... Hart will never quite be comfortable with who he is, where he is going or why he wants to get there."[1]

These words of his vagueness and his unwillingness to be transparent, written before his fateful weekend, show there was already a concern about his lack of openness and reservations about his total honesty. As we look at his description, we can assume he is a Perfect type of personality, deep, distant, diffident, somewhat detached and depressed. He is "impressionable, dismissive of ritual, relentlessly intellectual, in a perpetual state of becoming."[2]

In April 1987, when he announced he would try again for the presidency, he did not make a simple announcement from behind a polished desk, but instead chose a mountain side with snow-covered peaks in the background. He stood on a rock, above his wife and daughter, appearing as a towering giant, and stated clearly, "I intend as I always have, to run a campaign of ideas." *Time's* Walter Shapiro wrote about the $1.3 million still owed from the last campaign and the raids made by U.S. Marshals on two of Hart's Los Angeles fund-raisers, and then added, "Far more amorphous, yet potentially far more serious for Hart, are the lingering echoes from what is politely called the character issue. In 1984 underlying doubts about Hart's personality took the form of an overheated discussion of his name change and his frequent misstatements of his age. This time around Hart is plagued by rumors of womanizing, all advanced without a shred of credible evidence. ... Inevitably, Hart himself will become the issue."[3]

Little did the author know when he wrote these words that within a matter of days there would be more than a shred of evidence as the *Miami Herald* reporters took Hart at his word when he dared some *New York Times* staffers, "If anyone wants to put a tail on me, go ahead. They'd be very bored." But no one was bored, and Hart himself did become the issue.

The big weekend started with an anonymous tip to the *Herald* that Hart was having an affair, had been on a yacht trip with the girl and was about to meet her at his townhouse in Washington. On Friday, reporter Jim McGee hopped on a plane from Miami. Ironically, Donna Rice was on that plane also and McGee, when he saw her enter the townhouse with Hart, remembered having seen her on the plane. On Saturday evening the pair came out of the townhouse, sensed the reporters' presence and went back in. Hart came out alone and the questioning began. Although he denied any wrong actions, Hart was obviously nervous and refused to let the reporters talk to "the woman." The next day the scoop was in the *Herald's* Sunday edition, followed by confirmation of the yacht trip.

Within a few days the Washington *Post* got proof of a different "relationship," and Hart's campaign was over, although certainly not boring. An added touch was a video tape taken by an insurance salesman from Iowa while vacationing in Florida. CBS bought the tape for

$5,000 when they learned it showed Hart relaxing on the "Monkey Business" with a young woman in a white bikini. She wasn't Donna Rice and after the trip she entered a dockside beauty contest for the title of "Miss Hot Bod." Can you imagine this cutie as a president's wife? "Meet our First Lady, Miss Hot Bod!"

Tragic though the whole affair was there was continuous humor, if only in the names. Gary Hart had left his wife on Troublesome Gulch Road while he took secret trips to Bimini on a yacht named "Monkey Business" first with Miss Hot Bod and later with a part-time actress named Donna Rice. Even author Hart himself could not have created more appropriate titles for these people and places in one of his own novels.

One headline warned, "Too Much Rice Causes Hart-Attack." Some had Hart-murmurs and later were Hart-less.

David Letterman, referring to the stake out at Hart's Washington condo where he was caught with the then-unknown dish of Rice, offered the "Top Ten Gary Hart Pick-up Lines." One was, "If anyone asks, you're my niece."

Mark Russell proclaimed, "These days you need a degree in journalism to be a Peeping Tom." Everyone began to make up jokes. One questioned, "What is the new Hart campaign slogan?" Answer: "Just say NO!"

The *Boston Herald* headlined, "I'm not a Hart-breaker!" "Actress denies bombshell sex-tryst report."

Also humorous is that Donna was plain Rice until her rendezvous with Gary, an affair that has not condemned her but catapulted her into national prominence, covers of magazines and a *20-20* interview with Barbara Walters. She was signed on to model jeans, appropriately named "No Excuses," "I make no excuses, I only wear them," but her contract was soon cancelled.

Papers and magazines produced instant articles on the infidelities of past presidents. *Life* did a splashy display with pictures of FDR and Lucy and their "affair of the heart" that took place in his railroad car on a siding in Allamuchy, New Jersey. They also showed Warren Harding's illegitimate daughter and a cartoon of Grover Cleveland's "bastard son" from the *Buffalo Telegraph* in 1884.

A survey that *Life* reported showed that 32 percent of Americans would prefer a president who "has a charismatic, exciting personality and fools around a bit in his sexual life" to one who is "completely faithful to his wife but has a rather dull personality."[4]

A poll of vital presidential qualities showed honesty as the most important followed by ability to communicate and intelligence.[5]

A *Time* poll indicated "by a ratio of roughly 10 to 1, those polled said they would be more troubled by Hart's not telling the truth than by any extramarital sexual relations."[6]

Summing up these statements, the American public doesn't much care what you do, as long as you don't flaunt it and when you're caught, you tell the truth and repent.

Lance Morrow made it clear when he wrote, "If all the adulterers who ever served in the U.S. Congress were to have their lives and legislative works obliterated from history, America might revert to forest."[7]

The third problem that Hart demonstrated after the dalliance and the deception was the apparent denial that he had done anything wrong or that it was his fault. Morrow adds, "One sensed in him a territory of ignorance about himself. On the evidence of recent weeks, Hart has moments when he's overtaken by a denial of reality, a trait that might be dangerous in the Oval Office."[8]

In the same issue of *Time*, "Hart challenged the moralistic conventions of political behavior and ultimately paid the price for his apostasy. Until the very end Hart seemed oblivious to the reality that his actions had consequences."[9]

He has not been quite able to come out with a statement of Hart-felt repentance, and his weak apologies reflect his inability to look the facts in the eye, accept the truth, and put his introspective talents to work on examining the "why" of his mistakes.

Gary Hart's whole life is like a strand of brilliant beads strung together by a thin fiber of deception. The string has broken; the hopes have shattered. Will he ever put it all together again?

"Oh, what a tangled web we weave,
When first we practice to deceive!" [10]

From May to December, all the kings horses and all the kings men must have worked overtime for suddenly there was Humpty Dumpty put together again. In a surprise move, Gary Hart emerged from self-inflicted retirement and signed in for the New Hampshire primary to rewrite his last chapter. He claimed no candidate was addressing the issues and the Democratic Party needed his leadership. The survivors were infuriated over his inference that they had been doing nothing during his seven months of introspection.

Candidate Bruce Babbitt complained, "Well, that's just baloney and I resent it. I'm here to tell Gary Hart that he has a long way to go before he reaches the standard of honesty and creativity that I have been setting in this campaign."[11]

Derogatory comments were heard from far and wide: "Morally repugnant," "recklessly stupid," "ego trip," "another Johnny Carson routine," "another soap opera segment," "another Merry Month of May," "an exercise in futility," "a circus freak show."

In a field where "undecided" was leading the pack, the last thing the survivors needed was another entry to water down their weak broth.

Analyst Robert Beckel wrote from Washington, "Gary Hart is back. The Democrats are panicked and the analysts are dumfounded. Hart's entrance is likely to be the shortest running tragedy or the shrewdest campaign move in recent political history. It all depends on how long this revival lasts.

"Clearly it is a setback for his Democratic competitors, furious over Hart's decision. And not just because they have to run against an experienced, media-savvy candidate. Hart's presence underscores the current field's weaknesses."[12]

Former Reagan advisor Stuart Spencer commented, "What gives Hart his shot is the incredible political weakness of the six other guys who stayed in the Democratic race for president. Hart may fancy himself the 'white knight' that Democrats have been hoping would rescue them from their pedestrian field. In reality, he is the seventh dwarf."[13]

In a campaign compared to a Disney classic, the last thing the Democrats needed was to add another dwarf when they were longing for a jolly green giant.

Stephen Hess, an expert on presidential politics, said, "What you have to draw is an electability index — his rate of approval minus his rate of disapproval. For him to get nominated, the Democratic Party would have to have a death wish."[14]

"I have to look at this as a complete and total ego trip," said William Sweeney, a Democratic Party consultant. "He's putting his party and friends through another round of Johnny Carson routines."[15]

James Reston, in some brilliant words, summed up the situation in this way. "The only possible explanation of the Democrats' campaign for the Presidency is that somehow it's being run by the Republicans.

"They've made every mistake in the book except bringing back Senator Kennedy. Their best men won't run and their worst won't quit. It would be funny if it weren't so serious. ... Gary Hart is making a laughing stock of his party. He treats it the way he treats his wife; as a personal convenience. By returning to the race, he kicked it when it was down and proved for the second time that his judgement is as defective as his conduct ... the reappearance of Gary Hart on the scene, however, has been helpful in only one respect. He has created such a mess in his party that it will either have to wake up or give up for another four years."[16]

While pundits were amused, Democrats enraged and Republicans thankful, Hart was busy writing his own last chapter.

Gary Hart

Perfect (Melancholy)

Strengths

mysterious
mystical
visionary
literary, cool & cerebral
issue oriented
idealistic
controlled
bookworm
complexity of character
nostalgic
dared to be different
gifted mimic
imaginative author
well-organized
quixotic
spectral
haunting
loner
carefully outlined
crusading
must be the best
voluminous position paper
high flown rhetoric

Weaknesses

seemingly unstable
recklessly stupid
loner-outsider
odd
deceptive
indignant
unrepentant
bitter
self-serving
buried anger
confused about himself
self destructive psychology
pre-emptive annihilation
   of self
fails to come to grips
   with himself
elusive
apocalyptic
hypocritical
cynical
truculent & testy
seriously deluded
cool, aloof & enigmatic
has a death wish
oblivious to reality

22

Happy Talks Too Much

Joseph R. Biden, Jr.

Popular

Personality Principle: *The Popular personality never lets the truth stand in the way of a good story.*

Whether or not you remember Joseph R. Biden, Jr., he is worthy of reading about for his pure representation of the Popular strengths and weaknesses. At the start of the 1988 campaign, Joe was the best known and most impressive of the Democrat's Seven Dwarfs. Joe was born in 1942 but always talks of himself as a "baby boomer," waxes eloquent on "my generation" and boasts that he was the second youngest person ever to be elected to the U.S. Senate.

Wherever he is, he talks about youth and vigor. He touts himself as an orator and tells touching tales about what the American family used to be like in the good old baby-boom days when mother stayed home where she belonged, kissed you good-bye in the morning and met you at the school bus with warm cookies in her hand. By the time he paints this pretty picture, all of us who have ever had mothers who baked cookies are in tears of nostalgia.

But that doesn't last for long, for as soon as he pulls on our heart strings he jerks them up sharply and cries out "the world has changed. Only 19 percent of the children in America today live in a family, the so-called nuclear family, with mom and dad, mom at home and no divorce." Now all those who've been divorced are gasping in guilt.

And so it goes with Biden's oratory, a veritable roller-coaster of emotion.

Popular, talkative Biden regrets he can't run against the Great Communicator who would have met his match. Joe sadly laments, "It seems like dullness is in."[1]

The *New York Times* reviewing Biden's New Hampshire campaign said that he was not dull. "His extemporaneous speeches are like modern jazz, with intense little riffs on American idealism and the revolution in super conductivity and the failures of the Reagan Administration's policy in the Persian Gulf. When he connects with an audience, as he did in Keene, he can moisten eyes and set heads to nodding. ... He is buoyed by such moments, by those who show up to hear the 'hot' candidate, who come ready to be transported. Even in a living room at a modest house party, Mr. Biden seems incapable of giving a low-key speech."[2]

Senator Shoot-From-the-Lip, as he is sometimes called, is a Popular personality, with a few attributes of the Powerful driver, high-powered, hot, confident, impulsive, but not Powerful enough to get himself under control.

Biden is a clear example of the principle "strengths carried to extremes become weaknesses." As a Popular he has the ability to talk fluently, speak passionately, and use colorful examples. Carried to an extreme, he monopolizes any conversation he can, is considered a "gabby lightweight," exaggerates, is not concerned with the facts, makes careless remarks, and thinks with his mouth. He loves people and wants them to love him, but if they fault him, he jumps on the defensive.

The Populars frequently have a problem with the truth because they exaggerate so consistently that after a while they don't have any idea what the facts might once have been. They have little concept of statistics, frequently make up their own to fit their need, and will innately top whatever story has just been told.

Added to his natural personality is Biden's insecure childhood where he was teased by his classmates because he stuttered and was nicknamed "Impedimenta." He determined to overcome this handicap, practiced speaking whenever possible, memorized passages and poetry, and did so well in his self-improvement course that he went on to become a passionate orator.

With Biden, his mouth was "both his greatest asset and his greatest liability," according to a *Time* campaign portrait, asking, "Does Joe Biden talk too much?" The article goes on to say, "The contrast between his highly effective speaking style and his occasional giddy lapses is curious in a politician who thinks of himself as grounded in both his psyche and his message. All his Democratic competitors save Jesse

Jackson seem bland by comparison, technocrats who emphasize specific programs and highlight their resumés. Biden's long suit is his appeal to idealism, his promise to be a president who would lead by strength of will and uncompromising candor."[3]

This quote, written before Biden's campaign began to fall apart, predicts some instability along with his abilities, mentions others who "highlight their resumés," and commends his "uncompromising candor."

Another quote worth reading is his own summary of his direction given while he was in Iowa. "I believe the 1988 election, at its heart, can be reduced to a fundamental choice between two paths to our future: the easy path, in which we consolidate our current comfort and a quick and false prosperity by consuming our children's future; and another, more difficult path, that builds a more genuine prosperity for ourselves, while guaranteeing to our children their birthright."

In retrospect, Joe did not follow the easy path, or the difficult path, but the wrong path, a path strewn with mis-statements, exaggeration, anger and plagiarism.

Biden was riding happily down the wrong path until the *New York Times* printed a story telling that Biden had not only duplicated a touching tale originating with British Labor Party leader Neil Kinnock, but he had even copied the same gestures. The *Times* had parallel videos to prove their charge. Suddenly people were calling in to say Biden had used Robert Kennedy's and Hubert Humphrey's words as if they were his own and the nightly news showed Biden and his selected mentors side by side giving clear evidence to any doubters.

Next came the report that Biden had plagiarized parts of a law-review article while at Syracuse University in 1965. This news alone would not have been enough to derail him, but added to the other quotes, it was indicting. As Biden and his staff were trying to dig out from under the damaging details, news was phoned in that *Newsweek* was publishing a story about a cable-TV, C-SPAN, that had a film of Biden lashing out at an innocent man who dared to ask about his academic credentials.

"I think I probably have a much higher IQ than you do, I suspect," Biden told the man as he began a rapid-fire account of his credentials. "I went to law school on a full academic scholarship, the only one in my class to have a full academic scholarship. I decided I didn't want to be in law school and ended up in the bottom two-thirds of my class and then decided I wanted to stay, went back to law school and, in fact, ended up in the top half of my class. I won the international moot-court competition. I was the outstanding student in the political science department at the end of my year. I graduated with three degrees from undergraduate school and 165 credits — only needed 123 credits. And I would be delighted to sit down and compare my IQ to yours if you'd like."[4]

I'm sure this answer was far more than the man ever wanted to know, but the angry, defensive way in which Biden tackled him, with his finger pointed at the man, reflected his touchy nature and suppressed anger that took little to ignite. Had Biden been secure in the fact that he had followed his own principle of "uncompromising candor," he would have had no reason to react so strongly. But in examining the tape, the reporters had found some more-than-slight exaggerations, unfortunately so typical of the Popular personality.

Biden actually "attended law school on a half-time scholarship based on financial need and ... he graduated 76th out of a class of 85. His undergraduate academic records show he graduated from Delaware 506th in a class of 688 with a 'C' average and that he got his undergraduate degree with a dual major in history and political science, two majors, not three."[5]

In a year when character and honesty were considered key virtues, and Gary Hart had already self-destructed, Biden's collection of misstatements and plagiarism were more than the public could bear. The great orator had overspoken. Even when he had appropriated Kinnock's touching message on how his ancestors had worked eight hours a day in the coal mines before coming up to play football with the children, Biden, in making the story his own, expanded the time his old ancestors spent in the mines of northeast Pennsylvania to 12 hours a day followed by four hours of playing football with the children. How tired his supposed ancestors must have been! What a miracle it was they had the strength to procreate after 16 hours each day of mining and football! When reporters checked out the anecdotes on Biden's ancestors they couldn't find any evidence that they even knew where the coal mines were or cared much about football!

Joe Biden's Popular strengths were carried to extremes, and they caught up with him.

George Church sums this up: "Accusations of plagiarism thus hurt almost as nothing else could. They turned Biden's strong point, the passionate oratory that could bring a crowd to its feet, into a subject for ridicule and fed deep suspicions about his ability to be president."[6]

USA Today said, "Biden's plagiarism was not so easily overlooked, some theorize, because it underscored his basic flaw — that he had nothing to offer but hollow rhetoric."[7]

Meg Greenfield wrote, "There is something of the invincible high-school boy about Joe Biden. It is his manner — ingenuous, good-natured, self-absorbed, awkward, incorrigibly given to not-so-funny jokes and asides. His punishment has been sensible, mild and familiar: he is going to have to take the course again, for which, this time around, he gets an F."[8]

Observing that the Democrat's score at that point was two down and six to go, Jonathan Alter and Howard Fineman in the same issue of *Newsweek* showed concern for the others. "The more disturbing cautiousness, however, could come from the candidates themselves. With every coffee klatsch now turned into a potential campaign breaker, they may measure their words so carefully that they end up saying practically nothing at all."[9]

The others may measure their words and say nothing at all, but not Joe. He knew everyone would be watching his farewell message and he pulled out all the stops. With his beautiful wife Jill standing nobly beside him, he said in lofty words, "I made some mistakes. Now the exaggerated shadow of those mistakes has begun to obscure the essence of my candidacy and the essence of Joe Biden."

Remembering the legendary oratorical rules for a sermon, three points and a poem, "Biden finished his withdrawal announcement with 'the promise proclaimed' in an old communion hymn that was a standard element of his campaign stump speech: 'And he will lift you up on eagle's wings and bear you on the breath of dawn and make the sun to shine on you.'"[10]

Shakespeare's words could have been written about Joe Biden. "Nothing in his life became him like the leaving it."

In spite of having to withdraw from the '88 campaign, Joe Biden didn't lose his sense of humor, a key Popular strength. While touring England in January 1988, he made a point of getting acquainted with Neil Kinnock and offering him the use of his speeches with or without giving him the credit. Joe can laugh even about his own presidential demise.

Joe Biden

Popular (Sanguine)

Strengths

eloquent
oratorical passion
responsive to people
wants to be liked
extemporaneous
buoyant
high key
devilish grin
ingenuous
inventive
persuasive
genial
incandescent smile
gift of gab
senator "shoot from the lip"
confident
runs on Automatic Pilot
slick stand-up style

Weaknesses

unchecked impulses
gabby
unable to settle down
shifting from one theme to
    another
easily frustrated
too passionate
easily angered
poor memory
careless remarks
fading meteor
embellishes facts
flash in the pan
short attention span
style without substance
arrives late
questionable character
strays from agenda
self-absorbed
unstable
not concerned with facts
exaggerates

23

Waving Magic Wands

In our selection system, we often start with the person's looks. Before we know what he stands for, before we've heard him open his mouth, we have made a visual judgment based on his looks.

The reason that the Kennedy and Reagan regimes have been described as reigns, Camelots and Kingdoms, is because the rulers looked like kings. They both presented themselves as royalty, were ruggedly handsome on first glance, and had magnetic appeal that riveted attention. Each one came with a real queen who wore designer gowns, ate from gold-rimmed plates every day, and maintained a regal air of confidence even in drastic situations.

When I tune in the evening news and they mention we will be seeing the Reagans giving a state dinner for Gorbachev, I stay close just to see what Nancy's wearing. If she's featuring a new fashion, I want to be among the first to follow. Even though the press has fussed about the First Lady borrowing her wardrobe from Galanos and Adolfo, I personally think a lending library of designer fashions is a brilliant idea.

I never had an urge to look like Bess Truman or have little bangs like Mamie Eisenhower. I knew I could never look fragile and pensive like Pat Nixon, but I did admire Powerful Betty Ford because she seemed so much like me both in personality and in style and one time when I followed ex-President Ford off an airplane, I was mistaken for his wife.

As a voter with above average interest in the political theatre I love to look at the costumes and as much as many of us hate to admit it we often judge a person on his or her looks.

Nelson W. Polsby, a political science professor at U.C. Berkeley, writes, "It used to be you'd look at a candidate's record. You'd watch to see what the people around him had to say. It was a kind of peer review, and it provided valuable information. If a candidate had 40 congressmen working for him, that counted for something. With candidates judged on their ability to project an appealing screen presence, the old tests of political readiness have become largely irrelevant."[1]

When politicians first appeared on television, what you saw was what they were. The individual candidates came on live without being cleaned up, cosmeticized, or coached. If the suit was wrinkled, the hair wind-blown, or the tie crooked, we accepted that as a part of the vicissitudes of everyday life. When Adlai Stevenson sat in such a way to show a hole in the bottom of his shoe, we laughed and tucked our feet under chairs; however, when Richard Nixon supposedly lost the 1960 debate with Kennedy — and later the election — because he hadn't shaved closely enough and looked tired next to robust, healthy Jack, a cry went out for make-up and make overs.

A new career was created. Media managers and image consultants came bursting forth to make candidates camera ready. What a shame these fairy godmothers had not been around earlier to replace George Washington's wooden false teeth and camouflage President Taft's weight problems.

During the preparation for the Presidential Debates of 1984, Walter Mondale was carefully worked over to improve his looks on camera. Cartoons showed him with dark circles under his eyes, so heavy "concealer" was necessary. Because Reagan is such a natural on camera, Mondale's coaches suggested he create an image of conscious masculinity. Patrick Caddell came up with "the pivot" to help Mondale look in control and dominate the debate physically. This trick of stagecraft involved a pivot turn toward Reagan, creating the impression that he was about to step over and take him on. This "pivot" was Caddell's way, in his own words, "to counter Reagan's own natural mastery of a stage with his size and his skills at body language."[2]

Republican candidate Alexander Haig made this suggestion for the much maligned and defeated Supreme Court nominee Judge Robert Bork: "As much as I love and admire Bob Bork, if I had been his choreographer, I'd have taken him in to the barber, cut that beard, cut that hair and not have him look like the reincarnation of some of the extremists the history books have taught us to be wary of."[3]

We're no longer taking such chances with our candidates. Not only are we waving magic wands over each one, but we now have a new device to instantly measure public reaction to the make overs.

Bill Batoff has created the latest gimmick in hi-tech T.V. politics, producing a second-by-second, computerized printout of the PBS Houston debates.

Newsweek says: "It was quite a show. Superimposed on the screen were graphs, bar charts and number grids, giving the continuous reactions of 85 Iowa Democrats who had watched the event with electronic 'response' dials in their laps. When one of the candidates made a lame joke, the lines dipped down in negative reaction." When one said something positive, "the audience approval boosted the graphs like the heart beat spikes on a hospital monitor."[4] How exciting it was for the candidates to know which lines raised the pulse rates of the viewers.

Speaking of the seven Democratic contenders for 1988, *Newsweek* said, "Vox Pop Hit Parade ... will consist of what amounts to T.V. auditions by a chorus line of candidates before a press and public plumbed for on-deadline reactions."[5]

Senator Paul Simon even brought his "television press secretary" to the debates to check the camera angles and show him how to cross his legs.

Because of the close television scrutiny by the public, we now have the "wimp factor" for each candidate to consider. Do you come across as a strong, tough leader, or could you be thought of as a wimp? To counteract this possibility, the Democratic candidates of 1988 invested heavily in the "muscle factor."

Time summed it up cleverly by saying about the candidates, "Like novice sportswriters, they festoon their rhetoric with images denoting oomph. They strain to adopt positions that appear to be gutsy ... they do their Atlas act to impress independent voters."[6]

With this chorus line of candidates costumed and cued, how can we ever know what each one is really like when off the political stage? The answer is that we can't really know them; some of their mates may not really know them. We may see them on camera more often than their children see them at home. By watching the candidates, or any public person, however, we can get a sense of their personalities through their gestures, postures and responses. As we observe debates, forums and interviews on TV, we can see how each person reacts to attacks and whether or not he has a sense of humor, or any sense at all. We can see how they voted on issues that represent our values, thereby knowing with some accuracy how they will vote in the future.

Meg Greenfield cautions us against choosing our leaders by the method of "Herdthink," her term for going along with the opinion of the masses, "thundering mindlessly into the sea." She observes, "The more the great loudspeaker of our political culture tells me, the less I know."

In reviewing the blandness of the 1988 candidates, she suggested that we look for surprises in the person's record that show he has a working mind and is not a robot. He should have an individual philosophy and not just be responding to some interest group or "some bean-counting totter-up of liberal-vs.-conservative votes." He should be willing to take risks and not just walk the middle road of majority acceptability, and there should be signs of growth, personal progress not created by media hype."[7]

When it is time to choose a leader, a president, an actor or an employee, "remember that you are looking for a moral person, a courageous person, a strong person and one who is neither intellectually in thrall to somebody else's political ideas or, as seems so often to be the case, just intellectually dead."

In addition to Meg's wise counsel we can also know that when we understand a person's strengths, we can project where his weaknesses will lie and not be surprised when our Superman has no muscles. We can also try to understand a candidate's value system, his worldview, and what he pre-supposes to be truth. If we know what a person bases his beliefs on, we can know with some certainty how he will make his decisions and often what those decisions will be.

Kennedy was the first American President who seemed to be born camera ready. Because he, Jackie and the children were so photogenic, the public could hardly get enough of them. We watched their every move on television and became part of the family in a vicarious way that had never been possible before. Lyndon Johnson thrived on publicity and seemed to have a knack for tossing off a folksy homily just when the camera focused in on him. The Popular side of their personalities made both Kennedy and Johnson natural and at home before the TV cameras.

When Nixon ran for president in 1968, after losing to Kennedy because of his poor TV image, he was groomed for presentation by Roger Ailes, former executive producer of the *Mike Douglas Show* and 1988 media consultant for George Bush. Ailes told a reluctant Nixon that he had to change his hatchet-man image and warm up to the people. Nixon's suspicious nature and his remote detached feelings about intimate relationships made it extremely difficult for him to present a new personality of magnetic charm.

Initially he threw off Ailes' instructions and said to him, " It's a shame a man has to use gimmicks like this to get elected." Ailes responded quickly, "television is not a gimmick, and if you think it is, you'll lose again."[8]

Nixon gave in and allowed Ailes to recast him as "the man in the arena" warmly answering the questions of a well-coached studio audience. Nixon learned that knowledge alone was not enough to win power.

Ford with his Peaceful Personality never excited audiences and his coaches found he did better staying home in the White House than tripping along the campaign trail. Even though he was the most genuinely likeable president we'd had since Eisenhower, his TV image didn't denote power. Retirement and new financial security seem to have given Ford an air of authority, for as he spoke at the 1988 National Republican Convention he took charge and supported the nominee by stating dramatically that he wouldn't stand by and let anyone pick on his friend George Bush.

Carter came across as sincere and spiritual, but the TV coaches could not wipe out his melancholy look, his furrowed brow, and his worrisome, wearying ways.

After eight years of Popular President Reagan, ever camera ready, the 1988 campaign presented the media makers with two new challenges, two candidates who have little natural charm, no innate sense of humor, and no personality in a political sense.

By eliminating Popular Jackson, the only candidate with any flash of color, or charm, the Democrats found themselves with what Patrick Buchanan labeled a "Pure Vanilla Ticket." Speaking of Dukakis and his chosen Vice-President Lloyd Bentsen, Buchanan wrote, "When they get up and speak, they simply are not glowing. There are not two men in America who are less powerful and articulate than Dukakis and Bentsen.

"As President Nixon says, people still want poetry in their politics. But Michael Dukakis is a word processor, a 'Zorba the clerk.'"[9]

Knowing that he is short on magnetism and short of stature, Dukakis set out to lift his shoes. A banner held high at the Republican Convention said, "Beware of Greeks wearing lifts."

Roger Ailes, while working over the prospects of making George Bush appear presidential, was quoted as saying, "I know there are limits to what a coach can accomplish in improving speechmaking, unless the subject is a diligent student of himself. Dukakis is totally self-absorbed in that regard. He's spent hours reinventing himself in front of a television camera. Bush says, 'That's all bull. I am what I am.' He's not a narcissistic person, and he refuses to become one."[10]

Image impressions made a major difference in the 1988 election because there was no pressing issue to help people decide. In the long run Dukakis came across as risky and Bush as comfortable. If we couldn't have charisma we'd settle for comfort. George Bush won the likability sweepstakes and the election.

24

Senator Straddle

Robert Dole

Powerful

Personality Principle: *A Powerful may become depressed when some part of life is out of control.*

The most Powerful presidential candidate of 1988 was Bob Dole. As a born leader with driving ambition, Dole has spent a lifetime projecting an image of power and strength. Even though Dole didn't make it to the finals, he, like Roosevelt, is a clear example of the born-leader rising above crippling circumstances, and his Powerful profile shows both the strengths and weaknesses of the born leader.

From the time he was a child, Bob Dole knew he was going to make something of himself. Living in the dust bowl of Kansas during the Depression, he learned, as many of us did, that hard work was the only hope for success. Bob got up at 5:30, did his chores, exercised, lifted weights and delivered papers. He studied hard enough to be a member of the National Honor Society, he was captain of the basketball team, played end on the football squad, and was a winner on the track team. In his spare time, he was a soda jerk for the local drugstore in Russell, Kansas, where he frequently stayed to close up at 11:00 p.m.

Right from the beginning, he had the Powerful traits of wanting to be in control of his life, to be independent, and not owe anything to anybody. He kept himself in physical and mental shape, he had natural good looks, and even as a teenager he had an air of authority.

With $300 he reluctantly had to borrow from George J. Deines, a banker and drugstore customer, Bob headed off to the University of Kansas. He would become a doctor and show those hometown people what he could make of himself but, instead, World War II roared onto the scene and any real American man just had to join up. Those who copped out for any reason or were rejected when they applied, were designated "4-F," a label equal to wimp or nerd today.

Bob enlisted in the Army, was commissioned a second lieutenant and was sent to Italy. In typical Army style, they assigned the young man from the plains of Kansas to the Mountain Division. Three weeks before the end of the war in Europe, Bob Dole was hit by some mortar while helping a buddy on Hill 913, 40 miles south of Bologna.

Although he received two Bronze Stars for his heroism, the awards did little to cheer him on as he lay paralyzed for 39 months, through eight operations. Anyone would be depressed over such a devastating disruption of his life's plans, but a Powerful personality can't handle being dependent upon someone else for survival.

When we understand the basic personalities and their desires, we can see what causes depression in each type of person. Take away what we want in life, make us feel helpless to achieve our goals, and we will become discouraged.

The Populars get depressed when life is no longer fun and no one is giving them complimentary attention.

The Perfects get depressed when things aren't lining up properly and people aren't sensitive to their inner feelings.

The Peacefuls get depressed when they have to face conflict personally (they can always mediate other people's problems with a cool detachment) and no one is appreciating their worth.

The Powerfuls, like Bob Dole, become depressed when any part of their life is out of control, whether it is work, family, finances, health, or body.

Bob Dole, a young man who had great ambitions and who took pride in his excellent physical condition, lost hope in his future and found himself with a shattered body, unable to control the simplest functions of living. As a Powerful, he fought back but some of the bitterness and anger felt from this devastation and the realization that life isn't fair, still sit in the seat of his emotions and seep out in the form of sarcasm even today.

The New York Times, in a lengthy article, "The Contradictions of Bob Dole," said, "Mr. Dole resented his enforced dependence and it was at this time that his temperament as a self-reliant loner began to emerge."[1]

In our awareness of the four basic temperament patterns, we can understand that the Powerful must be in control and that his greatest fear is appearing weak. Dole was born with a personality that wanted to be in charge and be strong, so his incapacitating tragedy hit straight across his major desires, crippling him physically and draining him emotionally.

As a determined winner, he, like Roosevelt, underwent painful rehabilitation and has tried to bury his handicap from view. He keeps a pen
in his useless right hand, giving the appearance that he could write
momentarily, if he chose to, and keeping people from reaching out to
shake hands with him. He has trained himself to write with his numb
left hand and to button his shirt.

As a Powerful, he has done all he possibly could to overcome his
limitations and he has never used his Bronze Stars to win elections.
However, with George Bush parading his war record before the public
in hopes of overcoming his "wimp factor,"Dole reached into his past
and produced a new video "To The Stars Through Difficulties," playing
up his heroic feats and his small town beginnings, two pluses in the
1988 campaign.

The one word most frequently used about Dole by columnists and
critics is "contradictory." This word, literally, is "contra," against, "dict,"
speaking; speaking against, giving opposite signals. In Dole's case, his
contradictions confuse the public. He resents any help and yet he needs
support to win. He doesn't seek suggestions and yet he can't succeed
without the input of the others. He has strong opinions and yet he holds
back until he sees which way the wind is blowing. In one debate, when
Bush was supporting the president's arms agreement with Russia, and
the other Republican hopefuls were opposing it, Dole said he was
reserving judgment until he'd read the treaty. Since everyone knows
Dole is highly informed on the issues and, as one wag put it, "eats bills
for breakfast," his playing dumb was a ploy to wait until he could
assess the voters' desires. As the treaty and Gorbachev himself became
popular, Dole jumped on the bandwagon and even had smiling pictures
taken of himself with President Reagan, much to the consternation of
loyal George Bush.

U.S. News and World Report had an article, "Bob Dole: Ready to
lead, but where?" They quote a colleague who said, "He is the most
obsessively driven guy I have ever seen."[2] This drive is understandable
when you take his Powerful birth personality and add the tragedy which
led him to a fanatical desire to overcome, a feeling of 'I'll show them
I can do it.'"

The article goes on to point out that in his need to be a winner, Dole
takes both sides of issues, trying not to offend the right or the left and
ending up saying nothing. They quote a budget lobbyist who comments on Dole's unexplainable waffling. "His general political style is
to watch the way people are going, then get in front of them."[3]

Dole's style is like that T-shirt of mine that says, "I must hurry and
catch up with the rest, for I am their leader." Perhaps I should send it
to Bob Dole!

In 1988 the country was looking for direction, but a man without a national vision, one waiting for the audience to write his script, was not what we wanted for our leading man.

Dole is said to be a hatchet man, acid-tongued, an opportunist, friendless, a slasher and cutter, tactless and obsessive. But on the other hand, he has compassion for the handicapped and has quietly visited their homes, pushed for favorable legislation, and set up a foundation to train the disabled. Bob Dole is a man of contradictions.

People who know him will avoid doing anything to cross him up, no one wants to be on his "black list" and he seems to be perpetually looking down on the dummies. In response to a man who complained that Dole hadn't thanked him for his contribution, the senator replied, "It just drives me up a wall. You don't have to go out of your way to tolerate all the incompetents in the world just because you're in politics."[4]

One of his staffers, with tongue in cheek, said, "Being a senator means never having to say you're sorry."[5]

In the 1988 primary contest Dole made strong, bold statements against his Peaceful opponent, "Bush says [he's] been standing by the president for 7 years. Well I've been out there working for him."[6]

Dole used terms like "hard choices," "sacrifice," "end to self-indulgence" to predict what he felt needed to be done to get the country's economy on the move again. While Bush smiled and talked of "continued prosperity" and "peace through strength," Dole latched heavily onto the October 19, 1987 stock market crash as a precursor of gloom and doom.

In the *New Orleans Times-Picayune* they quoted Bush campaign manager Lee Atwater about Dole's negative predictions. "He's running for Dr. Feelbad, Dr. Pain. I think it's a loser."[7] And it was.

To counteract this thinking and verify that the public wants to know the bitter truth, they gave Dole's reply. "If you're looking for a feel-good candidate, I'm not it. I don't want to make you feel good. I just want you to be realistic."[8] The electorate wasn't ready for realism; they were still basking in Reagan's glow.

Laurence Barrett, in *Time,* wrote, "Bob Dole exudes a can-do aura that allows him to project toughness without resorting to overheated rhetoric. When he talks about being the one Republican willing to make tough decisions to reduce the federal deficit, his listeners may dislike his message implying austerity but they respect the messenger."[9]

In reference to Bob Dole, William Schneider writes, "Dole seems embarrassed by ideas. Dole seems interested in issues only for their strategic value."

As we have already seen, Dole has an uncanny sense for sitting on the fence until it's the right moment to move onto the winning side. In reviewing the dearth of deep thinking in all the candidates of 1988, Schneider concluded that those who try to be bold and unconventional become risky and unelectable.

"Ideas are rarely at the center of presidential campaigns. Next year should be no different. Ideas are risky, and in a close election, no one wants to take risks. Instead of a contest between old ideas and new ideas, 1988 is likely to offer voters a choice between old ideas (the Republicans) and older ideas (the Democrats)."

We have a new cast with a new image and new morals, but we don't have new lines; we're still reading the same old safe script.

During the primaries there seemed to be a new respect for Bob Dole. People talked about seeing changes in him. Some say he's softened. Has there been a real change? Has the hatchet-man buried the hatchet?

Time says that since 1976, Dole has "worked hard to shed his hatchet-man image ... 'I've done a lot of soul-searching,' he says. 'I think a lot of the criticism was unfounded. I don't dislike people. I'm a very friendly person, not mean or vicious. But you take a look at how you're perceived, and obviously you don't want that perception.' Friends agree that since his marriage to Elizabeth, he has mellowed, replacing the hatchet with a stiletto."[10]

His wife, Elizabeth, a born-again Christian, who resigned from her job as Secretary for Transportation, tones down his acid-tongue with her soft Southern charm, her tactful manner, and her spiritual insight. Since their 1975 marriage, Libby has had a positive influence on the Senator, although she would be the first to admit that no one tells him what to do. He calls her his "Southern Strategy," "the greatest resource in my campaign."

Ellen Goodman says of this brilliant woman, "Elizabeth Dole is not a model of Every Workingwoman whose husband has just gotten a job opportunity 1,500 miles away. If she isn't exactly co-piloting this campaign, she has her eyes fixed on the same destination: the White House. She is one woman who would turn the First Lady from a role into a job. Her resumé is hardly at risk."[11]

As to her influence on what some are calling the "New Bob Dole," Goodman continues, "When his image tips too far to the right wing, she pulls in the flaps. In the language of image-makers, she softens the senator's reputation, both politically and personally. Bob has a reputation for acidity; Elizabeth neutralizes it."[12]

Libby, who is herself both Perfect and Powerful, receives rave reviews everywhere she turns. She is bright, feminine, articulate, charming, convincing, skillful, and irrepressible. She is a "power broker," a tireless campaigner, a role model, a lawyer, a former cabinet member, and a national political figure on her own.

At the Republican convention Elizabeth Dole presented herself so well that many who had not considered the possibility of a woman for vice-president hoped George Bush would choose Libby. As temporary chairperson she handled her role with feminine charm without becoming cute, with softness and authority at the same time. When commenting on the Dukakis inconsistencies and indecisiveness she brought the conventioneers to wild applause with her statement, "We don't have Dukakis and Bentson, we have Bentson and Hedges."

Hugh Sidey calls the combination of the two Doles, Dole^2, Dole to the second power. "Senator Bob Dole has been nipping at Bush's heels for a long time. Now he has been cloned. Libby Dole is not only his wife; she is also a national political figure with presidential potential of her own. She left her Cabinet job as Transportation Secretary last Wednesday to join her husband's crusade. There has never been a combination like this in American history ... The task before the Doles now is to shape this new thing in politics. It won't be easy, but it certainly will be fascinating. And if it works, the next time a reporter sits down to play with the presidential equation, he may decide that the answer is Dole to the second power."[13]

This is certainly a Powerful couple, the tireless Minority Leader who has triumphed over tragedy and the former Duke University "Queen of May." With his formidable knowledge and her soft, unthreatening style, they could make an unbeatable team.

Because of Elizabeth's obvious Southern charm, her Powerful personality is not so obvious as that of her often abrasive husband; yet her tremendous drive toward whatever goal she has in sight is legendary. She may never be the First Lady but she could become at some point in the future, the first female vice-president or even president.

Her Perfect traits are easier to observe as she does everything perfectly. She looks perfect, has flawless manners, and smiles engagingly at the right time.

Gail Sheehy wrote of her, "Elizabeth Dole herself has struggled against a lifelong compulsion to do everything right, foresee every pitfall, turn every key twice, check and recheck. Anything less than perfection in her performance could upset her. Her fixation on work left her little time to be a friend."[14]

Is there really a new Bob Dole? Has the acid tongue turned to honey?

Newsweek says, "Dole is tough, combative, and decisive."

He has a dry wit that "can curdle into bitterness and anger. While he is compassionate toward the infirm and ailing, his patience is often wafer-thin with the shortcomings of people who are — as he puts it — 'whole'. When he ran for vice president with Gerald Ford in 1976 and in his abortive 1980 bid for the presidency, Dole sank armadas of advisers, occasionally flinging briefing papers at them."[15]

With Bob Dole, there are always contradictions. He will never be predictable but, he has, at some point in the last few years, taken time to assess his weaknesses and set out to overcome them. He has realized that his strengths, when carried to extremes, have become weaknesses and, with his wife's help, he seems to be making progress. If he can temper his driven combative nature, quit straddling fences for security, and trade in his sword for a plowshare, he could become the leader he was born to be although he may never grasp his most coveted position, that of the president of the United States.

Robert Dole

Powerful (Choleric)

Strengths

powerful
artful dodger
formidable foe
strong-minded leader
acute politician
skillful director
eats bills for breakfast
tough, combative, decisive
independent
triumphed over injuries
wants to be top dog
mastered pragmatic art of
   I.O.U.
record of wartime bravery
hands-on person
bold & daring
a survivor
extraordinary energy
master deal-worker
projects toughness
can-do aura
dominating
strong leadership

Weaknesses

acidic
sarcastic
impatient
shifting with the wind
grabbing opportunities
fears delegating authority
easily angered
bitter & resentful
ruthless
more disciplinarian than
   visionary
workaholic
incorrigible
embarrassed by ideas
mean-spirited
cold-blooded politician
opportunist
a slasher & cutter
combative
partisan
tactless
style is attack

25

The Amazing Race

Pat Robertson and Jesse Jackson

Both Popular-Powerful

Personality Principle: *Personal faith gives hope for the future and brings passion to politics.*

Up until the time of Kennedy, religion was seldom an issue in politics. Candidates were assumed to be respectable citizens who went to church regularly and their spiritual values weren't questioned. With the strong Irish Catholic beliefs of the Kennedys came a fear that the Pope might end up in the White House in some kind of an advisory position, a fear that never materialized.

During the time of Richard Nixon, reared as a Quaker, Billy Graham was brought in to the White House to preach and counsel. A personal faith was openly talked about, but the unsavory end to the Nixon regime dimmed any spiritual influence that Graham might have had.

Gerald Ford talked of a Christian commitment but evangelicals winced at Betty's strong stand for the Equal Rights Amendment. Jimmy Carter brought the term "Born Again" into the political arena, gave his personal conversion testimony and taught Sunday School in a Baptist church. Ronald Reagan fought for conservative Christian causes and reversed many liberal trends. Gary Hart, raised as a strict Nazarene and enrolled in Yale Divinity School, left the faith to follow himself. "I am who I am. Take it or leave it," he once said. He has turned to Eastern mysticism and lately has been involved in New Age practices. Mike Dukakis adheres to his Greek Orthodox traditions and Episcopalian George Bush passed the spiritual test when questioned in *Christianity Today.*

During the long battle of the 1988 primaries, the question of religion and politics was brought to the fore. With morals at an all-time low, people began to look for candidates who didn't lie about their age or credentials, who were faithful to their mates, and who believed in something.

Attempting to answer the call were two charismatic preachers: Jesse Jackson and Pat Robertson, both men who have personal magnetism, evangelistic fervor, missionary zeal, and patriotic preaching. Although the press, right from the beginning, gave neither one a chance of becoming president, they followed them closely for their colorful personalities and for the "nuisance value" in the campaigns. Because of the dedication of their diverse supporters and the emotional drive to succeed, each one arrived at the conventions with committed blocs of delegates which they used as bargaining tools to chisel away at the platforms and as influence in the selection of the party nominee. No one seemed to know what to do with these two master showmen. Each party quietly wished they would go away, but neither side dared to tackle them. It's as if there is a secret belief that if you touch one of God's anointed that He just might strike you dead.

Although they are both similar in their Popular-Powerful personalities, their differences are as obvious as black and white, Democrat and Republican, liberal and conservative, civil-rights and moral-rights, rejected minority and Moral Majority; yet they both have a touch of martyrdom about them.

Time's Walter Shapiro says criticism only consolidates their supporters who revere them and will defend even their mistakes. Robertson's press coverage "may have enhanced the image of him as martyr. Evangelicals could view Robertson as crucified by 'secular humanist' reporters."[1]

Together they have brought moral issues to the fore, although they have emphasized different points of view.

William Schneider wrote in the *L.A. Times,* "What we have is two politicized minorities, roughly equal in size, moving in opposite directions, each concentrated in one party. ... Jackson and Robertson undeniably add something to American political life. They address issues that have largely been excluded from modern U.S. politics, namely, class and religion. ... They bring a moral energy to public life. ... They also appeal to people not ordinarily involved in politics."[2]

How unusual it is that we have two preacher-politicians, two Popular-Powerfuls, who are fervently leading opposite groups of "dispossessed and resentful" people who feel they've never had a real voice in politics in the past.

In a field of bland candidates and dwarfs, Jackson and Robertson stood out and stood up for something. They presented clear-cut choices, black and white, for those who have complained of a dull grey slate in '88.

Jesse Jackson, who has become an icon to blacks and an inspiration to some disaffected whites, is noted for his passionate oratory, his magnetic charm, and his ability to bring even a skeptical crowd to its feet. He can address a pot-smoking auditorium of teens and have them walking the aisles in repentance. He can go to the Mideast and free up a Navy flier. Jesse is daring and dynamic; Jesse has a Popular personality with a touch of the Powerful.

But with his formidable campaign skills, his obvious platform strengths, come accompanying weaknesses. As is typical of his personality, his ability to organize is missing, he is often functioning in chaos, and he does little advance planning. He is a charmer on the stage receiving applause but his temper flares when someone questions his loose facts or his fidelity. He's a song-and-dance man creating his own music, but he's a loose cannon on deck rolling wildly from one idea to another. He operates his finances out of an offering plate, yet his ability to pull money out of people who don't have any is without compare.

As Ambassador Joseph Kennedy had a compulsive need to show the Boston upper class that an Irishman could become president, so Jesse Jackson has an evangelical fervor to become "legitimate" and show the country that a black could be considered presidential.

Born of a statuesque black beauty who wanted to be a singer and fathered by the man next door, a mulatto with some Cherokee and Irish blood, Jesse was, in his own terms, "a bastard and rejected." He determined from childhood that he would show his people he could defy all odds and make it in the big, white world.

His father, Noah Robinson, Sr., had five preachers in his previous generation and Jesse declared he would be one also.

As Gail Sheehy said, "Jesse believed he was set aside by God for a purpose — one of the hallmarks of the victorious personality. ... Those who suffer shame as children often cover it up with a false superiority. A sense of shame drives some people to build an inflated self-image through the pursuit of fame or excessive amounts of money, hoping to convince themselves of their lovability. The emotion, ignored by psychology until very recently, is now seen as a 'master emotion'. If it is carved in early, it is father to all the other emotions. For Jesse, its child was envy."[3]

Spurred on by envy and not held back by humility, Jesse states triumphantly, "I'm a man on a mission. I was born to lead. ... Jesus was never anybody's patsy. Nobody pushed him around."

Popular-Powerful Jesse Jackson has electrified the crowds and inspired indifferent people to action; yet he is considered "unelectable" by the political pundits.

Coming in second to Mike Dukakis on Super Tuesday, March 8, 1988, gave Jesse an unprecedented boost from the South. In 1984 he received 55 percent of the black Southern vote and three percent of the white vote. On Super Tuesday he won 96 percent of the black and 10 percent of the white. The self-described "underdog with the big bite" spent little money compared with his opponents and gloated "I had a poor campaign with a rich message."

Most important of all in Jesse's drive for legitimacy were headlines proclaiming "Jackson has gained full respect, status in the Democratic Party."[4]

In the magazine *Black Enterprise* the cover story in July 1988 showed a confident Jackson and told of "the Power and the Glory," of Jesse's rise from poverty to presidential possibility, of his transformation from outspoken activist in 1984 to a polished and seasoned politician in 1988. "Jackson has seized the nation by the lapels and forced it to take notice of his historic quest for the Democratic presidential nomination."[5]

Although neither Jackson nor Robertson won the nomination, they both gave their mutual conventions a dramatic shot in the arm. The Democratic gathering, the least watched convention in history, had its most exciting and emotional moment when Jesse Jackson came to the platform and cried out "Keep hope alive!" With his electric personality sparkling, Jesse turned on the crowds and wags wondered if there was any point in low-wattage Dukakis showing up at all. Jesse seemed to be the fulfillment of Martin Luther King's "I have a dream."

USA Today called Jackson the star of the show and said that his "charisma shone brighter than any TV star's. From his stunning speech, to numerous interviews in all anchor booths, the appearance by his children, his sense of drama, the magic that surrounds him—he's a master of the medium."[6]

At the Republican Convention, Popular Ronald Reagan was the obvious master of the medium, but coming in a close second was Pat Robertson. Having buried the hatchet with the Bush forces over the lingering dispute regarding the Michigan delegation, Pat was awarded a spot on the platform. His supporters provided posters for every delegate who was willing to hold one and when Robertson appeared the huge Superdome was filled with waving signs which said "Robertson for Bush." At first glance it looked as if Robertson was the nominee and Bush the vice-president, but what the placement of the words intended to communicate was a healing of relationships and Robertson's support for Bush.

As Pat Robertson was introduced the crowds went wild for this charismatic leader who stood there beaming proudly and nodding affirmations to his screaming supporters. He hadn't won the prize but he'd run a good race and everyone knew it. He stood with the stature of a statesman and dispelled the myth that he was only a country preacher.

Jesse Jackson achieved his status by climbing from humble beginnings to a platform of prominence; Pat Robertson started out with a political background and base. His father A. Willis Robertson was a U.S. Congressman for 14 years and a Senator for 23. A typical southern gentleman, he paved the way for Pat's classical education at Washington and Lee and his military discipline at Virginia Military Institute. Pat went to Yale Law School with an idealistic mind and was disillusioned to the point he didn't study for his bar exam and flunked it. He was always in search of some crusade and when a minister named Cornelius Vauderbregger shared his faith with Pat, he accepted Jesus Christ into his life and found his new direction.

Pat Robertson, a Popular-Powerful like Jesse Jackson, had been a "gregarious party animal" who supposedly pinched the Korean maid who cleaned the barracks where Pat was stationed in the Marines; yet when he dedicated his life to the Lord he, like the Prodigal Son, gave up wasting his life on riotous living and had a complete change of attitude and desire.

Some feel his new zeal went a bit too far when he left his pregnant wife and toddler to go to a rustic retreat in Canada to commune with the Lord. He told his wife Dede that God would take care of them. When she begged him to return and called him a "fanatic" he wrote, "this is God who is commanding me."

Pat went to New York Theological Seminary and after his graduation he felt called to minister to the poor. He moved Dede, the granddaughter of an Ohio state senator, into a one-room ghetto apartment, gave away their possessions and subsisted on a soybean diet.

In his autobiography *Shout it From the House Tops,* Robertson tells about his friend George Lauderdale who had "a vision ... one of God's coincidences." In his vision Lauderdale found a defunct television station for sale and brought it to Robertson's attention. Pat raised $37,000 and bought the station.

When questioned by Kevin Menida at the *Dallas Morning News,* Lauderdale admitted that there was no vision, but it made a good story. "In other words, it wasn't all that mystical an experience as it comes out in the book."[7]

One of the key weaknesses that the Popular personality has is their lack of concern over details. They sometimes remember incorrectly and colorfully and after they've told about an event a certain way for awhile they really believe that's how it happened.

One of their key strengths is their ability to charm those around them, inspire others to join and donate to their movement, and to attract volunteers who will lay down their lives for their leader.

Using the Popular appeal and the Powerful drive, Robertson in 25 years built the Christian Broadcasting Network, now the nation's fifth-largest cable network, an accredited university, and broadcast operations in 24 countries.

Menida comments, "In addition to business acumen, Robertson brought to his role as television evangelist a magnetic public persona that helped attract viewers and fueled the growth of his electronic ministry. On the campaign trail, the man who lists his heroes as George Washington and Abraham Lincoln is an engaging figure who spins a good yarn and keeps a broad smile ...

"In private, he can be ever the commander in chief, displaying his temper and rejecting challenges to his way of thinking."[8]

As with each type of personality, Robertson has both strengths and weaknesses. His Popular side is what makes him so appealing and refreshing. He says whatever comes to his mind knowing from experience that most of it will be well received and unworried about possible inaccuracies.

He assumes everyone will love him, and most do. One day on the TV he confessed that he occasionally "misspeaks and forgets," but, in spite of his mistakes, Robertson is the only Republican candidate who can generate wild enthusiasm and revival-meeting rapture upon entering a room.

His beaming countenance and electric charm transmit power on an equal voltage with Jackson.

Newsweek said, "Robertson's relentless smile seems eerily unrelated to any external referent, so his continuous chuckling is no laughing matter, but it is nice to see a man happy in his work."[9]

Robertson obviously loves his work and it is his Powerful side that has been able to create the grand plan, dare to dream so ambitiously, organize so efficiently, travel with such energy, keep the standards high, motivate supporters to work and maintain intense loyalty.

Because I know Pat Robertson personally and have appeared on the *700 Club* show many times, I can speak from experience as to his gracious manner, his magnetic appeal, and his control over his empire.

He is highly respected by his co-workers and two that I interviewed gave me reports of a man who has all strengths and no weaknesses. He can inspire people to work for him for little or no pay and be grateful for the opportunity.

He has motivated people who never voted before to register, people who never got involved in politics, to run for office. He is the first leader of the Christian conservatives to have the ability and the power to organize a serious political machine, and to have the Popular personality to keep the people motivated and enthusiastic.

When questioned as to whether his failure to win the nomination would wipe out the evangelical interest in politics, Pat Robertson replied, "My goal all along was to bring evangelical Christians, conservative Roman Catholics, people who were pro-family Americans, into the political process. ... I wanted them to be knowledgeable, trained and active. That was the long-range goal, regardless of what I do personally. But I do think by being a highly visible candidate for president, I accelerated the process dramatically."[10]

Robertson is fighting for a revival of patriotic spirit, a renewal of spiritual values, and a return to old-fashioned moral values. More people agree with him than the votes show. Isn't it a shame that we have gone from being a country where "In God We Trust," to a land where many fear that their president might be too religious?

Both Jackson and Robertson have the Popular charismatic magnetism laced with some throw-away lines and both, for different background reasons, have the Powerful drive to succeed and the supreme self-confidence to keep them going in spite of adverse circumstances.

US News and World Report, in a cover-report called "The Amazing Race," says that Jackson and Robertson have come along so far because of the national problems with drugs, violence and immorality. Those voting for either of the two are not so concerned with whether the facts are correct as they are with the fervor of their convictions.

"Robertson speaks eloquently to a sense of American unease that is both deep and abiding. His followers are not particularly concerned whether his secular political prescriptions hang together. They are with Robertson because they are worried that America is in spiritual decline. ... Yet most of the Robertson faithful see the government as the problem, and they follow his call to arms to topple the dreaded 'secular humanists,' the 'Eastern liberal establishment' and the 'radical, militant homosexuals' because they believe what Robertson has told them for years in his television ministry. They believe, as he says, that there are evil forces abroad in the land that, without their consent, have turned their world upside down. And naturally, they don't like it."[11]

Just before Super Tuesday, Robertson's director for the state of Kentucky, Philip Thompson, said his candidate appealed to people concerned about America's "moral decay." "He is a person who mirrors their own values. He is someone they can rally behind and assist."[12]

During the last few months of the campaign Jesse Jackson was kept busy and out of trouble in order to show the white Reagan Democrats that they could safely come back to the fold, but when polls predicted fewer blacks planning to vote for Dukakis than for Mondale in '84, the Duke moved Jesse up to the front of the bus and asked him to collect markers from anyone he could find there. The telegenic preacher, when asked what he really thought about the Dukakis campaign, admitted that the candidate was not inspirational and that he understands "why the Duke has to play it cool with me." In a typical Jackson pronouncement, he explained, "We the people can provide the passion. He can provide the priorities."

Neither Jackson nor Robertson was able to win, but with their God-given Popular-Powerful personalities, they will not soon be forgotten.

The Reverend Austin Ray of Lexington's Wesley United Methodist Church stated from his pulpit, "Maybe Jesse Jackson will never get to be president, but it will instill in other young black kids' minds, perhaps 20 years from now, the thought that 'maybe I can be president.' They will have a positive image of themselves."[13]

The Amazing Race of 1988 has given Christian believers of any color, church, or political party a chance to be heard, a chance to feel good about themselves. The memories will surely "Keep hope alive."

Pat Robertson

Popular (Sanguine)

Strengths

magnetic public personality
generates revival-meeting rapture
beaming countenance
constant chuckle
rhythmic cadences of a polished
    preacher
ready smile
patriotic fervor
missionary zeal
charismatic magnetism
ability to draw people to him
sophisticated performer
disarming sincerity
Reagan's equal as a charmer
stops for chats
moving & mystical
gregarious party animal

southern gentleman
visionary
engaging figure
spins a good yarn

Weaknesses

colorful nuisance
loose tongue
talks without thinking
cannot remember
    sources
creative statistics
has flights of rhetoric
unabashed &
    unapologetic
misstated facts
mispeaks & forgets
relentless smile

Powerful (Choleric)

Strengths

natural commander-in-chief
supreme self-confidence
organizational energy
ability to ambush critics
determined to succeed
fights for principles
pragmatic
strong leader
true to his word
demands excellence
remembers people
anticipates problems
requires action
knows when he is right
quick to action

Weaknesses

some tough cookie
short fuse
narrow view
irritated at disruptions
drives himself relent-
    lessly
bristles at criticism
chews up underlings
privately shows a temper

marine discipline
motivates supporters
    to work
draws intense loyalty
sharp intellect

Jesse Jackson

Popular (Sanguine)

Strengths
country preacher
master showman
melts people with charm
great sense of humor
can shift language quickly
dramatic presence
quicksilver politician
can fill a church to
  overflowing
speaks in evangelistic
  cadences
stages media events
flashy media image
mercurial career
professional talker

Weaknesses
craves respect
begging for acceptance
rhetorical excesses
reckless rhetoric
can't remember what he said
hopelessly disorganized
oblivious of time
unaccountable
enlarged view of self
crowds into pictures
sense of chaos
promises mean nothing
little confidence in his
  word
childish & immature
more rhetoric than reality
endless quest for
  recognition

Powerful (Choleric)

Weaknesses
impatient, frenetic
berates opponents
bristles at slights
angry outsider
superheated maverick
edge of anger
pushy, snappish
risk addicted
thrives on defying odds
drives himself to exhaustion
wants to be treated like
  a monarch
sneers at opponents
overly ambitious

Strengths
imposing
penetrating gaze
always tries harder
tries to demystify
politics
a protest candidate
master manipulator
was born to lead
vaunted ambition
competitor's iron will

26

Cool Is Hot, But Not Hot Enough To Win

Michael Dukakis

Peaceful-Perfect

Personality Principle: *Opposites attract in marriage.*

Prior to the 1988 presidential election, satirist Mark Russell was heard to say, "There may not be enough caffeine in America to keep the country awake during the coming campaign." That statement would be true if we were looking for creative genius, political innovation, or heroic statesmen.

With the Democrats producing Gary Hart, a fallen and reborn mystic, and Seven Dwarfs who shrank down to Six Survivors, and with the Republican six-pack somewhat lost in the Bushes, and the press shooting Quayle, there appeared to be no Giants atop the political beanstalk; however, if you happened to be interested in political personalities, self-destruction, media scrutiny, or sadistic humor, you could have sipped herb tea and stayed awake.

The big question during Joe Biden's undoing was: "Who did it?" Who squealed on Happy Joe? Did Gary Hart attack? Did Gephardt gossip? Or was it the GOP elephant that never forgets old law school records? It couldn't be Michael Dukakis, a Peaceful-Perfect Dwarf known for his rock-solid integrity and hands-on management.

A lackluster campaigner, the Duke had drawn attention not on his personality, but because of his ability to raise money, a constant necessity for presidential candidates. In his first three months of fund-raising, Dukakis collected $4.2 million (doubled by October, 1987), two-thirds of it coming from Massachusetts. Although it is widely acknowledged that the state's rebirth was well on its way before the Duke took over as governor and he just fell into a lucky situation, he has claimed credit for the economic climate.

L.A. Times' Ronald Brownstein said that Dukakis has "poked his head out of a pack of Democratic contenders best known for being unknown."

"This elevation of Dukakis from the ranks of the 'seven dwarfs' can be attributed to the natural rhythm of a presidential selection process which can endure only so much equality. Among the press and the political insiders already engrossed in the race, there is an enormous need — bordering on a primal urge — to establish a designated front-runner, or at least a first among dwarfs."[1]

Being first among dwarfs is hardly an honor, but the Dukakis campaign was grateful for any positive designation. The staff Dukakis had put together had seasoned political veterans John Sasso and Paul Tully in charge. Sasso was so close to Dukakis as to be considered by insiders as his alter ego or his brother. With this unified relationship and reputation for strong business ethics, it seemed unlikely that this team would be involved in trying to shoot down Joe Biden, one of their own party, especially on the eve of the Judge Robert Bork hearings which Joe was about to conduct.

When Sasso reported to Dukakis that *Time* was printing a story saying the videos of Biden and Kinnock had come from their camp, the Duke didn't even ask if it was true. He held a press conference on Monday to deny any involvement and righteously reported, "Anybody who knows me, and knows the kind of campaigns I run, knows how strongly I feel about negative campaigning." That should have been the end of the matter except that the press kept after the team until Tuesday afternoon when John Sasso confessed to Dukakis that he was, in fact, the person who sent the tapes to the New York *Times,* the Des Moines *Register,* and NBC News.

Had Dukakis been a Powerful personality, he would have fired him on the spot. But being Peaceful, he had the typical reaction: Don't make hasty decisions and avoid conflict as long as possible. Dukakis went to a party that night to celebrate raising $8 million, twice as much as any other candidate.

Time in an article entitled "The Dwarfs in Disarray," told of that party. "Dukakis, an amateur trumpet player, tooted — of all things — 'Happy Days are Here Again.' But by Wednesday morning he had to face a different kind of music."[2]

The governor admitted his men had sent the video, but he claimed he'd known nothing about what they were doing. This admission was a hard one for a man to make who'd boasted about his hands-on management and who had ridiculed Ronald Reagan for being out of touch with his administration. Again, because of his Peaceful nature, Dukakis, even with hot evidence in hand, couldn't bear to fire his alter ego and so he gave him a two-week leave in which to reform his strategy.

The public, in a state of disbelief, caused enough of an uproar within the next four hours that the beleaguered governor had to reconsider and dismiss both Sasso and Paul Tully, who had been aware of what was going on and hadn't told Dukakis. With his two campaign strategists gone, Dukakis, the hands-on CEO, had no close aides to keep his hands on.

Newsweek called it the "Dukakis Fiasco," and the whole Democratic race "politics by subtraction." They also quoted Chris Howel, Iowa campaign manager for Bruce Babbitt, as saying, "Our goal is to be the last campaign left standing."[3] It wasn't!

USA Today recorded the statement of 1984 Mondale-Ferraro chairman Robert G. Beckel, "If the Democrats were a bottle of wine, it'd be a bad year."[4] Also from Biden's Iowa chairman Lowell Jurkins, "Democrats are lining up the firing squad in a circle, shooting their brothers and sisters. ... This craziness has got to end."[5]

Time said "that the party's race is becoming a demolition derby that will be won by the last battered survivor."[6] And they quoted Will Rogers who announced that he didn't belong to an organized political party: he was a Democrat.

While some of the press assumed loss of the Dukakis top strategists might derail his campaign, they did not count on his underlying will of iron, a hidden Peaceful trait, or his Perfect ability to regroup efficiently with or without his staff. The Duke kept his peace throughout the difficult days following the disclosure and didn't resort to name-calling or blame shifting.

In contrast to Biden's contrived coal-mining ancestors, Dukakis's father really was a Greek immigrant to this country when he was 15, and within eight years he was in Harvard Medical School. His mother was the first Greek girl to go to college after graduating from Haverhill High School — my *alma mater* and where I taught for four years.

As the Kennedy family had a driving desire to lift themselves from low-class Boston Irish to the highest position in the land, a force that pushed Jack into political pursuits, so the Dukakis family has a need to continue demonstrating that immigrants from Greece can become doctors, governors and even the president.

Meg Greenfield commenting on what she calls the "Immigrant Mystique" asks, "Are we really still in the funny looking foreigner phase of our politics?" She compares the Kennedy's reminiscence with old grandpa Honey Fitz and the Dukakis nostalgia over Father Panos and notes that those of us who use our ethnicity as a positive reference can't do so until we've completed Harvard and won political office.

Time calls the Dukakis parents "textbook cases of the hard workers who turn opportunity into achievement."[7]

"The trouble is not just that we romanticize our immigrant past, straining out the family scoundrels as the dirt and pestilence and the ethnic and religious hatreds that were generated in us, not just endured by us; it is also that so many of us only tend to this romance once we are safely aboard that jet to Moscow, all dressed up, every trace of immigrant status gone. By the time we start reveling in the mischief of old Honey Fitz, we are naming our yacht for him. We boast of being immigrants, that is, when we no longer are subject to the immigrants ordeal, after we have become certifiable natives and, often, at a time when we and our kind are busily closing the door to others."[8]

Michael Dukakis, hardly the typical poor immigrant, grew up in Brookline outside of Boston. The family had a strict moral code and high standards, and Mike became president of the student council and lettered in three sports. His high school yearbook labeled him "Big Chief Brain in the Face." He became a lawyer and entered politics, but he never was the Popular, hail-fellow-well-met, typical politician.

USA Today described the 1988 Democratic Convention as "starring an electrifying preacher, a bland governor."[9]

An *Insight* cover story on Dukakis headlined "Cool is Hot" and compared the similar personalities of Dukakis and Bush. "It is surely the most profound phenomenon of this campaign, and the one least acceptable to the media hounds, that the two blandest in the field will be the finalists in the fall general election. It speaks volumes about what is going on in the mind of the American voter this year.

"The third-term governor of Massachusetts has the oratorical skills of the fellow who has been announcing the arrival and departure of the trains from the depots of America for the past hundred years, and he faced Vice President George Bush, a man rendered faceless in the comic strips."[10]

The Duke's Peaceful, bland nature has kept him consistently quiet, reserved and well-liked. In his campaigning he didn't seem to have any obvious weaknesses, a trait known only among the Peacefuls, and he has always been able to keep his feelings hidden. In fact many people found his lack of emotional response in the campaign to be too cold and aloof.

His Perfect side makes him appear organized, disciplined and detail conscious and his bushy eyebrows help him look deep, thoughtful, even brooding.

His friends say he is both sensitive and frugal and some go so far as to call him stingy. He buys his suits in Filene's basement, drives a Dodge Aspen and still lives in a modest duplex. In winter he keeps his thermostat at 58 at night and at 63 in the daytime and when his daughters complain, he tells them to put on more sweaters.

Dukakis is called "Meticulous Mike" a Perfect name. He likes to cook, he follows the recipe exactly, and he cleans up as he goes along. His daughter Kara was heard to say, "He's very careful in the kitchen, never spills or dribbles anything. You don't even know he's been cooking."

This Peaceful-Perfect combination gives Michael Dukakis a cool, laid-back look that is supposedly appealing to women with a serious businesslike manner that impresses men.

U.S. News and World Report summed up the Dukakis Peaceful-Perfect personality. They said he has an "icy calm." He doesn't get excited over good or bad and he insists on "business as usual in his no-wasted-motions march through the process of governing." They feel he is so dedicated to politics that he is a "government priest practicing a kind of civil religion." They compare him to Perfect President Jimmy Carter and ask if he would be "another technocrat governor given to picking nits and focusing his considerable intellect on the most sparrow-small aspects of public policy?"[11]

Knowing that opposites usually attract, it is no surprise that Peaceful-Perfect Dukakis married a strong, dynamic, active Powerful personality with some Popular traits. Kitty, a divorced Jewish girl with one child, fell in love with Mike, and they were married. Her ambitious and persistent personality helped push her low-key, somewhat reticent husband along in his career, and the Boston papers that call her a spoiled Jewish princess refer to him as "henpecked," a term frequently used to describe Peaceful husbands married to Powerful wives, whether or not it happens to be true.

While Mike is cautious, Kitty charges forth and doesn't care what anyone thinks about her. This forthright attitude has not always been an asset to her husband, and she has been called the proverbial loose cannon.

As the *Dallas Morning News* reveals "she is the antithesis of her husband. He is mechanical and technical; She is emotional and dramatic. Shopping for clothes is a chore for him; to her it's a birthright."[12] When asked if Kitty would borrow clothes if she became First Lady, Dukakis replied, "No, she'll buy them in Filene's basement."

The *Boston Business* magazine writes of both her strengths and her weaknesses. "The Commonwealth's First Lady has been praised for her candor, intelligence and charm. She's applauded for using her considerable clout, real and perceived, to effect policy and legislative change.

"But Kitty Dukakis has also been criticized for overstepping her bounds in public affairs. For being too much of a State House presence, for throwing her weight-by-association around too heavily. She's been called steely, pushy, manipulative."[13]

Her friends say you can expect the unexpected with Kitty. She's independent, strong-willed, unorthodox, volatile, and impulsive. No one knows what she'll do next and the Dukakis staff assigned a "Kitty Litter Patrol" to clean up behind her. She doesn't let public opinion sway her and she states clearly "I am what I am." When asked, " How would you describe yourself?" Kitty replied, "I'm intense, impatient to get things done. I always think everything should have happened yesterday."[14]

This typical description of a Powerful woman shows why she has been able to accomplish so much, and also why she comes across a little too strong for some. She directs a project she created, Public Space Partnerships, at Harvard's Kennedy School, and she is a tireless and outgoing campaigner.

Because of the media mania for examining the tiniest little skeleton in the 1988 closets, Kitty decided to bring out her own secret before it was discovered. She publicly confessed to 26 years of mild amphetamine dependency overcome after a stay in a drug rehabilitation clinic in 1982. There was no negative reaction from her announcement, and *Time* said she had "enrolled in the Betty Ford school of political candor."[15]

Because Kitty is aggressive, intelligent, candid and impressive, some have wondered if she should have been the candidate, but she is content to pursue her own career and be supportive of her husband, the Governor of Massachusetts.

If Mike Dukakis had won and he and Kitty had moved into the White House they would have followed many pairs of opposites:

Ronald Reagan, Popular	**Nancy, Perfect**
Jimmy Carter, Perfect	**Rosalyn, Powerful**
Gerald Ford, Peaceful	**Betty, Powerful**
Richard Nixon, Perfect-Powerful	**Pat, Peaceful**

Although the purpose of this book is not to discuss the marriages of the Personalities in Power, it is important to note that we do usually fall in love with a person who is quite different from ourselves. Opposites do attract. Looking at this illogical truth from a positive point of view we can see that ideally each partner's strengths should fill in the other's weaknesses making a whole. "The two shall become one."

In our marriage of 35 years, Perfect Fred plans all of our schedules and manages the office; I teach seminars and write books, and direct CLASS Speakers using my Popular-Powerful skills. Looking at the negatives, we would seldom agree on anything, but using our opposite strengths we make a complimentary whole. In my 20 years of speaking and counseling on marriage, I have found that a simple understanding of why we are different and the knowledge that the other person isn't out to get you, can change relationships immediately without months in therapy.

In observing the Dukakis marriage on the Personality Profile, it is quickly obvious that they are very different. Kitty is Powerful with a Popular touch and Mike is the opposite, Peaceful and Perfect. Noting that there are apparently no Popular traits in Mike and only a few in Kitty indicates a strong serious family pattern with little time for fooling around or playing trivial pursuits. Friends say Mike has almost no sense of humor and is only a fair joke teller.

As you map out your family Personality Profile, you will see perhaps for the first time, your differences on paper and resolve to accentuate your positive relationships and eliminate your conflicts.

After the conclusion of the Democratic convention *USA Today* writer Judy Keen described a Peaceful-Perfect presidential bid when she called the convention, "A week of perfunctory enthusiasm."[16]

It appeared that what "we the people" were looking for in 1988 was a practical business-minded man without flash or flair: Dukakis had become the Democrat's leading man. He had somewhat eliminated the old politics of patronage. In his first term as governor he went so far away from the award system that even his loyal supporters deserted him, that along with giving the state the highest combined tax increase in its history, led to his defeat in the following election. The opposition criticized his patriotism by reminding us that he vetoed a bill calling for Massachusetts' school teachers to lead their classes in the Pledge of Allegiance, and they ridiculed him for allowing convicted murderers to have a weekend leave from prison.

At the Republican Convention the national committee distributed "get out of jail free" cards exactly like those from the Monopoly game. Dukakis was also well known for his strong support of abortion. The *Boston Herald* comments, "It's doubtful that any politician is more inflexible, more dogmatic, more doctrinairily pro-abortion than he. ... A Dukakis administration would set the right-to-life movement back a decade."[17]

His support for homosexual rights had earned him the applause of Jean O'Leary, the Executive Director of the National Gay Rights Advocates, "We have in Michael Dukakis a candidate who is instinctively supportive, who has a good record on gay rights, who wants our support and who can win."[18]

Mike is by nature extremely thrifty and in his first term he rode the subway to the State House to be one of the people. He still does much of the family grocery shopping because Kitty is not price conscious enough to suit him. He has been known to share his brown bag lunch with important visitors to his office rather than take them out to eat.

With his Peaceful strengths of a quiet, cautious, sensible nature and the Perfect assets of a detail-conscious, disciplined business mind, come some weaknesses that would have been a handicap for any president. He had no grand vision, no lofty programs, little knowledge of foreign affairs, no sweeping statements, no color, flair, humor, or drama.

Three weeks before the election an NBC *Wall Street Journal* poll showed George Bush with a 17 point lead over Dukakis. The poll also showed that Dukakis' negative rating was going up. The election was obviously over. Although the point spread closed as the election neared, it was a clear win for traditional values.

At the Democratic convention, Dukakis had given the most dramatic speech of his long political career. His writers produced unusually lofty thoughts which he delivered without his metronomic gestures. He reminded us of Martin Luther King as he said, "I have a dream, a dream so powerful that no distance of ground, no expanse of ocean, no barrier of language, no distinction of race or creed or color can weaken its hold on the human heart." Impressive words, but Michael Dukakis did not have the opportunity to translate them into everyday action.

Michael Dukakis

Peaceful (Phlegmatic)

Weaknesses

uninspiring
unimaginative
apathetic
bland
cold-fish
barely escapes monotone
no fireworks
inability to act decisively
tendency to self-righteousness
avoids hard questions
holier-than-thou
cold, unemotional, insensitive
hesitant & wavering
henpecked
stubborn will
no charisma
detached & indecisive
tuned out
dull & unexciting
chilly and awkward figure
clipped cool cadences without
 a sliver of a soul

Strengths

balanced
no spurts or gulps
undemonstrative
contained air
consistent
adroit negotiator
non-bellicose
serene
conformist
cautious leadership style
low-key personality
strong, sensible and silent
grinning Greek
quiet & honest
too principled to practice
 politics
ingenuous smile
few obvious weaknesses
soft, shy & sensitive
uncomplicated & decent
hides his hurts
no extremes
emotional solidity

Perfect (Melancholy)

Weaknesses

stingy
brooding
parsimonious
unsocial
cerebral
accountant-like
sanctimonious
insufferable
know-it-all
soul-less
preachy & pedantic
too high standards

disciplined & sacrificial
tearful ethnic
musical & talented
frugal

Strengths

calculated achievements
gives no political favors
has integrity
altruistic
walking pocket calculator
button-up standards
well-prepared
mythical
measured intensity
substantial
managerial skills
technocratic
attention to detail
private
withdrawn
earnest
reflective

27

A Kinder and Gentler Nation

George Bush

Peaceful

Personality Principle: *The Peaceful's greatest strength is the lack of obvious weaknesses.*

One week before the 1988 election the *New York Times* summed up the two candidates as bland and colorless. They did not analyze the Peaceful personalities of Bush and Dukakis that kept them from exhibiting the Popular personality we have come to expect from Ronald Reagan, but they did quote Professor Larry Sabato. "Could it be that it's been a passive campaign and that fits television perfectly? The candidates are not emotional. They don't arouse passion. It's a campaign that's well suited to spectatorship. It's the ideal couch potato campaign."[1]

What better way to describe a duel between two Peacefuls than as a "couch potato campaign." We all know by now that a Peaceful blends in anywhere, adapts to differing circumstances, and avoids conflict at all costs.

The Peaceful does not have a flashy personality like the Popular, obvious skills like the Powerful, or deep strengths like the Perfect. The Peaceful's greatest strength is an invisible one. He has no obvious weaknesses. He will always try to do the right thing and avoid problem situations. As George Bush said at the Republican Convention, "I am that man."

James David Barber, author of the book *Presidential Character*, wrote of George Bush, "He wants to do the right thing, and, above all, not do the wrong thing. He defines his virtue by what he does not do. By restriction."[2]

Both Presidents Eisenhower and Ford were chosen not for their outstanding political strengths or innovative programs, but for the fact that they had no obvious weaknesses. Ike could win on a grin and tread water for two terms, Ford could keep everybody happy and heal the wounds of Watergate, both without getting in trouble. They were men for their hour; they gave us Peace when we were tired of conflict.

George Bush is a Peaceful Personality whose biggest challenge at the beginning of the campaign was fighting the "Wimp Factor," but with careful planning of his daily photo opportunities his handlers helped overcome this misperception and when he appeared on T.V. next to Dukakis, Bush looked tall and athletic.

After Super Tuesday, March 8, 1988, when both Peacefuls surged ahead, Columnist Richard Reeves headlined:

"Bush vs. Dukakis? Yawn ... George Bush vs. Michael Dukakis for president? What could be more predictable? More boring? I don't say that only because Super Tuesday's big winners are not particulary exciting fellows, but because the Republican vice-president and the Democratic governor are such faithful and orthodox representatives of their parties.

"Bush is the classic Republican — much more than that Wild Westerner, Ronald Reagan — a pure old-line defender of Yankee patriotism and the high-church Protestant values the Grand Old Party has sworn to protect and preserve. He's a country club chap who rolled up about 60% of the Republican vote Tuesday in beating back the rougher populist pitches of Robert Dole and Pat Robertson.

"Dukakis is the son of immigrants, a pure post-Cold War liberal, who removed any doubts about his national appeal to Democrats by prevailing in the parts of the country most likely to be suspicious of Massachusetts messages."[3]

Even though Dukakis was the big primary winner, he never did come up with any brilliant ideas. In fact he has been so bereft of fresh thoughts that he hired a "vision doctor" to dream for him. Unfortunately for his party, some of these dreams became nightmares.

The Democrats did not have a total monopoly on non-new ideas. In George Will's commentary on the Republican November 1987 mini-debate in Houston, he wrote, "The debate resembled the Lincoln-Douglas debate, except there was no Lincoln, no Douglas and precious little debating. Lincoln and Douglas, having nothing better to do, argued, at length. They would rattle on for three hours, just the two of them. But what can six fellows do, now that the national attention span has shrunk? In Houston they were sometimes allowed to ramble on for 45 seconds."[4]

And sometimes it seemed even longer.

William Schneider wrote an insightful article entitled "New Ideas Will Never Nominate the Next U.S. President." He predicted that Bush would be the next president because he had successfully stayed away from big ideas. "They only get you in trouble."

Bush has never been noted for clever phraseology and as Schneider says, "Bush has a tendency to do foolish things ... the Republican campaign consists of a bunch of candidates waiting for Bush to say something really stupid." But he kept jogging and repeating his one good line, "Loyalty is not a character flaw."[5]

In the 1988 campaign, the "wimp factor" became a new measuring stick of candidates and was focused, primarily, on George Bush, our Peaceful vice-president. Because he was put in the awkward position of supporting the President and being loyal, while at the same time trying to establish a strong identity of his own, the press pictured him as weak and vacillating, a view not backed up by the facts.

While other candidates had to scrounge for credentials and exaggerate their abilities, George was quietly living an exemplary life. As a Peaceful person, he has been willing, from childhood, to put the other person first and not insist on his own way. He has been generous, well-mannered and gracious. As a child, he was nicknamed by his mother "Have Half" because whenever she gave him a cookie, he would turn to the person beside him and say "have half."

His family background was similar to that of Franklin Roosevelt, in that he grew up with solid financial footing, patrician social standing, classical education, and a desire to serve those less fortunate. Like FDR, his parents both came from exceptional stock, with each mother being the dominating influence in the children's lives.

Dorothy Walker Bush, daughter of George Herbert Walker, champion polo player, founder of golf's Walker Cup, and head of the New York State Racing Commission, was and still is a Powerful-Popular personality, who disciplined the children firmly while making the whole experience fun. As a mother she was a warm, religious woman who read Bible verses at breakfast and then challenged the family to a seasonal variety of athletic pursuits: tennis, boating, football, hunting, golf, baseball, backgammon, and charades.

Where FDR spent much of his sheltered childhood alone, reading books on history and recreating naval battles with toy ships, Bush was engaging in athletic events proving him the opposite of a wimp.

In contrast to the Kennedy clan who emphasized sports and were taught to win for the sake of always being first, the Bushes were encouraged to be the very best they possibly could, without gloating over the victory. As the Kennedys collected trophies, the Bushes were trained to say, "I was lucky." When George would tell his mother he had won, she would ask, "How did the team do?" Individual pride was discouraged and being a team player was essential.

The Los Angeles *Times* titled their article on the Vice-President, "Team Player Bush: A Yearning To Serve." Writer Barry Bearak stated, "Games — far more than literature or the arts — prepared one for life, or so went the premise. The goal was to be the best, though never to brag about it.

"In victory, there was only one proper thing to say: 'I was lucky.' Humility, politeness, sociability: These were insisted upon, applied purposefully day after day, like a sculptor's pats."[6]

The word "good," a typical Peaceful adjective, has been used to describe George from childhood on. His teachers remember him as a good boy and his family as a good brother. As a teen, he stayed out of trouble without being a sissy or being preachy about being good. Everyone enjoyed his company and while he liked a good joke or a good prank, he was never mean or vulgar. He was never a goody-goody, and he was always strong enough and concerned enough to protect those who were weak.

As Bearak wrote, "George Bush always had about him a sense of bearings. It kept him from going astray. He was a good boy from a good family, headed for good things."[7]

I remember Prescott Bush, George's father, as he was our senator from Connecticut when Fred and I lived there in the late '50s and '60s. Senator Bush was a Perfect patrician person of pedigree and the press had to push to find anything wrong with him. He was tall, dignified, refined and gracious, and there was never much point in anyone running against him. He was a Perfect prototype of the Eastern Establishment, investment broker, and civic leader. While he made money, he never talked about it as a path to power, as Joseph Kennedy did. He was not dying to climb hastily to the top; he was already there. He was never trying to "show them"; they could already see his genuine character and quiet success.

Lust for money was a sin and Senator Bush instilled in his children that financial substance required civic service. With privilege come obligations; give generously with no desire for credit.

From this family background, George grew up as a fair and decent person with the desire to serve his fellow man and his country. At Phillips Andover Academy, he was the all-purpose person and was president of almost everything he joined. Not because he craved position, as a Powerful would, but because he was so likeable, inoffensive and willing to work for the benefit of others.

Even though he could have escaped military service in World War II, by going to college or using his father's influence, he chose to enlist on the day of his 18th birthday, June 12, 1942. He worked diligently to learn to fly and was the youngest pilot in the Navy to receive his wings. George never held back or looked for favored treatment, but he plunged into the war with dedication to duty and piloted TBM Avengers. While flying into enemy territory and daringly dodging the flak, Bush was twice thrown into the sea and narrowly escaped death. On the second crisis, as he bailed out of a plane about to explode, the Japanese sent gunboats after him and he swam desperately for 90 minutes before an American submarine emerged and swept him to safety.

George Bush's wartime record is hardly that of a wimp! With customary modesty, Bush never points out his patriotic deeds. It was just part of his obligation to serve.

After his time in the Navy, George entered Yale in 1945. As an economics major, he sped through his requirements in 2 1/2 years, made Phi Beta Kappa, and graduated with the necessary credentials to enter the blue-blooded financial fields so readily open to the son of Prescott Bush.

But once again, George didn't opt for the easy life, he didn't want to be pulled along on his father's coattails, he didn't want to settle into the safety of the status quo. He and his wife, Barbara, daughter of the president of McCall's publishing empire, drove off to Texas, where he learned the oil business from below ground up. Before he was 40, George had become an oil-millionaire, an established Texan and an accepted leader in the Republican party.

In 1966, when he was 42, he was elected to Congress, one of only two Republicans from Texas. Because of his easygoing nature and friendly attitude, he fit in quickly with the establishment and, with some influence from his father, he was soon assigned to the Ways and Means Committee.

Bearak wrote of him, "He made friends as fast as a small boy collects baseball cards. Sunday afternoons at the Bushes drew a crowd: congressmen, ambassadors, a Supreme Court justice. He seemed to know the whole town."[8]

During the Nixon-Ford era, Bush served as ambassador to the United Nations (22 months), chairman of the Republican-National Committee (20 months), chief of the liaison office in Beijing (16 months), and director of the CIA (12 months).

Nixon admired Bush's humility, good-nature, and willingness to be a team-player. George never had the smell of mutiny about him and Nixon was drawn to obvious loyalty.

In all of George Bush's diverse areas of public service, he was considered as a kind, encouraging, soothing, understanding, amiable, witty person, who listened politely to all opinions, tried to take the middle-road, and didn't need to get the credit.

George personifies the old adage, "there's no limit to what you can accomplish when you don't care who gets the credit."

All of these Peaceful strengths are quiet low-key attributes that don't make headlines. When Bush took over the CIA, the agency was trying to recover from exposés and excesses. His "don't-rock-the-boat" attitude calmed the troubled waters, and steadied the reeling spy-ship. He testified in Congress without drawing attention to himself and he quietly healed the hurts of the agency.

He and President Ford, both Peacefuls, worked to bring harmony to the government but, because of their low-key natures, neither one came across as a powerful leader, neither was credited with any life-changing ideas or legislation and they both proved the principle that the Peaceful's greatest strength is his lack of obvious weaknesses. This often unseen and unaccepted strength doesn't carry the excitement and glamour that the public envisions as leadership, so Ford, Mr. Clean, lost to Carter, and Bush, Mr. Nice Guy, lost in the 1980 primaries to newcomer Ronald Reagan, the very image of what a president should be like.

Bush was a war hero, but Reagan looked like one. Bush had a solid marriage with devoted supportive children, Reagan talked movingly of family values. Bush took speech lessons and worked on his gestures, Reagan opened his mouth and produced story after story, charmingly and naturally.

Nice guys sometimes finish last. Bush had manners and dignity, Reagan had machoism and dazzle.

"That was the difference," Bearak said. "One man had antennae for showmanship, the other for gentility. Any smart studio would know how to cast them. They were the cowboy and the dude."[9]

We the American public prefer the cowboy every time.

When Reagan offered Bush the Vice-President's position, he accepted. Because of George's Peaceful personality, his willingness to moderate his positions, and his ability to play second fiddle in a new symphony, he was able to become a loyal Reaganite.

Had Bush been a Popular, he might have tried to steal a spot in the sun, but instead he stayed quietly in the background. Had he been a

Powerful, he might have tried to exert control and get his personal points across to the President, but instead he supported positions he had formerly opposed and didn't propose any policy shifts.

Had he been a Perfect, he might have held grudges against Reagan for comments he'd made about Bush in the primary campaign and subtly sought revenge, but instead he accepted the negative as part of politics and was able to put the past behind him without rancor.

Only the Peaceful is naturally able to play the role of the bridesmaid when he wanted to be the bride; only the Peaceful can sit in meeting after meeting and not need to make a comment; only a Peaceful can support other people's ideas continually without insisting they adopt a few of his.

These Peaceful attributes were appealing to a President who loved center-stage and who didn't like conflict. Bush's soft sense of humor appealed to Reagan and he would often ask George to repeat a joke he'd particularly enjoyed.

Writer Gail Sheehy, commenting on the Bush personality, says, "Some of the world's unfunniest people suddenly feel, in Bush's presence, like true wits. The secret to his sense of humor is that he plants the punch line in someone else's mouth. ... George Bush has made a career out of nicing people to death."[10]

George is everyone's Mr. Nice Guy, every woman's first husband, and he brought to the '88 campaign the most impressive credentials in a field of generally unexciting candidates. He is relaxed, at peace with himself, and naturally polite and gracious. It is often noted that on the day after his 3-year-old daughter's death from leukemia, George Bush returned to the hospital and personally thanked each nurse and doctor who had cared for her. He is known for handwriting personal notes to friends and underlings to congratulate, console, or encourage.

Bush is a qualified political servant who modestly refuses to blow his own horn, a decent man who hasn't made major mistakes and who, under press scrutiny, has opened a closet holding no skeletons.

On the afternoon when George Bush was to make his entrance to New Orleans on the riverboat Natchez, I was given two formal invitations that would allow me to enter the VIP area where I pictured I would be seated in some restricted viewing section.

As I followed the crowds through the French Quarter toward the waterfront I wondered what important people would be in the VIP lounge and whether there would be refreshments. Surely, with the engraved invitation would come some special treatment.

As I moved along I looked over the crowd to spot some lady of a similar age and style who would be thrilled to accompany me into this prestigious position of prominence. Spotting a solitary soul, I spoke to her and offered her my extra ticket. We had much in common and my excitement grew as I knew I had someone to share it with.

By the time we got to the dockside, Pie Hebert and I were firm friends. We followed the signs for "VIP Viewing" and found ourselves in a long line standing still in the hot August sun. After a half hour hardly moving we got inside a flat, roped off area and found that these tall people were all VIPs. From a position like a child at the Rose Bowl Parade I tried to stand on tip toes and focus on finding the river. I knew it was there but I couldn't see it. I began to apologize to my new friend for my failure to get her up front with the Bush family as I had inferred we might be. Surely I had not imagined that everyone in New Orleans was a VIP with an engraved ticket.

As I stretched my neck up I spotted the corner windows of Abercrombie and Fitch jutting out over the crowds. Since we had nothing to lose in leaving this far from intimate gathering, I suggested we push our way out of the throng and go into Abercrombie and Fitch. We weren't the first to think of standing in the store window somewhat like a pair of plaster dummies but we managed to get our faces up to the glass with our backs against a table of polo shirts in assorted colors.

During those two hours we stood in the Abercrombie and Fitch shirt department we became well-acquainted with our new close friends and I even picked out a few shirts for Christmas presents. Finally the Natchez came down the river preceded by a barge shooting up fountains of red, white, and blue water. Our clear, unobstructed view through the store window let us see the Bush family as they stood waving on deck and gave us almost a front row position for the surprise debut of Dan Quayle.

At the end of the festivities George Bush walked off the stage toward our window and a limousine drove in between us and the river to pick him up. We couldn't believe we were in the only spot to see him closely. As he and his sons came in our direction, he noticed us waving and jumping as animated mannequins in the Abercrombie and Fitch window. He laughed at the sight, paused and called out, "thanks for coming." As the Secret Service Agents walked beside the limo, George Bush waved good-bye to this special group of front row fans.

I paid for my selection of shirts and sweaters and felt grateful that I had been at the right place at the right time to see the relaxed and natural personality of the future President of the United States.

At the time of the 1988 election the Bushes had been married for 43 years, had five living children out of six, and had 10 grandchildren. The family obviously enjoys each other's company and they exemplify the values they want for America.

Barbara is a Powerful personality balancing and completing George's Peaceful nature. She is open, candid, and expressive and isn't worried about what people think of her. She has been the disciplinarian of the family, the caretaker of the home, while her husband has been traveling and working long hours. Before the White House they had lived in 28 houses in 17 cities and it was Barbara who found each new home and moved into it.

Her son Marvin calls her "the enforcer" and she agrees she was the one who carried out the family rules.

USA Today said of her, "Barbara Bush is down-to-earth and outspoken, always lets you know what she thinks and where you stand, is confident enough to know there are more important things in life than being a perfect size 6 or dying your hair."[11]

Many of us women will be glad to have a First Lady who is a size 14 and doesn't look like a dresden doll. Perhaps the '88 to '92 years will be the era of the average woman. Perhaps we can stop starving ourselves and be proud of the natural look God gave us.

Barbara has the strengths of the Powerful Personality without the abrasiveness that often accompanies these characteristics. Her son George says of her, "I predict that my mother will be the most loved First Lady this country has ever had. Everyone who knows her, loves her."

Of his father he admiringly stated, "If my father died tomorrow, as his soul ascended to heaven, he would be content, knowing he'd never done anything he wasn't proud of, to accomplish his aims."[12]

How fortunate this country is to have a person of honor and integrity in the White House even if he is not a charismatic platform personality.

Bush speaks in what George Will calls "verbal fender-benders" and his most memorable phrase was when years ago he called Reagan's financial plans "voodoo economics." I heard him interviewed one night and when this term was mentioned, he replied, "It's the only thing I've ever said that people remember, and I wish I'd never said it."

Time writes, "Bush's campaigning skills have improved notably in recent years. In the 1980 primary, he had a Jimmy Carter-like tendency to numb audiences with superfluous detail."[13]

Robert Ajemian comments, "Bush has long been a dangerously awkward speaker. He often sets off in one direction at the beginning of a sentence and wanders off in another before it ends. ... Excitable on his feet, a man who lunges for political bait, the Vice-President is a high risk in debates."[14]

Indeed, stylish rhetoric is not natural to George Bush. One of his statements is this confusing paragraph quoted in *Time:*

"There will be a reordering of priorities and it isn't inconceivable, in the future, that there will be more emphasis (on government's role). I do think there is a certain feeling concerning tolerance, compassion, understanding, caring. I think there's a re-awakening in those areas."[15]

"Fighting the Wimp Factor," a cover article for *Newsweek,* says that Bush has "enviable advantages — high-name recognition and strong voter ratings for experience and competence. ... Yet Bush suffers from a potentially crippling handicap — a perception that he isn't strong enough or tough enough for the challenges of the Oval Office. That is, in a single word, a wimp."[16]

The *LA Times* political writer, Robert Shogan, wrote, "At the root of the Bush campaign's organizational weakness, his rivals say, is the lack of something money can't buy — the emotional juices that are needed to fuel even the best designed political machinery."[17]

Somehow the sparkle is missing and when the *New Republic* called Bush "Vice-President Sunbeam,"[18] they were referring to him not as a bright shining light, but as a beam that can't be touched."

In the Iran/Scam Tower Commission report, Bush was barely mentioned and Brent Scowcroft said, "He wasn't a player, just an advisor to the President. There was no evidence on him at all, other than attendance at a couple of meetings, and sometimes people weren't even sure he was there. Given that, we just left him out."[19]

Ted Kennedy led the Democratic convention in Bush-bashing when he called the vice-president a "hear-nothing, see-nothing, do-nothing" candidate. In reviewing administration scandals, Kennedy asked a question that quickly caught on, "Where was George?"

However, President Reagan received a rousing response at the Republican Convention, when mentioning George Bush's good works and accomplishments. The 40,000 attendants enthusiastically chanted in unison, "George was there!" And whenever a convention speaker mentioned George Bush's accomplishments, the crowds spontaneously erupted into "George was there!"

The one positive in the negative wimp campaign, is that once the press picks on a decent person, there's usually some backlash in his favor. The letters to the editor in *Time* in response to the "Fighting The Wimp Factor" article were affirming. One said "wimpery might be a refreshing change." Another said, "I hold George Bush in high regard for his loyalty to his boss and for his consideration of others."

One asked, "If a man is soft-spoken and intelligent but does not look like Hulk Hogan, does it necessarily mean that he is a 'wimp?'"

Most creative was Karen Wickens, who wrote, "After years of listening to political candidates who cheat in college and at home, embellish their records and wallow in emotion on TV, it was refreshing to read about a man who is honestly educated, competent, experienced, competitive, modest and loyal to family, friends and employers. Perhaps 'wimp' stands for: <u>W</u>ar hero, <u>I</u>ntelligent, <u>M</u>ature and <u>P</u>residential."

George Bush is the political model of a Peaceful leader. He is able to mediate between contentious people and moderate hot tempers while staying calmly above the fray.

Bush advisor and Secretary of the Treasury Nicholas Brady "marvels at how Bush has kept that potentially combustible group of strong-minded aides from blowing up." As a prediction for how this Peaceful talent would help Bush in the future Brady said about the campaign, "It's a peek behind the veil. You'd have many strong personalities, but they'd work as a team."[20]

In the major positions Bush has held, he has come in at a time of trouble, calmed everyone down, brought harmony out of chaos, made differing opinions into unity, and built an effective team, all without drawing attention to himself. These may not be flashy traits, but they could well be what we need in the post-Reagan era.

"Bush has never been known as a bold leader. He has always been an accommodating sort, managing by consensus and conciliation, skirting conflict. He advanced by being a good soldier: someone who goes where he's told, tidies up and smooths things over, and then moves on. He was a stabilizing influence, former employees say, not one to shake things up."[21]

George Bush has been known for skirting conflict and for his stabilizing influence. He has been and will be a Peaceful leader and, like Gerald Ford, he arrived at the White House with few enemies. His affable nature, expressing no extremes of opinion, adjusts according to each situation and keeps him from offending anyone.

Dan Quayle showed an understanding of the different personalities when he said in a *Time* interview, "People are swayed by Reagan's personal charm. That's part of the greatness of Reagan. George Bush will achieve greatness, but it's not going to be the same as it was with Reagan. He doesn't have that engaging speaking manner, and there is no use trying to project it if it's not there."[22]

Wouldn't we rather have a leader who functioned in his natural strengths than one who tried vainly to imitate someone else?

During the 1988 campaign Bush became a master of his personality strengths and even the Democrats were not able to find anything of significance wrong with him. Bush didn't try to be something he isn't but kept his middle-of-the-road, easy-going, pleasant personality before the public who finally accepted him as an honest person, a decent moral man, who might not ever be exciting but who would wear well. Even though his managers tried to turn him into a Powerful to enhance his leadership image, he held true to his nature and came through as sincere and genuine.

New Jersey Governor Tom Kean in his keynote address at the Republican Convention summed it up this way, "George Bush is a decent man — and he shouldn't have to defend his being one. If defending values such as loyalty, family, or belief in God is no longer fashionable, then I fear for our country."[23]

Just prior to the election, *The Wall Street Journal* summed up what I believe to be the reason George Bush won in a landslide, "Mr. Bush has built his lead through his success at painting Mr. Dukakis as out-of-step with mainstream America, and through rising voter satisfaction with Mr. Reagan and with staying on the path of his policies.

"The poll suggests that Republicans' attacks on the Massachusetts prison-furlough system, Mr. Dukakis' membership in the American Civil Liberties Union and his veto of a pledge-of-allegiance bill appear to have taken hold with the voters. Seventy one percent of likely voters believe that Mr. Bush 'represents traditional American values'. ..."[24]

Well-known writer William F. Buckley, Jr. wrote of George Bush, he is "A man of intelligence and common sense, a public man of conservative temperament."

Bush brings "good-nature, intelligence and an abiding faith in high standards to serve his country. George Bush in his early 20's was always a center of the admiring and affectionate attention of his peers, modest, bright, engaging man, thoughtful and considerate, tough and competitive. ... I have seen and judged his reactions in myriad situations. ...

"He has been tested by more varied experience of national government than any other applicant for the presidency in this century. Bush knows in his bones what a President Dukakis could learn only by an arduous tutelage at high potential cost."[25]

In the second presidential debate where the Duke needed a sure victory, Bush came across as a kind and serene statesman who was willing to overlook the accusations of his opponent, forgive his transgressions and move quietly beyond him to the Oval Office. Bush held himself as a gentle giant smiling benignly from the top of his beanstalk to a little Jack frowning below wondering how to make the climb.

Once George Bush had been overwhelmingly elected, winning 40 states with 426 electoral votes to Dukakis' 10 states with 112 electoral votes, the press began to view him through new eyes. They used descriptive words typical of the Peaceful Personality: Extending the peace-pipe, minimizing problems, bi-partisan person, reaches out to all, heals wounds, slow-starter, too neutral, lacking depth, abstinate, opaque and elusive.

Fred Greenstein, a political scientist at Princeton, summed up the Peaceful Personality when he said, "He's never moved quickly to put his mark on a new job. He's been like a chameleon that takes its colors from its environment. Bush may have a substantial period of sitting in neutral."[26]

One thing everyone agreed upon was that Bush would have his work cut out for him and that sitting in neutral wouldn't solve the nation's problems. With the huge deficit and the bulk of the bills for the military build-up coming due in 1990, Bush needed miracles along with peace pipes and bandages.

Michael Nelson, author of *Presidents, Politics and Policy,* explained the 1988 election in terms of recurring political cycles: Preparation, achievement and consolidation. He considers Ronald Reagan to have been an achiever along with Woodrow Wilson, Franklin Roosevelt and Lyndon Johnson, because he was politically skillful and could move Congress with his rhetoric, because he had ideas new to his time and was able to convince the public he was right, and because he was empowered to action by a landslide victory accompanied by Republican control of the Senate for the first time since 1955.

Nelson points out that while Reagan had all the essential qualities and circumstances to be an achieving President, George Bush campaigned on continuity of what was right and competence to heal what was wrong. As a president of consolidation, Nelson wrote, Bush will "give the American people a desired respite from change after a presidency of achievement. ... and work through some of the unresolved problems. ... Mr. Bush seems perfectly willing to govern in the shadow of Mr. Reagan's achievements."[27]

George Bush certainly has the Peaceful Personality needed to be a president of consolidation.

After years of being number two and winning the election because he tried harder, George Bush became number one, was put in the drivers seat and headed over bumpy roads in hopes of consolidating the electorate and making the United States "a kinder and gentler nation."

George Bush

"Inspiration is not his talent"

Peaceful (Phlegmatic)

Strengths

a sweetheart of a human being
relaxed & funny
uncommonly nice man
looks for the best in others

Weaknesses

acts insecure
makes few bold statements
uses if's & maybe's
lacks emotional juices
Mr. Boring
not at ease in spotlight
numbs audiences
difficulty expressing deep
    feelings
no independent identity
vaguely admirable
verbal dyslexia
obstinate
opaque and illusive

ultimate team player
crisis manager
unpretentious
unfailingly courteous
thoughtful to a fault
never challenges others
keeps low profile
no meanness about him
defuses tense situation by
    being funny
not interested in getting even
not a bitter bone in his body
at peace with himself
emotionally self-controlled
makes witty asides
astonishingly resilient &
    persevering
a blue-chip individual
unquenchable loyalty
vastly self-assured
squeaky-clean image
good in crisis
steady-handed and tempered
comfortable and consistent
passes the peace pipe
heals wounds

28

Odd Couples

The choice of vice-presidents in the 1988 election was a surprise on both sides.

Liberal Dukakis chose a tall, lean conservative Texan who looked as if he belonged with George Bush. Lloyd Bentsen has a bland Peaceful personality and he didn't try to overshadow Dukakis in anyway but height. When considering the ideological differences between the two Democrats, columnists immediately labeled them as the "odd couple."

Time's Richard Stengel wrote, "For Dukakis, who has been likened to a walking pocket calculator, the choice was shrewd. If Bentsen wins Texas, Dukakis may win the whole enchilada."[1]

Stengel then commented on how Bentsen's classic conservative style does nothing to attract Jackson's followers. He contrasted the two candidates on their political beliefs. "The Texas Tory and the Brookline Bantam make a sitcom-like odd couple. Bentsen is more Bush's twin than Dukakis'. Bentsen supports the contras; Dukakis reviles them. Dukakis mocks the policies of Reaganomics; Bentsen backed them. Bentsen boosts new missiles; Dukakis denigrates them."[2]

By putting a moderate on the ticket who has opposite views, Dukakis hoped to eliminate the Republican labeling of him as a liberal. Although in the last two weeks of the campaign, when all else had failed, he fashioned himself as a reborn liberal like FDR and JFK. Dukakis has tried to appear as a friend of the poor by riding subways, living in a duplex, driving an '83 Dodge, and buying suits on sale. He artfully concealed the potential inheritance he will receive on his mother's demise and listed his net worth as $500,000. By adding Bentsen to the ticket Dukakis lost some of his parsimonious profile.

Lloyd Bentsen, born with the proverbial silver spoon in his mouth, drives an '88 Lincoln Continental, buys designer clothes from the same company in Houston as George Bush and owns a seven-room Washington townhouse, a condominium in Houston, a 10,000- acre ranch in Texas, and a farm in Virginia. Bentsen, who goes quail-hunting in his spare time, is hardly the personification of the average American.

Former Secretary of State, Alexander Haig, the Powerful "I am in control" General and ex-presidential candidate, said of the Democratic team, "Atlanta was good theatre. It was an off-Broadway revival of *The Odd Couple,* starring the diminutive clerk from Massachusetts and the tall stranger from Texas."[3]

The similarities between Dukakis and Bentsen are that they are both Democrats and that they both have a Peaceful personality providing little excitement or emotion. In a joint campaign appearance with Jackson, Bentsen received little applause while Jesse was interrupted with 15 standing ovations.

George Bush, another Peaceful with few emotional juices, surprised the Republican Convention with his dramatic choice of Popular Dan Quayle of Indiana and provided the country with another "odd couple." Instead of selecting Powerful Bob Dole or any of the other well-known and available Republicans, Bush chose a relatively unknown senator. Typical of the Peaceful personality, Bush had delegated the research of the candidates to underlings, had taken their recommendation and was stunned when Quayle's dutiful service in the National Guard became an instant hot potato. Bush, whose nature keeps him from facing controversy, suddenly found himself defending his choice of what appeared to be a draft dodger who had used his wealthy family's influence to keep him out of Vietnam. No credible evidence was ever produced and the furor died down when polls showed that around 80 percent of the American people thought the media was out of line in its attacks on Quayle and that few people really cared about what Quayle had done 20 years ago as more than half the people surveyed would have done the same thing if given the opportunity.

On the afternoon of August 16, 1988, as George Bush alighted from the riverboat Natchez, he stood before cheering crowds on the Spanish Plaza under impending thunderclouds, and announced his choice for the Republican vice-presidential nominee. The decision had not been anticipated until later in the convention and the Bush announcement took the people by surprise. Many had no idea what George had said or who Quayle was. Murmurs grew to shouts, "What did he say?" "Dan who?" "Who's a quail?" "Let's see him?"

Suddenly a handsome young man smiling in wild disbelief emerged from the crowds and bounded toward the vice-president. He whipped off his jacket and joked, "Actually, I was just in the area and stopped by."

With his boyish charm and Robert Redford looks, Danny brought out maternal instincts in many of us and gasps of admiration in others. When he turned to give George Bush an appreciative hug, he almost knocked him over with enthusiasm and eagerness to get on with the campaign.

As with every personality, each one comes equipped with both strengths and weaknesses. The media did instant studies on Dan Quayle and found him to have the Popular engaging attributes: sunny, affable, talkative, humorous, charming, magnetic, eager to please, exuberant, rambunctious, energetic, engaging, naive, trusting, ingenious, wholesome, loveable, and sparkling.

Within 24 hours of his selection, Dan Quayle displayed some of the Popular weaknesses. At times when he opened his mouth he seemed to put his foot in it. When faced by a probing and aggressive media he looked confused and upset.

Time gave both his positive and negatives in one paragraph. "Quayle radiates the same bumptious enthusiasm, the same uncritical loyalty, the same palpable gratitude and the same malleable mindset that Bush brought to the G.O.P. ticket in 1980. But by appointing Quayle, Bush also stepped into deep boo-boo. Within 24 hours of his selection, Quayle became a political bumper car careening from one public relations crack up to another."[4]

The Bush team did not believe the news media would make such a mountainous storm out of so little a mole hill, thus Bush's aides did not prepare Quayle for what he was about to face.

Even though Quayle kept a low profile toward the end of the campaign, he certainly added color to the gray months of 1988.

Comedians said Bush chose Quayle as "impeachment insurance" and in the Fall of 1988, while Dan Quayle was trying to find his political soul, Lloyd Bentsen was looking presidential and in the debate he appeared to sneer down at "Danny Boy."

When Quayle stated that he had just as much experience as Jack Kennedy did when he ran, Bentsen pulled himself up to an imposing height and uttered the most quoted line of the night, "Senator, you're no Jack Kennedy."

Immortal though the line became, some of its brilliance faded when Ohio Representative Dennis Eckart admitted that during the debate preparation he played Quayle and threw out the Kennedy line as a possible Quayle comment. This triggered the retort in Bentsen's thinking and when Quayle made the hoped-for comparison Bentsen was ready.

Patrick Thomas, political writer in Washington, happily stated that

Quayle passes the "sidekick test" in that he would certainly not over-shadow Bush. Conversely, "Bentsen makes a very unconvincing Sancho Panza, Tonto or Ed McMahon to the Democratic presidential nominee. ... Affection for the courtly Senator is not transferable to the prickly Massachusetts governor."

And so it wasn't. Bentsen demonstrated his own lack of confidence in the ticket by simultaneously running for re-election to the Senate under a Texas law tailored for Lyndon Johnson 30 years ago. For Johnson it was only insurance, for Bentsen it was political salvation.

Dan Quayle got an unlikely boost toward the end of the campaign from Democratic Senator Ted Kennedy who said the press had not been fair to Dan who is much better at the "give and take of the Senate" than he appeared to be on the political stump.

Quayle's favorite movie is *The Candidate* starring his look-alike Robert Redford. His life parallels the plot line of the show but hand-some Dan Quayle is no longer a candidate; he's the Vice President of the United States.

Time is on Quayle's side now and, as Populars often do, he will probably turn his negatives into positives.

Postscript:
Personal Application

— 29 —

Presidential Personality Profile Overview

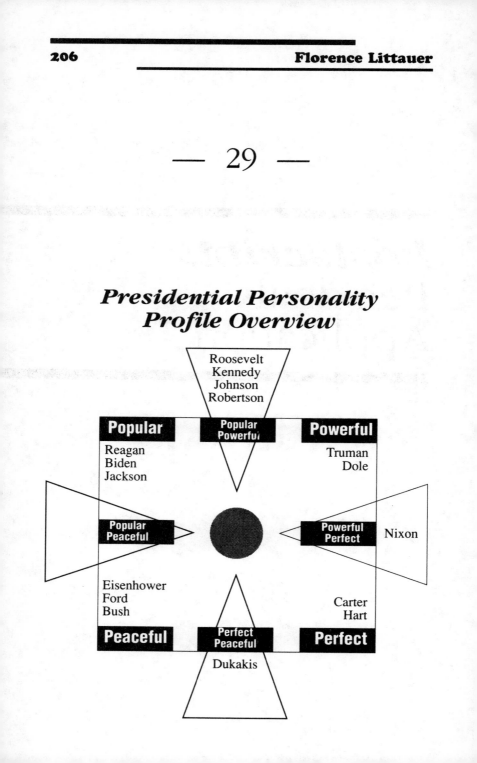

What Makes A Great Leader?

As we have reviewed our cast of Personalities in Power from 1932 through the fascinating campaign of 1988, we have seen that each person is born with a basic temperament pattern.

Gail Sheehy in her insightful book on presidential *Character* writes:

"Inborn temperament also influences the way people turn out. Certain broad characteristics of one's temperament — the tendency to be sociable or withdrawn, optimistic or depressive, open to change and risk or given to following rules and staying within safe bounds — now appear from studies of identical twins raised apart, to be profoundly influenced by heredity."[1]

As we accept that each one of us was born with a personality pattern, we need to find a way to understand ourselves and others.

Oswald Chambers defines personality as "that peculiar, incalculable thing that is meant when we speak of ourselves as distinct from everyone else. Our personality is always too big for us to grasp."[2]

In this book I've tried to break our personalities down into bite size pieces so that it will no longer be too big for us to grasp. By using the strengths and weaknesses of the four personalities, I've given you a measuring device that Fred and I have taught for over 20 years, an explanation that changed our marriage, helped us raise our children as individuals, gave us insight into the behavior of co-workers, and provided us with a basic understanding of each person's leadership potential.

Once we comprehend the personality pattern which predetermines a person's reactions, we are able to add on their childhood experiences which have either increased their strengths by parental affirmation or have decreased their feeling of worth by repeated put-downs and rejections.

As we have looked at the personalities of our leaders and seen their strengths and weaknesses, I hope this information has added a new dimension to your own sense of worth and challenged you to become a leader. No matter what our personality pattern is, when we understand it, we can develop our abilities, talents, and gifts to achieve our leadership potential.

If you are a Popular-Personality like Ronald Reagan, Joe Biden, and Jesse Jackson, rejoice in your communication skills, use your sense of humor to lighten serious situations, warm up the crowds with your engaging smile and infectious laugh; but be sure to do your homework, base your grand statements on fact and don't be caught using creative statistics.

If you are a Popular-Powerful combination, you are like so many successful leaders. You have the power to influence other people and the charm to make them want to do it. Roosevelt, Kennedy, Johnson, and Robertson, although different in looks, background, and moral values, all had the charisma and drive to mount a campaign, inspire people to work for them, keep smiling in adverse circumstances, and create lasting leadership legends. If you have a similar personality pattern be grateful for your inborn motivational skills, but be careful to temper your eagerness with a loving concern for those around you, to put the interests of the group over your own personal pleasure, and to appreciate and compliment the devoted workers who helped you become a Personality in Power. You may meet them face to face on the way back down.

If you are the Powerful-Personality like Truman and Dole you have a single-minded purpose to succeed and you don't care what anyone thinks about it. Control, direction, and correction come as naturally to you as breathing. You don't stand at the door of opportunity and wonder if you should turn the knob, you push the door open wide and stride into the control position. With you the impossible just takes a little longer and tragedies cause you to say, "I'll show them."

All of these leadership skills will move you up the ladder quickly, but remember that no one likes a person they perceive to be bossy, manipulative, angry, and impatient. Remember those pawns on your chess board of life are real people, with real feelings and they really count.

Don't let your direction and correction lead them to insurrection!

If you are a combination Powerful-Perfect like Nixon you have the best attributes for leadership because you easily take control of each situation and you want to do everything correctly. You can make quick decisions without being impulsive, lead strongly without being insensitive to the needs of the people, have a quick grasp of the facts without getting bogged down in details. The caution is to guard against letting the end justify the means and compromising your standards in order to win the game.

If you are a Perfect person, deep, thoughtful, analytical, remote, and mystical like Carter and Hart, you can be an inspirational leader. You can make the ordinary things of life seem beautiful, poetic, and majestic. You can raise people's expectations of themselves to new heights and articulate people's inner needs in spiritual terms, but you must not put the standards for yourself and others so high that you can't hope to meet them or rise to such an intellectual level that your feet don't reach the ground, you're out of touch with reality, and you reside in the remote reaches of your ivory tower. Dare to dream, but don't get depressed when your hopes get dashed against the big rock of reality.

If you are a combination Perfect-Peaceful like Dukakis, you are a cool and detached leader whose skills are in management rather than inspiration. Your Perfect side gives you the ability to plan, chart, and add up columns, but allows you to become discouraged and disheartened when life doesn't balance out perfectly. Your Peaceful part provides impartial judgement and an ability to mediate in sticky situations, but keeps you indecisive and unenthusiastic. As a leader you will be faithful and loyal to your troops and expect the same from them, you will keep your head while those all about you are losing theirs, but you may appear to be cold and unemotional.

If you are a Peaceful Personality, inoffensive and noncontroversial like Eisenhower, Ford, and Bush, your greatest leadership skills will be keeping people happy, and producing few enemies. You can bring the Popular people into serious thinking, the Powerfuls into a sense of humility, and the Perfects into an attitude of joy. You are the great balancer of life, the one person we can count on to keep us out of trouble. You may not come up with grand plans or innovative legislation, but you will hold true to your quiet beliefs and no one will have a bad word to say about you. You won't jump into impulsive decisions, but will weigh the possible consequences of each action before taking the first step. You may be considered bland or even boring, but we can count on you to keep the peace.

If you are a Peaceful-Popular, like Quayle, you have a cool allure and low-key sense of humor that attracts people to your side. You don't turn others off with an intense drive for either achievement or perfection, you're content to be relaxed and happy and you take the easy road if at all possible. You're not as loud or desperate for attention as the Popular, but you have their wit and charm blended with the Peaceful, easy-going nature. As a leader you will draw people's support and admiration for your pleasing personality, but you will need to discipline yourself to do the dull work and to keep going until the goal has been reached.

As you have analyzed your own abilities and learned to keep yourself and others functioning in their strengths instead of plodding through their weaknesses, you have come to see your potentials as a leader and have found new ways to get along with others. You don't need to hurry to catch up with the rest; you are already out in front.

— 31 —

Choosing A New Cast

Personality Principle: *With every set of strengths there come corresponding weaknesses.*

We have already looked at the four personalities, their basic strengths and weaknesses. We have read of the presidents of the past and reviewed those who are still living at the present. We have seen that what the public wants is an impossible dream with the strengths of all and the weaknesses of none, but we must remember that with each set of strengths there come corresponding weaknesses. We want what we've liked about Reagan, but without the flaws.

In the 1988 campaign, we saw the Democrats self-destructing and the Republicans sitting safely on fences. We reviewed the demise of Popular Joe Biden and the Hart-attack of Perfect Gary who, after some self-surgery, got up and about, in and out, round and round and out for the second time in one campaign — somewhat of a record.

For our personal use, let's look at some simple steps of objective analysis.

1. Realize that politics is viewed as a game of personalities because few people read the platforms or care to. As soon as we can establish the strengths of a candidate for office or employment, we can project his probable weaknesses. This plan will apply to the selection of any public personality and can be done even more accurately with anyone available to take the Personality Profile on page 217.

2. To get acquainted with the person in question, read as many articles, books, resumes or references as possible on the individ-

ual and look for descriptive words that give you some insight into his emotions, strengths and weaknesses, his gut-level reactions. But remember, after determining a candidate's personality you must look at his voting record. Where does he stand on the issues that are important to you. His past record is a clear indication of what he will do in the future. Don't read too much into his speeches as these are prepared to suit the needs of the people, and since they frequently are written by somebody else, these messages may give no clue as to his real feelings.

3. Watch the candidates on television to assess their reactions to circumstances. Observe their glances, movements and responses when they aren't "up front." In interviewing, watch body language for clues to personality type.

4. Check off their strengths on the Candidate's Chart (or have them take the Personality Profile if they are available). Remember that each set of strengths is quietly accompanied by weaknesses that will emerge later. Check off any weaknesses that are apparent.

5. When using this material for potential employees, have them take the Personality Profile and then you, or an assistant, transfer the marks to the scoring sheet and add up the columns. This will give you a quick analysis of their strengths and weaknesses and help you to place them properly. Read page 221 on Interpreting Scores.

By following these steps you can predict where the candidate for office or employment will shine and what problems may arise in the future so that you will not be caught unaware.

We all love to be amateur psychologists and analyze those other people. We can easily see how Mrs. Popular would be more so if she just knew when to stop talking. Mr. Powerful could be more effective if he weren't obsessed with controlling every person he met. Mr. Perfect would be easier to get along with if he'd just realize that nobody's perfect. Ms. Peaceful is so pleasant and inoffensive but if she could only make up her mind once in a while and act as if she cared.

How easy it is for you and me to see the faults in others and know how they could improve. This talent for objective analysis is a strength in our human make-up when properly channeled. This instinct for quick evaluation and intuition for the nature of others can be put to powerful use in our human relationships if we first recognize we have this ability, and second, know how to harness it so as to lead this intuition in the right direction.

We are not to become junior psychiatrists or set out to be spies and sleuths, but to use our new understanding to give us a productive edge over those people who blunder through life wondering why the Populars are always "turned on" and excited, why the Powerfuls grab control even of the seating arrangements at someone else's dinner party, why the Perfects can never give a compliment without tagging on, " ... however, the next time you do this ... " and why the Peacefuls always manage to escape the blame and come out clean.

Now that we understand the basic differences in human nature and realize that just because he's different doesn't make him wrong, we can quietly practice our skills and become the one person who seems to get along with everyone. By using political personalities for our examples, we are not taking sides but are practicing analytical skills on public people who will never know or care. By watching people we can view frequently on television and read about in the newspapers, we can find new enjoyment in observing public personalities with whom we might have nothing in common. This parade of political people across our living room screens takes on new meaning when we look at it as a practice time in developing our relationship skills.

Dr. Eli S. Chesen in his book, *President Nixon's Psychiatric Profile,* based his analysis on the public view of Nixon. "The profiles in this book are not secret, and for the most part were compiled in my own living room as I watched my own television set, using methods that are completely open to question and scrutiny ... my television set served me well as a surrogate for opportunities not otherwise available to me or anyone else. ... I have taken great pains to listen carefully to the words of all these men, to watch for displays of emotion — or lack of emotion. Patterns of dress, use of humor, candor and general attitude were scrutinized most carefully."[1]

Although Dr. Chesen based his analysis on the performance of Watergate participants as they passed across the screen, we can do the same with each season's parade of public personalities whether it be the local mayor, the potential president, or the characters in situation comedies.

How quickly we all did amateur analyses of Oliver North, based on nothing but his TV appearance! At the beginning of the Ollie Show, few of us knew anything about him and expected to see some schizophrenic spy who would wilt under the scrutiny of the sophisticated senators. Surely, his advance press was far from positive, yet when he looked straight into the camera and began to speak, friends and foes were fascinated with what he had to say and how he said it. He combined the Powerful military presence with the innocent humor and quavering voice of a beguiling little Popular boy. Suddenly, senators seemed insensitive and the lawyers were picking on Tom Sawyer. The press did an about-face and began to march to the beat of a new drummer: "Ollie Captures the Hill," they headlined.

As Dr. Chesen said, we "can make valid judgments by analyzing the facial expressions and words of a man being televised. In other words, not only can a psychiatrist glean insights by observing someone on television, but so can the layman. ..."[2]

We can use the mediums of TV, newspapers and magazines to train us in analyzing others, not to be their critics, but to benefit our relationship skills with our mates, our children, our friends and our co-workers. We can use the simple principles of Personalities in Power and practice on the public figures ever before us, remembering that with every set of strengths there will be corresponding weaknesses. We can analyze our own leadership skills while watching others rise and fall and we can do as that old popular song suggested, "Accentuate your positives, eliminate your negatives."

— 32 —

Candidates Chart
Strengths

Popular (Sanguine)
Talker

___ Magnetic personality
___ Storyteller
___ Sense of humor
___ Entertaining
___ Charming
___ Inspiring
___ Talkative
___ Friendly
___ Creative and colorful
___ Dramatic
___ Optimistic
___ Enthusiastic

Powerful (Choleric)
Worker

___ Commanding personality
___ Controlling Leader
___ Straight talker
___ Goal oriented
___ Business minded
___ Motivational
___ Logical
___ Persistent
___ Risk-taker
___ Practical
___ Quick organizer
___ Authoritarian

Peaceful (Phlegmatic)
Mediator

___ Low-key personality
___ Good listener
___ Patient
___ Conservative
___ Agreeable and adaptable
___ Competent and steady
___ Team-oriented and loyal
___ Administrative ability
___ Moderate
___ Prefers status quo
___ Cooperative
___ Diplomatic
___ Easy going

Perfect (Melancholy)
Thinker

___ Analytical personality
___ Detail-conscious
___ Serious and thoughtful
___ Deep and intellectual
___ Likes charts and graphs
___ Sees problems
___ Schedule-oriented
___ Holds high standards
___ Organized on paper
___ Artistic, musical
___ Philosophical and mystical
___ Sensitive to others
___ Long-range goals

Candidates Chart

Weaknesses

Popular
(Controls by charm)

___ Compulsive talker
___ Exaggerates
___ Rather talk than work
___ Can't remember details
___ Surface, little depth
___ Poor follow-through
___ Undisciplined
___ Loses things
___ Needs rewards
___ Messy surroundings
___ Easily distracted
___ Interrupts
___ Irresponsible

Powerful
(Controls by anger)

___ Angers easily
___ Impatient
___ Bossy and pushy
___ Intolerant
___ Workaholic
___ Rude and tactless
___ Manipulating
___ Demanding
___ Makes rash decisions
___ No time for research
___ Not a team player
___ End justifies the means
___ Blames others

Peaceful
(Controls by procrastination)

___ Indecisive
___ Not self-motivating
___ Procrastinates
___ Compromises standards
___ Underlying will of iron
___ Stubborn
___ Lazy and laid back
___ Dull and bland
___ Resists change
___ Passive
___ Low self-worth
___ Shy
___ Unenthusiastic

Perfect
(Controls by moods)

___ Easily depressed
___ Bogged down in details
___ Too much preparation
___ Too slow to action
___ Too perfectionistic
___ Emphasis on negatives
___ Inflexible
___ Pessimistic
___ Suspicious
___ Moody
___ Standards too high
___ Critical
___ Too mysterious

Personality Profile

DIRECTIONS — In each of the following rows of four words across, place an X in front of the one word that most often applies to you. Continue through all forty lines. Be sure each number is marked. If you are not sure of which word "most applies", ask a spouse or a friend.

STRENGTHS

1	Adventurous	Adaptable	Animated	Analytical
2	Persistent	Playful	Persuasive	Peaceful
3	Submissive	Self-sacrificing	Sociable	Strong-willed
4	Considerate	Controlled	Competitive	Convincing
5	Refreshing	Respectful	Reserved	Resourceful
6	Satisfied	Sensitive	Self-reliant	Spirited
7	Planner	Patient	Positive	Promoter
8	Sure	Spontaneous	Scheduled	Shy
9	Orderly	Obliging	Outspoken	Optimistic
10	Friendly	Faithful	Funny	Forceful
11	Daring	Delightful	Diplomatic	Detailed
12	Cheerful	Consistent	Cultured	Confident
13	Idealistic	Independent	Inoffensive	Inspiring
14	Demonstrative	Decisive	Dry humor	Deep
15	Mediator	Musical	Mover	Mixes easily
16	Thoughtful	Tenacious	Talker	Tolerant
17	Listener	Loyal	Leader	Lively
18	Contented	Chief	Chartmaker	Cute
19	Perfectionist	Pleasant	Productive	Popular
20	Bouncy	Bold	Behaved	Balanced

Personality Profile

WEAKNESSES

21	Blank	Bashful	Brassy	Bossy
22	Undisciplined	Unsympathetic	Unenthusiastic	Unforgiving
23	Reticent	Resentful	Resistant	Repetitious
24	Fussy	Fearful	Forgetful	Frank
25	Impatient	Insecure	Indecisive	Interrupts
26	Unpopular	Uninvolved	Unpredictable	Unaffectionate
27	Headstrong	Haphazard	Hard to please	Hesitant
28	Plain	Pessimistic	Proud	Permissive
29	Angered easily	Aimless	Argumentative	Alienated
30	Naive	Negative attitude	Nervy	Nonchalant
31	Worrier	Withdrawn	Workaholic	Wants credit
32	Too sensitive	Tactless	Timid	Talkative
33	Doubtful	Disorganized	Domineering	Depressed
34	Inconsistent	Introvert	Intolerant	Indifferent
35	Messy	Moody	Mumbles	Manipulative
36	Slow	Stubborn	Show-off	Skeptical
37	Loner	Lord over	Lazy	Loud
38	Sluggish	Suspicious	Short-tempered	Scatterbrained
39	Revengeful	Restless	Reluctant	Rash
40	Compromising	Critical	Crafty	Changeable

NOW TRANSFER ALL YOUR X's TO THE CORRESPONDING WORDS ON THE PERSONALITY SCORING SHEET AND ADD UP YOUR TOTALS.

Personality Scoring Sheet

STRENGTHS

#	SANGUINE POPULAR	CHOLERIC POWERFUL	MELANCHOLY PERFECT	PHLEGMATIC PEACEFUL
1	Animated	Adventurous	Analytical	Adaptable
2	Playful	Persuasive	Persistent	Peaceful
3	Sociable	Strong-willed	Self-sacrificing	Submissive
4	Convincing	Competitive	Considerate	Controlled
5	Refreshing	Resourceful	Respectful	Reserved
6	Spirited	Self-reliant	Sensitive	Satisfied
7	Promoter	Positive	Planner	Patient
8	Spontaneous	Sure	Scheduled	Shy
9	Optimistic	Outspoken	Orderly	Obliging
10	Funny	Forceful	Faithful	Friendly
11	Delightful	Daring	Detailed	Diplomatic
12	Cheerful	Confident	Cultured	Consistent
13	Inspiring	Independent	Idealistic	Inoffensive
14	Demonstrative	Decisive	Deep	Dry humor
15	Mixes easily	Mover	Musical	Mediator
16	Talker	Tenacious	Thoughtful	Tolerant
17	Lively	Leader	Loyal	Listener
18	Cute	Chief	Chartmaker	Contented
19	Popular	Productive	Perfectionist	Pleasant
20	Bouncy	Bold	Behaved	Balanced
TOTALS				

Reprinted by permission from How To Get Along With Difficult People by Florence Littauer © 1984 Harvest House Publishers, Eugene, Oregon 97402

Personality Scoring Sheet

WEAKNESSES

	SANGUINE POPULAR	CHOLERIC POWERFUL	MELANCHOLY PERFECT	PHLEGMATIC PEACEFUL
21	Brassy	Bossy	Bashful	Blank
22	Undisciplined	Unsympathetic	Unforgiving	Unenthusiastic
23	Repetitious	Resistant	Resentful	Reticent
24	Forgetful	Frank	Fussy	Fearful
25	Interrupts	Impatient	Insecure	Indecisive
26	Unpredictable	Unaffectionate	Unpopular	Uninvolved
27	Haphazard	Headstrong	Hard-to-please	Hesitant
28	Permissive	Proud	Pessimistic	Plain
29	Angered easily	Argumentative	Alienated	Aimless
30	Naive	Nervy	Negative attitude	Nonchalant
31	Wants credit	Workaholic	Withdrawn	Worrier
32	Talkative	Tactless	Too sensitive	Timid
33	Disorganized	Domineering	Depressed	Doubtful
34	Inconsistent	Intolerant	Introvert	Indifferent
35	Messy	Manipulative	Moody	Mumbles
36	Show-off	Stubborn	Skeptical	Slow
37	Loud	Lord-over-others	Loner	Lazy
38	Scatterbrained	Short tempered	Suspicious	Sluggish
39	Restless	Rash	Revengeful	Reluctant
40	Changeable	Crafty	Critical	Compromising
TOTALS				
COMBINED TOTALS				

— 34 —

Interpreting Scores

Scoring for you or the person you are testing:

If you come out predominantly in one category with a scattering among the others, read the page on your basic personality.

If you are high in one with a close second in another, read both pages and coordinate. For example, if you are a Popular and Powerful, you want to have fun while doing the work. If you are a Powerful and Perfect, you want to get the work done and have it right. If you are Perfect and Peaceful, you want things to be right but not if it will cause conflict. If you are a Peaceful and Popular, you want fun but not if you have to go somewhere to do it.

Any of the above combinations is a natural blend.

If your score splits somewhat evenly between two of the opposites (Popular/Perfect or Powerful/Peaceful), this indicates one of several possibilities: you may have taken or scored the profile incorrectly, so go back and check the directions, you may not have a clear view of yourself, so have a close friend or partner discuss it with you, or you may have had a past problem that caused you to put on a mask over your birth personality. This problem could be childhood abuse, emotional neglect, extreme deprivation, sexual molestation or parents who were alcoholics or on drugs. Any of these could have caused a covering of the original personality. Another reason could have been deep insecurities as a teen causing you to try to be someone you weren't in order to be popular, and thus creating a false personality. Another possibility is that you may have married someone who tried to change you and in an effort to be pleasing you wiped out many of your genuine feelings, leaving you somewhat confused about your identity. Multiple marriages increase this confusion.

If your scores were even all the way across, this may indicate you had difficulties with the definitions of the words, you are a Peaceful who has trouble making decisions, or you have spent your life trying to be all things to all people to such an extreme that you have obliterated your real personality.

If any of these questions arise, try to think back to your childhood desires. Did you always want fun, control, perfection or peace? Talk with parents or relatives. Try to find your birth personality and begin to function in it. We are never comfortable with ourselves or secure with others when we are playing a role or trying to be what someone else felt we should be.

For further study on emotional or residual problems, read *Your Personality Tree* by Florence Littauer and *Freeing Your Mind From Memories that Bind* by Fred and Florence Littauer.

Footnotes

The Populars
1. *Newsweek,* November 21, 1988

The Perfects
1. *Newsweek,* November-December, 1984

The Powerfuls
1. *Newsweek,* June 22, 1987
2. *Newsweek,* January 12, 1987

The Peacefuls
1. *Wall Street Journal,* date unavailable
2. *LA Times,* August 14, 1988

Personalities of the Powerful
1. O'Neill, Tip with William Novak, *Man of the House,* Random House, 1987.
2. Ibid

The Fireside Chat
1. Perry, Enos J., *The Boyhood Days of Our Presidents,* Enos J. Perry Publishers, 1971
2. Lash, Joseph P., *Eleanor and Franklin,* W.W. Norton & Co., Inc., 1971
3. Shapiro, Walter, *Time,* November 9, 1987.
4. Carson, Clarence B., *The Welfare State 1929-1985,* American Textbook Committee, 1986
5. October 31, 1936 Madison Square Garden Address
6. Lash, Joseph P., *Eleanor and Franklin,* W.W. Norton & Co., Inc., 1971
7. Teamsters Dinner, September 23, 1944
8. Tully, Grace, *F.D.R. My Boss,* Charles Scribner, 1949

Give 'em hell!
1. Donovan, Robert, *Tumultuous Years,* W.W. Norton & Co., 1982
2. Ibid
3. Ibid
4. Isaacson, Walter, *Time,* August 31, 1987.

We Like Ike
1. Weigley, Russell F., *New York Times Book Review,* December 20, 1987
2. Eisenhower, David, *Eisenhower: At War, 1943-1945*
3. Morris, Charles R., *A Time of Passion — America 1960-1980,* Harper and Row, 1984
4. Montgomery, Ruth
5. White, Theodore H., *The Making of a President,* Atheneun, 1961
6. Ibid
7. Ibid
8. Ibid
9. O'Neill, Tip with William Novak, *Man of the House,* Random House, 1987
10. Ibid
11. Ibid
12. Ibid

Nature vs. Nurture
1. *Journal of Personality and Social Psychology*
2. Ibid

Camelot
1. White, Theodore, *The Making of a President,* Atheneun, 1961
2. Ibid

3. Morris, Charles, *A Time of Passion — America 1960-1980,* Harper and Row, 1984
4. Dickerson, Nancy, *Among Those Present,* Random House
5. Clinch, Nancy Gager, *The Kennedy Neurosis,* Grosset and Dunlap
6. Buck, Pearl, *The Kennedy Women*
7. Ibid
8. O'Neill, Tip with William Novak, *Man of the House,* Random House, 1987
9. Clinch, Nancy, *The Kennedy Neurosis,* Gosset and Dunlap
10. White, Theodore, *The Making of a President,* Atheneun, 1961
11. Dickerson, Nancy, *Among Those Present,* Random House
12. Will, George F., *The New Season,* Simon & Schuster, 1988
13. Carsen, Clarence B., *The Welfare State 1929-1985,* American Textbook Committee, 1986
14. Tindall, George Brown, *America, A Narrative History, Vol. 2,* W. W. Norton & Company, 1984
15. Buchanan, Patrick J., *Right From the Beginning,* Little, Brown, & Co., 1988
16. Clinch, Nancy Gager, *Among Those Present,* Random House
17. Tindall, George Brown, *America, A Narrative History, Vol. 2,* W.W. Norton & Company, 1984
18. *New York Times,* August 30, 1987
19. Carsen, Clarence B., *The Welfare State 1929-1985,* American Textbook Committee, 1986
20. Tindall, George Brown, *America, A Narrative History, Vol. 2,* W. W. Norton & Company, 1984

All the Way with LBJ

1. Dickerson, Nancy, *Among Those Present,* Random House
2. Healy, Diana Dixon, *America's Vice-Presidents,* McClelland and Steward LTD., Baltimore, MD, 1984
3. Goodwin, Doris Kearns, *Ford and Carter*
4. Dickerson, Nancy, *Among Those Present,* Random House
5. Pierpoint, Bob, *Parade Magazine,* November 27, 1977

Knowledge Is Power

1. Chesen, M.D., Eli S., *President Nixon's Psychiatric Profile,* Peter H. Wyden/Publisher, New York, 1973
2. Detoledano, Ralph P., *One Man Alone, Funk and Wagnalls,* New York, NY 1969
3. Chesen, M.D., Eli, *President Nixon's Psychiatric Profile,* Peter H. Wyden/ Publisher, New York, 1973
4. Morris, Charles, *A Time of Passion — America 1960-1980,* Harper and Row, 1984
5. Ibid
6. Chesen, M.D., Eli S., *President Nixon's Psychiatric Profile,* Peter H Wyden/Publisher, New York, 1973
7. *Time,* May 4, 1987
8. Ibid
9. Ambrose, Stephen, *Nixon: The Education of a Politician,* Simon and Schuster, 1987
10. Ibid
11. Ibid
12. Ibid
13. Dickerson, Nancy, *Among Those Present,* Random House
14. Chesen, M.D., Eli, *President Nixon's Psychiatric Profile,* Peter H. Wyden/Publisher, New York, 1973
15. Morris, Charles, *A Time of Passion — America 1960-1980,* Harper and Row, 1984
16. *Newsweek,* May 19, 1986
17. Dickerson, Nancy, *Among Those Present,* Random House
18. Goodwin, Doris Kearns, *Ford and Carter,* Ladie's Home Journal, November, 1976
19. *Signature,* June, 1987

A Time of War and a Time of Peace
1. Goodwin, Doris Kearns, *Ford and Carter*, Ladie's Home Journal, November, 1976
2. Ibid
3. Ibid
4. *LA Times Magazine*, February 15, 1987
5. Ibid

Jimmy Who?
1. Goodwin, Doris Kearns, *Ford and Carter*, Ladie's Home Journal, November, 1976
2. Ibid
3. Rapp, Frederick, *Associated Press*, 1976
4. Baker, Ross, *LA Times*, May 7, 1983
5. *Newsweek*, September 27, 1982
6. *Newsweek*, July 23, 1979
7. Ibid
8. Ibid
9. Ibid
10. Ibid
11. Morris, Charles R., *A Time of Passion — America 1960-1980*, Harper and Row, 1984
12. *Newsweek*, November 16, 1987
13. *An Outdoor Journal*
14. *LA Times*, August 18, 1988

Let Reagan Be Reagan
1. White, Theodore H., *The Making of a President*, Atheneun, 1961
2. *Newsweek*, Nov/Dec 1984
3. Ibid
4. Ibid
5. Ibid
6. Ibid

The Great Communicator
1. Will, George F., *The New Season*, Simon & Schuster, 1988
2. Clives, Francis X, *NY Times*, August 20, 1984
3. Rusher, William A., *The Rise of the Right*, William Morrow & Co.
4. Kempton, Murray, *LA Times*, Sept. 11, 1984
5. *Newsweek*, Feb 6, 1984
6. Ibid
7. Lance Morrow, *Time*, July 7, 1986
8. Ibid
9. *Time*, August 24,, 1987
10. *Time*, March 30, 1987
11. Buchanan, Patrick J., *Right from the Beginning*, Little, Brown & Co., 1988
12. *Newsweek*, August 27, 1984
13. *Newsweek*, August 27, 1984
14. Tindall, George Brown, *America, A Narrative History, Vol 2,_ W. W. Norton & Co., 1984
15. *Newsweek*, August 27, 1984
16. Morganthau, Tom, *Newsweek*, August 27, 1984
17. Mosse, Richard, *New York Times*, August 22, 1984
18. Lynch, Lorrie, *USA Today*, Review of *Hold on Mr. President*, Donaldson, Sam, Random House, 1987
19. *Sun*, San Bernardino, CA, March 16, 1984
20. *New York Times*, August 21, 1987
21. *Time*, November 24, 1986
22. *Time*, December 30, 198623. *Time*, March 20, 1986
24. *Time*, April 6, 1987

25. *Time*, August 24, 1987
26. *The People, Press and Politics, Times Mirror,* September 1987
27. *Newsweek*, June 8, 1984
28. Buchanan, Patrick J., *Right From the Beginning,* Little, Brown, & Co., 1988
29. *Newsweek*, October 19, 1987
30. Will, George F., *The New Season,* Simon & Schuster, 1988

Searching for a Superman

1. Shapiro, Walter, *Time,* July 13, 1987
2. Ailes, Roger, *Newsweek,* September 7, 1987
3. *Time*, May 18, 1987
4. *Newsweek*, August 3, 1987
5. *Insight*, December 28, 1987
6. *LA Times,* December 27, 1987
7. *Newsweek*, October 31, 1988

Choosing A New Cast

1. Chesen, Eli S., *President Nixon's Psychiatric Profile,* Peter H. Wyden/Publisher, New York, 1973
2. Ibid

Hart Attack

1. *Newsweek*, April 13, 1987
2. Ibid
3. Shapiro, Walter, *Time,* April 27, 1987
4. *Life*, August, 1987
5. Ibid
6. *Time*, May 18, 1987
7. Ibid
8. Ibid
9. Ibid
10. Scott, Sir Walter, *Marmion,* 1808
11. *Sunday Oregonian,* December 20, 1987
12. *New York Times,* December 20, 1987
13. Ibid
14. *Oregonian,* December 20, 1987
15. Ibid
16. *New York Times,* December 20, 1987

Happy Talks Too Much

1. *New York Times,* August 31, 1987
2. Ibid
3. *Time,* June 22, 1987
4. *The Honolulu Advertiser,* September 22, 1987
5. Ibid
6. *Time,* October 5, 1987
7. *USA Today,* September 24, 1987
8. *Newsweek,* October 5, 1987
9. Ibid
10. Ibid

Cool is Hot

1. *LA Times,* August 30, 1987
2. *Time*, October 12, 1987
3. *Newsweek*, October 12, 1987
4. *USA Today,* October 1, 1987
5. *Time*, October 12, 1987

6. *Time*, July 20, 1987
7. *Time*, July 25, 1988
8. *Newsweek*, August 8, 1988
9. *USA Today*, July 2, 1988
10. *Insight*, May 9, 1988
11. *U.S. News & World Report*, April 18, 1988
12. *Dallas Morning News*, July 17, 1988
13. *Boston Business Magazine*
14. *U.S.A. Weekend*, July 15-17, 1988
15. *Time*, July 20, 1987
16. *Vanity Fair*, November, 1987
17. *U.S.A. Today*, July 22, 1988
18. *Boston Herald*, August 1, 1988 (Michael Dukakis a peril to the unborn)
19. *Michael Dukakis — The Great Dissimulator*, Don Feder, September 1988

Waving Magic Wands

1. *L.A. Times*, July 25, 1987
2. *Newsweek*, November/December, 1984
3. *Newsweek*, January 4, 1988
4. *Newsweek*, August 10, 1987
5. Ibid
6. *Time*, August 10, 1987
7. *Newsweek*, July 13, 1987
8. *Time*, August 22, 1988
9. *U.S.A. Today*, July 21, 1988
10. *Time*, August 22, 1988

A Kinder and Gentler Nation

1. *New York Times*, October 30, 1988
2. *New Orleans Times-Picayune*, August 18, 1988
3. *The Charlotte Observer*, March 11, 1988
4. *Newsweek*, November 9, 1987
5. Schneider, William, *New Ideas Will Never Nominate the Next U. S. President*
6. *LA Times*, November 22, 1987
7. Ibid
8. Ibid
9. Ibid
10. *Vanity Fair*, February 1987
11. *USA Today*, October 21, 1988
12. *Vanity Fair*, February 1987
13. *Time*, August 27, 1984
14. *Time*, January 26, 1987
15. *Time*, March 30, 1987
16. *Newsweek*, October 19, 1987
17. *LA Times*, September 21, 1987
18. *New Republic*, March 30, 1987
19. Ibid
20. *Time*, March 21, 1988
21. *New Orleans Times-Picayune*, August 18, 1988
22. *Time*, August 29, 1988
23. *USA Today*, August 17, 1988
24. *Wall St. Journal*, October 18, 1988
25. *Atlantic*, October 1988

Odd Couples

1. *Time*, July 25, 1988
2. Ibid

3. *USA Today,* August 17, 1988
4. *Time,* August 29, 1988
5. *LA Times,* October 9, 1988

Senator Straddle

1. *New York Times,* November 8, 1987
2. *US News and World Report,* November 16, 1987
3. Ibid
4. Ibid
5. Ibid
6. Ibid
7. *New Orleans Times-Picayune,* November 12, 1987
8. Ibid
9. *Time,* August 10, 1987
10. Ibid
11. *LA Times,* September 19, 1987
12. Ibid
13. *Time,* October 12, 1987
14. Sheehy, Gail, *Character,* William Morrow, 1988
15. *Newsweek,* November 16, 1987

True Confessions

1. *LA Times,* August 15, 1988
2. Goodwin, Doris Kearns, *Ladies Home Journal,* November 1976
3. *Newsweek,* January 4, 1988
4. *Time,* May 18, 1987
5. *Time,* September 7, 1987
6. *USA Today,* September 24, 1987
7. *Time,* May 18, 1987
8. *Newsweek,* May 25, 1987
9. Ibid
10. Johnson, Gerald White, *American Heroes and Hero Worship,*

The Amazing Race

1. *Time,* January 11, 1988
2. *LA Times,* June 22, 1986
3. Sheehy, Gail, *Vanity Fair,* January, 1988
4. *Louisville Courier-Journal,* March 9, 1988
5. *Black Enterprise,* July 1988
6. *USA Today*
7. *Dallas Morning News,* November 8, 1987
8. Ibid
9. *Newsweek,* November 9, 1987
10. *The Times-Picayune,* August 16, 1988
11. *US News and World Report,* February 22, 1988
12. *Lexington Herald-Leader,* March 5, 1988
13. Ibid

What Makes Great Leaders

1. Sheehy, Gail, *Characters,* William Morrow, 1988
2. Chambers, Oswald, *My Utmost for His Highest*

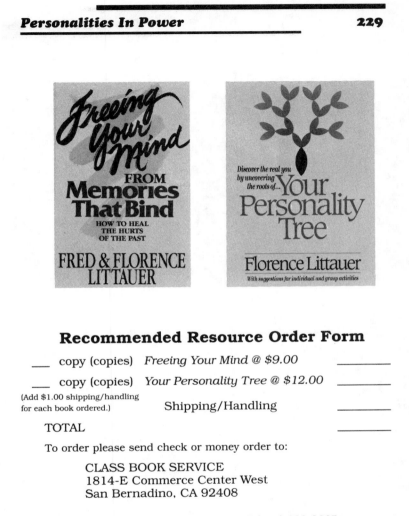

Recommended Resource Order Form

___ copy (copies)   *Freeing Your Mind* @ $9.00   _____

___ copy (copies)   *Your Personality Tree* @ $12.00   _____

(Add $1.00 shipping/handling
for each book ordered.)   Shipping/Handling   _____

TOTAL   _____

To order please send check or money order to:

> CLASS BOOK SERVICE
> 1814-E Commerce Center West
> San Bernadino, CA 92408

For faster service use VISA/Mastercard, call (714) 888-8665.
INTERNATIONAL ORDERS–Please send check in U.S. funds only, and add
$3.00 per book for shipping by Air.

Enclosed is $ _____ including postage.

Card type: VISA/Mastercard # _____ Expiration Date _____

Name _____

Address _____

City/State/Zip _____

OTHER BOOKS BY FLORENCE LITTAUER

The Best of Florence Littauer
(coming August 1989)
Pursuit of Happiness
Blow Away the Black Clouds
After Every Wedding Comes a Marriage
Out of the Cabbage Patch
It Takes So Little to Be Above Average
How to Get Along With Difficult People
Shades of Beauty co-authored with Marita Littauer
Christian Leaders and Speakers Seminar
(tape album and manual)

Personality Plus

Hope for Hurting Women
Your Personality Tree
Looking for God in All the Right Places
Raising the Curtain on Raising Children

ORDER THESE BOOKS FROM HUNTINGTON HOUSE!

___ America Betrayed.......Marlin Maddoux .... $6.95=_____
___ Backward Masking Unmasked.....Jacob Aranza .... 6.95=_____
___ Backward Masking Unmasked Audiotapes....Jacob Aranza .... 6.95=_____
___ Computers and the Beast of Revelation..Webber & Hutchings... 6.95=_____
___ *The Deadly Deception: Freemasonry ....Tom McKenney .... 6.95=_____
___ Devil Take the Youngest...................Winkie Pratney .... 7.95=_____
___ *Exposing The Aids Scandal..................Dr. Paul Cameron .... 6.95=_____
___ The Great Falling Away Today..............Milton Green .... 6.95=_____
___ Hand of Death-On Cults & Satanism.....Max Call .... 12.95=_____
___ Hidden Dangers of the Rainbow............Constance Cumbey .... 6.95=_____
___ Jubilee on Wall Street.......................David Knox Barker .... 6.95=_____
___ Last Days Collection.........................Last Days Ministries .... 8.95=_____
___ Lucifer Connection...........................Joseph Carr .... 6.95=_____
___ *Plague in Our Midst.........................Dr. Gregg Albers .... 7.95=_____
___ A Reasonable Reason To Wait.............Jacob Aranz .... 5.95=_____
___ *Responsible Parent's Guide to T.V......Colonel V. Doner .... 6.95=_____
___ *Personalities in Power......................Florence Littauer .... 8.95=_____
___ Twisted Cross...............................Joseph Carr .... 7.95=_____
___ Where Were You When I Was Hurting?....Nicky Cruz .... 6.95=_____

*New titles

Shipping and Handling _____

AVAILABLE AT BOOKSTORES EVERYWHERE or order direct from: Huntington House, Inc., P.O. Box 53788, Lafayette, LA 70505.
Send check/money order. For faster service use VISA/Mastercard, call toll-free 1-800-572-8213. Add: Freight and handling, $2.00
for the first book ordered, and $.50 for each additional book.

Card type: VISA/Mastercard # _____ Expiration date _____

NAME _____

ADDRESS _____

CITY/STATE/ZIP _____